FISH
AND
GAME
COOKING

Newest, easiest, most exciting
recipes and menus for

FISH
AND
GAME
COOKING

using standard kitchen equipment
plus energy-saving crockpots,
pressure cookers, outdoor grills,
microwave and convection ovens.

JOAN CONE

EPM Publications

To

ALISON, DAMON, ARTHUR III, STEPHEN AND WENDY

Library of Congress Cataloging in Publication Data

Cone, Joan.
   Fish & game cooking.

   Includes index.
   1. Cookery (Fish)   2. Cookery (Game)   3. Kitchen
utensils.   I. Title.
TX747.C76   641.6'91.   80-29220
ISBN 0-914440-45-4 (pbk.)

Cover and Book Design
by Ice House Graphics

Table of Contents

i

Foreword

After thirty-three years, I well remember meeting Joan. Maybe that's because she wore only a small bathing suit and a big smile. Timidly, I invited her to come fishing, and her refusal was a crushing blow. However, I persevered, to the extent that Joan's great aunt, deep in her nineties, perceived this young lady was being "rushed." It eventually came as a surprise to discover my blue-eyed blonde with the fantastic figure was also a remarkable cook. That was something I'd never even considered.

Now, more than three decades later, Joan's appearance at the beach causes fewer heads to swivel, but the meals she prepares create an enormous impression because, speaking frankly, they are wonderful. One of our children, a successful chef, admits he would rather not compete against his mother. She's a fantastic cook!

I should also mention that my wife is an expert angler and an excellent shot. She can hold her own with rod and reel, shotgun, bow or rifle in any company. We spend as many hours as possible hunting and fishing together in locales as varied as Scotland, Newfoundland, Virginia, Maine and Nebraska. Realizing how much skill is needed to provide the ingredients of a fish or game meal, Joan is determined to serve each type of meat or seafood at its very best.

If you have read *Easy Game Cooking*, or any of Joan's many magazine articles, or seen her on televison, you know she has the fine knack of making things simple. Joan can cook anything from an armadillo to a zebra. Best of all, she works her culinary wonders without pretense, nonsense, or any need to spend long hours over a hot stove. An honest, practical person, she has personally tested every one of the recipes in this book. That is more important than you might realize. Many cookbook authors, taking advantage of the fact that it is virtually impossible to copyright a recipe, simply plagiarize the work of others, often with weird results. I recall seeing a recipe which involved two woodcock, total weight of both birds about eight ounces dressed, to be prepared with half a pound of bacon! Why not just dump them in a pot of lard?

Joan's recipes make sense. They foster the saving of energy, calories and time too. How can a fish and game cookbook promote conservation? Easily. Nothing gets wasted! Joan believes in eating everything you bring home. After all, you are hardly an ethical sportsman if you shoot game or catch fish and stuff them in the garbage. So along with trout, salmon, venison, quail and rabbit, we eat raccoon, snapping turtles and bullfrogs. If you have ever been to the Carribean, you have probably eaten conch stew and enjoyed it. A conch is nothing but a whelk that you can pick up on many beaches. It is excellent.

So this book aims at conserving natural resources. It also saves you calories because fish, seafood and game are low in fats and cholesterol. It saves energy due to Joan's use of convection ovens, pressure cookers, microwave ovens, toaster ovens and crockpots, to reduce utility bills.

Perhaps you cook with wood or coal as fuel? That is what everyone used from the Stone Age until the Victorian era. Joan's recipes work just as well with solid fuels as they do with gas, electricity or propane.

Too many of us are nervous about cooking game or doing anything with fish beyond frying it. The word *gourmet* conjures up a need for powdered truffles, heavy whiping cream and other ingredients we either cannot buy or do not need. Joan's recipes can stand against any so-called gourmet assemblage of esoteric substances and difficult sauces. Taste and you will agree.

You are invited to settle down and enjoy this cookbook. You will not be harassed by having to go through sixteen steps for a single dish or buy some incredible number of spices before starting to prepare dinner. Joan explains everything, and each recipe has ingredients listed in the same order you will use them.

You'll find this book a wonderful timesaver too. The idea is to spend as little time hovering over a stove as possible. All that hovering and peeking does is waste fuel. It should be avoided. Everything here can be prepared in short order, or, if you use a crockpot, you can leave your meal to prepare itself while you go fishing.

You will enjoy this book! You will find everything in it is both good and good for you. Having eaten it all, I honestly feel that Joan has written a classic. You will not find any fish and game cookbook that can match it for simplicity or satisfaction.

Arthur L. Cone, Jr.

How to Save Energy When You Cook

Serving fish and game to your family can save both energy and money. It takes oil to run the farm equipment needed to raise food for cattle, chickens and other domestic animals. More oil and electric power are used to catch and freeze seafood commercially. Additional energy is required to package store-bought foods.

Granted that hunting and fishing generally mean some travel and a certain amount of expense. Yet most families need recreation, and, as the old saying goes. "You can't eat tennis balls."

One thing you can do, no matter what you serve, is to save energy and money in your kitchen by using efficient cooking methods and appliances. Minimum heat loss and energy-saving recipes in your kitchen will save money and energy two ways. First of all, you'll use less fuel. Second, a smaller amount of heat will escape into your house to be wasted, particularly in summer when air conditioning could be affected. All the recipes in this book are written with these aims in mind.

Here are some suggestions for better cooking habits, in these energy conscious times, from the Home Economics Department of Oster Corporation:

1. Use pots with tight fitting covers to prevent heat from escaping. Keep pots and pans tightly covered

while cooking so all heat and moisture are retained.

2. Use heavy metal utensils, since these are most efficient in spreading heat evenly and cooking uniformly. Heavy aluminum and cast iron make maximum use of energy.
3. Use cookware with flat bottoms to make maximum contact with your heat source.
4. Always use the proper size pan for your burner. Your utensil should also match the amount of food you are preparing. If it is too large, you will use more energy than you need. If too small, heat will escape.
5. Use minimum heat for the job at hand. The less water you add, the shorter your cooking time will be. Frying should be done uncovered, using only enough heat to brown properly.

Of course, what you cook also has something to do with energy savings. Substituting a pound of fish for a pound of beef once a month does not seem like much, but if all families did this, it would save 117 million barrels of oil annually, according to Dr. Mary Rawitscher of Tufts University Nutrition Institute.

Something else that can make a real difference in your energy dollars is the use of modern small appliances, including pressure cookers, and microwave, convection and toaster ovens. The Sunbeam Corporation has done studies comparing small appliances with an electric range. The studies claim that it takes three times as much energy to cook a pizza on an electric range as in an electric frypan; about two and a half times as much energy to bake a cake in an electric oven as in an electric frypan; and even cooking hamburgers, you'll save one and a half times the amount of energy with the electric frypan. It takes less than half the energy to use an electric coffeemaker than to heat water in a teapot on your range. And it takes more than four times as much energy to poach eggs on your stove than you would need with an electric egg cooker. Even toaster ovens use a third less energy than their larger counterparts. The reason is simply that, being smaller, there is less volume of air to heat.

Let's discuss some of these energy-saving appliances.

Pressure Cooker
You can prepare a meal for a family of four in an electric pressure cooker for 0.4¢. The same meal in a conventional electric oven would cost 7.6¢, according to Anita Wilson of the University of Wisconsin-Stout. Both portable electric and conventional pressure cookers save a great deal of energy and obviously cost far less than microwave ovens.

Crockpot
It's an energy saver because it uses only about as much current as a 75-watt bulb.

Electric Frypan
This saves money and energy because it uses regular 110-volt household current instead of a 220-volt line and a thermostat prevents the waste of heat.

Toaster Oven
Efficient, especially for the small family, it saves money by limiting the space that is heated. It can toast, broil, bake, reheat, and slow cook.

Convection Oven
This is a terrific money saver because it is designed to keep hot air in your oven, not in your kitchen. As an article by Elizabeth Schatjian in *Cuisine*, November, 1979, explains, convection ovens cook faster and more evenly at a lower temperature. Cooking temperatures are reduced by 25° to 75°. As a result, you save one third to one half the cost of normal oven operation, and your food loses less volume while cooking. You can use your convection oven to dehydrate fruits and vegetables. If you own a convection oven, use it for the broiling and baking recipes in this book.

Microwave Oven

The microwave is efficient because the heat goes directly into the food, and the air around it stays cool. In the South, where summertime heat is a problem, this is an especially fine energy-saving feature. You will find it wonderful with seafood and for reheating foods from the refrigerator. It uses about the same amount of energy as a conventional surface burner. The amount of food and cooking time determine the extent of fuel savings.

Most of the recipes in this book will work with any fuel, including wood and coal. If you supply your own wood, or can buy coal reasonably, a solid fuel stove saves money. The disadvantage is the amount of work involved in splitting wood, shoveling coal and removing ashes; and you are bound to have more soot and dirt to clean up.

Yet there are some worthwhile advantages to cooking as our ancestors did. Modern wood and coal stoves have thermostats, and their ovens bake and roast. They offer you something other stoves do not; a free crockpot! A Dutch oven left to simmer on your stove will do anything a crockpot would, and maybe better.

As with other conventional stoves, the best cookware for wood and coal stoves is flat-bottomed, heavy metal, cast iron and aluminum. If you can use the utensils your grandparents employed, you're ahead of the game for they are already broken in. Unused cast iron needs seasoning. Coat the inside with unsalted oil and heat in a 300° oven for two hours. Then let it cool and wipe off any excess oil.

Of course you can use heavy enamelware or copper bottom pots and pans. Your only problem is one of aesthetics. Cast iron, being black, never shows soot marks. If you own a heavy metal wok, it will do a good job on your wood or coal stove. Season it just like the cast iron.

Solid fuel stoves offer a very hot fire for stir-frying and rapid boiling; hot fire for deep frying; moderate heat for sautéing; and a steady simmering heat for slow cooking in crockpot style.

Wood stoves are wonderful with fish and game and especially good for stews and other crockpot recipes. With oven recipes, you'll have to check your thermostat regularly and probably make some minor adjustments in timing. Something else you can do economically with a wood stove is to place the carcasses of ducks, pheasants and other game birds in a deep pot with celery tops, carrot scrapings, onions and so forth, and simmer several hours to make wonderful stock or soup. On gas and electric ranges, the cost of this would be high, but stock-making utilizes the continous warmth that solid fuel provides. Yes, you can make fish stocks too. Just be sure they continue to simmer, because lukewarm seafood may produce bacteria.

Field Care and Freezing of Game

Some people are not all that enthusiastic about eating game. Their attitudes are based on either of two reasons. The first is a deep-seated psychological aversion to trying anything new or different. You can't do much for these unfortunates except pity them.

You can do something, however, about the other primary reason for not eating game: A prior experience with unpleasant flavor, toughness or a disagreeable odor. For game, properly handled in the field and turned over to a competent cook, will be delicious, tasty and smell so wonderful that no one can turn it down.

That so-called gamy flavor comes mostly from spoiled meat and occasionally because a deer was not killed cleanly by a single shot. Toughness and unfortunate odors can be handled by proper cooking, but meat that has been hung too long or cleaned out too late will not be easily salvaged.

Of course, some people's objectionable gamy taste is what others may prefer. In Europe, pheasants and other game birds, rabbits and hares are hung (until we'd want to throw them in the garbage) to develop what cultivated tastes say is the proper flavor. As far as I'm concerned, they can have it! I asked one of my husband's British cousins why he hung pheasants until they were strong, and he replied: "Otherwise they'd taste just like chicken." Poor

Bobby has since gone to his reward, not for eating his almost rotten pheasants, but because his foot on the accelerator knew only one position— full speed ahead.

Prior to actual cooking, getting good game on the table is just common sense. Prompt field dressing, cooling, skinning, and removal of all surface fat are essentials. Deer and other large game animals can then be hung at a temperature of less than 40°, but still above freezing. And while mammals should always be skinned, game birds should *never* be skinned, with two exceptions: clapper rails and sea ducks. Both of these must be skinned before cooking.

Another point in these days of home freezers is that your frozen game must be properly wrapped. Game birds and small animals, such as rabbits or squirrels, must be double-wrapped to insure that sharp bones will not cut through the wrapping material and let in air, with consequent freezer burn. For extra protection, I suggest you double wrap all cuts of big game as well. Be sure seams are taped and all game packages marked with type of meat and date.

Something else I want to stress here is that game should *never* be soaked. Soaking before freezing lets the meat absorb water that then forms ice crystals. These ice crystals expand while freezing and turn your good game into mushy meat. Just cut out badly shot areas, wash well and dry with paper toweling. Old methods, such as soaking in vinegar, make your game taste like vinegar, what else? Soaking in salt water removes the blood and juices which you need for an appetizing game meal. So leave the soaking to those misguided souls who don't know any better or who feel that meat tasting strong of vinegar is delicious. If people tell you game should be soaked, tell them to go soak their next supermarket steak and see what happens!

As for cooking—now that we're getting around to it— game is generally drier and less fatty than commercial meat sold at stores. The reason is easy to understand. Game birds and animals forage for themselves and do not have some keeper throwing corn, oats or hay at them all day long. Besides, they are active and rarely lie around.

Therefore, you'll find that many of the following recipes call for some sort of moist heat as found in a Dutch oven, a covered casserole, oven cooking bags, aluminum foil or a crockpot.

Try these new recipes and you'll discover game is wonderful, heathful, delicious, nonfattening and a real treat for everyone.

New Ways to Cook Upland Birds

You feed a dog, maybe a pair of them, year round. You have a beautiful shotgun that costs as much as jewelry these days. Maybe you go to Maine for woodcock and grouse, to the Carolinas for quail and the Plains states for pheasant and sharptail. Hunting upland game birds can be expensive. But there is nothing like the sight of a good dog on point, or the exciting roar of wings when the covey explodes.

Another reward comes later when your friends and family enjoy these delicious birds. Most of them are closely related to chickens but have retained all the delicate flavor that domestic fowl have somehow lost.

To enjoy them at their best, you should field dress your birds at the earliest possible moment, and be sure they are plucked and cooled quickly when you rack your guns after a day of walking through nature's beautiful autumn weather. In warm weather, carry a portable ice chest to speed cooling and protect your birds against spoilage during the trip home.

It's easier to pluck game birds while they are warm. If you can't do it then, clean them out and pluck them after they've cooled down.

I'm emphasizing plucking because, whether it be woodcock, snipe, dove, partridge or any other upland bird,

11

skinning can ruin them, because what little fat they have is right under the skin itself. The only exception would be clapper rails, which are actually better when skinned. Sora rails, smaller than clappers, are better plucked.

When game birds reach your kitchen, cut off the wings, which are difficult to pluck and have little on them to eat. After plucking, smaller birds, including woodcock, snipe, dove, quail and partridge, should be split up the back with kitchen shears and completely cleaned out. By removing lungs and blood clots, you eliminate a potential cause of disagreeable flavor.

Wrap your birds for the freezer so they will not be ruined by freezer burn. This means you should place each bird in an individual bag or wrap in heavy plastic film. Then put your individually wrapped birds in a good heavy duty plastic freezer bag, squeezing out all air and closing tightly. The second bag insures against freezer burn if sharp bones puncture the initial wrapping and lets you assemble your wrapped birds. You can then defrost the exact number needed. Be sure to mark the date and number of birds on each outer freezer bag. You can store game birds that are properly cleaned and wrapped up to one year in your freezer.

Never freeze anything in aluminum foil. The reason is that in cold temperatures aluminum foil becomes very brittle, punctures, and develops pinholes. Do not use breadwrappers for freezing. They won't protect your birds properly. After all you've gone through, including an investment in shotgun shells, licenses and everything else, it doesn't pay to cut corners with your game.

You can cook a variety of small game birds together, or use the same recipe for all. Just use birds of about equal size, so they will be ready together. Quail and woodcock, snipe and dove, are good combinations. All four can be prepared together if you allow slightly less cooking time for the dove and snipe, which are smaller.

Woodcock, Rail, Dove and Snipe

Woodcock are surely crazy birds. The legs are white meat, and the breast is dark! They are one of my real favorites because of the memories they bring—wonderful days in northern Maine with Wiggie Robinson in a land filled with spruce and white birches—and the whine of chainsaws. Once the Maine Public Broadcasting people wanted to have Wiggie, his dogs, my husband and me on television without the sound of chainsaws in the air. If you've ever been to northern Maine in the fall, you know there is no escaping the sound, except maybe in downtown Bangor. No matter how far off the roads you go, someone is out there, over the next ridge, chainsawing firewood for the winter. The buzz of chainsaws always reminds me of woodcock, and here is a great recipe for them. Quail, dove or snipe can also be used.

Woodcock, Dove or Snipe Amandine

6 woodcock, or 12 dove
  or snipe, split down
  back
¼ cup flour
  Salt and pepper

4 tablespoons butter
½ cup white table wine
2 tablespoons lemon
  juice
¼ cup blanched, sliced
  almonds

Dust birds in flour seasoned with salt and pepper. Melt butter in a heavy skillet or electric frypan and sauté birds until nicely browned. Add wine and lemon juice. Cover and continue cooking slowly for 15 to 20 minutes. Add almonds and cook for 5 to 10 minutes longer or until birds are fork tender.

(Allow 2 quail or woodcock per serving; 4 dove or snipe)

Curried Rail or Woodcock

This curry-flavored recipe is excellent with rail birds, woodcock, dove or snipe.

4 clapper rails or woodcock, split down back
2 tablespoons butter
1 teaspoon instant minced onion

1 tablespoon flour
1 can (10³/₄ ounces) chicken broth
1 teaspoon curry powder
Salt to taste

Melt butter in skillet or electric frypan and brown birds, breast side down. Turn and brown on opposite side. Remove birds from skillet. To drippings in skillet add instant minced onion and flour. Mix well and then gradually add chicken broth, stirring constantly. Add curry powder and salt. Return birds to skillet, cover, and simmer for 15 to 20 minutes or until fork tender.

(Allow 2 birds per serving)

Quail

Any mention of "birds" in a general store south of the Mason-Dixon Line refers to bobwhite quail. So many corner crossroads, now isolated by the Interstates, retain the rural flavor of bygone days, along with shelves filled with such staples as sorghum syrup, chewing tobacco and shotgun shells.

Bobwhite quail are probably my favorite bird. There's nothing more wonderful than seeing both our Brittany Spaniels on solid point and wondering whether a huge covey will suddenly go rocketing away. Sometimes it's a single or a double that gets up, and once in a while I see a cottontail rabbit sneaking off. Dogs will point rabbits, that's for certain! And while old timers can have a fit if you shoot a rabbit in front of their dogs, it doesn't bother our Britts at all. They go right back to finding birds.

Quail make wonderful hunting for many reasons: the weather, the fall leaves, the need for skillful shooting. Surely they have the most delicate flavor, which makes them versatile, as in the following dish.

Zesty Quail in Skillet

6 quail, split down back
2 tablespoons butter
2 tablespoons cream
   sherry

$^1/_2$ cup soy sauce
1 can (8 ounces) tomato
   sauce
$^1/_2$ cup sugar

Melt butter in a heavy skillet or an electric frypan. Place quail in skillet, breast side up. Cook quail, covered, at medium to medium high heat for 10 minutes. Combine remaining ingredients in small saucepan and bring to a boil, stirring until sugar dissolves. Pour this sauce over quail and simmer, covered, for 15 minutes. There is no need to salt and pepper as soy sauce contains adequate seasoning.

(Allow 2 birds per serving)

Quail Tahitian

Another excellent way of preparing quail is with an oven cooking bag. If you don't want to clean up when company is gone, a cooking bag guarantees no mess. The gravy makes itself in the bag, and your roasting pan won't even need wiping.

1 tablespoon flour	1 teaspoon ginger
6 quail, split down back	1 teaspoon soy sauce
1 can (6 ounces) frozen pineapple-orange concentrate, thawed*	2 tablespoons butter

Shake 1 tablespoon flour in an oven cooking bag and place bag in a 2-inch deep roasting pan. Place quail in bag, breast side up. Combine fruit concentrate, ginger and soy sauce; pour over quail. Dot birds with butter. Close bag with twist tie and make 6 ½-inch slits in top of bag. Roast in a 350° oven for 1 hour. Split bag open and baste quail with sauce. Turn oven to 425°, and brown birds for 10 to 15 minutes. Serve with gravy from bag.

(Allow 2 birds per serving)

*Or use ½ 6-ounce can each of pineapple concentrate and orange concentrate.

Quail Casserole

Perhaps you'd like to bake quail in a casserole for that special gourmet touch. If so, here's a fabulous way to do it.

6 to 8 quail, split down back
Salt
6 tablespoons butter, divided
Paprika
1/2 pound mushrooms
1 can (16 ounces) artichoke hearts, drained (optional)
2 tablespoons flour
2/3 cup chicken broth
3 tablespoons cream sherry

Sprinkle quail with salt. Melt 4 tablespoons butter in a large skillet. Place quail, skin side down, in skillet and brown on both sides. Remove quail from skillet; place in a large, deep casserole and sprinkle with paprika. Place artichoke hearts between quail. Add 2 more tablespoons butter to skillet and sauté whole mushrooms for just a few minutes until browned. Add 2 tablespoons flour to mushrooms in skillet; stir and then add chicken broth gradually, stirring constantly. Cook for a few minutes and then stir in sherry. Salt and pepper this gravy to taste. Pour the mushrooms and gravy over the quail. Cover casserole and place in a 350° oven for 1 hour or until birds are fork tender.

(Allow 2 birds per serving)

Pigeon

Often on abandoned farms, and sometimes where farmers want to get rid of them, you may have the chance to shoot some barnyard pigeons. You might also find plenty of them at your next dove shoot. You should ask permission to hunt if you are on private property or suspect they are someone's tame birds. These pigeons, actually European rock doves, are delicious yet tough. This means they are best cooked either in a crockpot or in a pressure cooker. Out West, there are also band-tailed pigeons, wild American birds that are comparable in size and require the same cooking methods as their European cousins. With these recipes, you can use either pigeon or quail.

Savory Pigeons for Crockpot

4 to 6 pigeons or quail
Salt
4 strips bacon
1 onion, thinly sliced
2 large carrots, thinly sliced

2 ounces mushrooms, sliced
1 bay leaf
1/4 teaspoon thyme leaves
1 tablespoon chopped parsley
1/2 cup white table wine

Salt pigeons or quail inside and out. Cook bacon until crisp; remove and chop. Fry vegetables in bacon fat until lightly colored. Transfer vegetables to crockpot and place pigeons on top of vegetables. Add cooked, chopped bacon, bay leaf, and sprinkle birds with thyme and parsley. Pour wine over all ingredients. Cover and cook on low heat for 8 to 9 hours. (Allow 2 birds per serving)

20

Pigeon in White Wine for Pressure Cooker

4 to 6 pigeons or quail
2 tablespoons fat or
  cooking oil
  Salt and pepper
$^1/_2$ cup white table wine

$^1/_2$ teaspoon instant
  chicken bouillon
$^1/_8$ teaspoon thyme leaves
1 teaspoon chopped
  parsley

Melt fat in cooker and brown birds on all sides. Season
with salt and pepper. Combine remaining ingredients and
pour over birds. Close cover securely and cook under 15
pounds of pressure for 12 minutes or longer for tougher
pigeons. Quail will only take 8 minutes. Cool cooker at
once. The delicately flavored gravy in the cooker can be
thickened if desired before serving over birds.

(Allow 2 birds per serving)

Pheasant, Partridge and Grouse

Pheasants and partridges are Eurasian birds. Yet pheasants are America's most popular game bird, and partridges, both chukar and Hungarian, flourish in some areas. In addition, we have prairie chicken, plus sharptail, ruffed, blue and spruce grouse, along with sage grouse nearly the size of a turkey.

They all add up to wonderful sport and excellent eating, although some, ruffed grouse particularly, are better than others. Pheasants, because they are naturally very dry birds, are probably the most difficult to cook properly. Over the years, more people have asked me for help in cooking pheasant than anything else. They're supposed to be delicious, and are. But they will not turn out that way unless you know which recipes work. I include the pheasant recipes here, because if a recipe works well with pheasant it will be excellent with partridge, prairie chicken and grouse as well. Being smaller, these birds take less cooking time.

When I started hunting, my very first shot was a pheasant. It fell, seemingly stone dead, and I'm still looking for it! This is why we have bird dogs today. They find the birds, point them and retrieve. Retrieving a pheasant can be a problem. Our youngest Brittany, Wiggie, tracked a wing-shot pheasant more than a half-mile this past season before finding it in a blackberry bramble thicket. Pheasants are tough birds, which is how they survive Nebraska winters and North Dakota summers. They can run at amazing speed, fly fast and far, and generally escape or scare off predators. Many a house cat, having tangled with a cock pheasant, never wants to approach one again.

Living in the open and running and flying constantly, wild pheasants accumulate little fat. This is why it is a mistake to open roast a pheasant as you would a chicken. Instead, when cooking pheasants keep them covered and moist by using a Dutch oven, aluminum foil, crockpot or oven cooking bags. Cock pheasants (it is illegal to shoot hens almost everywhere) average about two pounds each and will be done with 1¼ to 1½ hours of cooking time— slightly more than you would take for a chicken. Pheasants should be field dressed as quickly as possible. Do them at once, if you can, or during a rest break. Carrying them uncleaned for hours will not help their flavor.

Pouring a small amount of almost boiling water over a pheasant makes plucking much easier and lets you leave the skin intact to keep whatever fat there is. When freezing pheasants, be sure the body cavity is washed clean and all blood removed. Then wrap twice in freezer paper or place within two heavy freezer bags. If air cannot reach your birds, they will stay in fine condition for many months.

Most grouse and partridge are not quite as dry as pheasant, yet the same rules apply. You'll find ruffed and sharptail grouse average about a pound or slightly more, and the partridge species, chukar and Hungarian, weigh between half and three quarters of a pound. If you can obtain grouse, you're in for a really special treat. They are the most tender and delicious of all the upland birds.

Roast Chukar or Partridge with Brown Rice Stuffing

4 chukars or partridges	1/4 cup butter, melted
1 recipe Brown Rice Stuffing	Salt and pepper

Stuff birds and wrap each in a piece of heavy duty aluminum foil, sealing edges tightly. Place birds in a shallow roasting pan and bake in a 350° oven for 1 hour. Unwrap birds; brush with melted butter and bake in a 425° oven for 10 to 15 minutes or until browned. Prepare gravy from drippings. Salt and pepper to taste.

(Serve 1/2 bird per person)

Brown Rice Stuffing

1 cup brown rice	1 can (4 ounces) sliced mushrooms, drained and liquid reserved
1/4 cup butter	
1 medium onion, finely chopped	1/2 teaspoon salt
1/2 cup celery, diced	1/2 teaspoon marjoram leaves
	1/8 teaspoon pepper

Cook rice about 5 minutes less than directed on package. Melt butter in a skillet and sauté onion, celery, and mushrooms until tender. Add vegetables to cooked rice. Mix in seasonings and add mushroom liquid as needed. Mixture should be moist and hold together well.

Pheasant Oriental

Here is an absolutely delicious dish. It is always a big favorite with our guests and includes a marvelous sauce made in the oven cooking bag.

1 tablespoon flour	2 tablespoons honey
1 large or 2 small pheasant, cut up, or 3 grouse, halved	$^1/_2$ teaspoon ground ginger
Paprika	$^1/_4$ teaspoon garlic powder
$^1/_4$ cup soy sauce	1 can (4 ounces) sliced mushrooms, drained
	$^1/_3$ cup water chestnuts, sliced

Shake flour in a large size (14″ × 20″) oven cooking bag and place in a 2-inch deep roasting pan. Season pheasant pieces with paprika and place in bag. In a small bowl, combine soy sauce, honey, ginger and garlic powder; pour over pheasant in bag. Add mushrooms and water chestnuts to bag. Close bag with twist tie. Marinate in refrigerator 6 to 8 hours or overnight; turn bag once. When ready to cook, make 6 $^1/_2$- inch slits in top of bag. Cook in 350° oven for 1 to 1$^1/_4$ hours or until pheasant is tender. Cook grouse 1 hour or less. Serve sauce over birds.

(1 large pheasant serves 3)

Braised Pheasant in Crockpot

If you are going to be busy during the day and want to
return to an outstanding meal, here is one guaranteed to
please.

1 pheasant, quartered	1 tablespoon grated
3 tablespoons butter	orange peel
6 stalks celery, cut into 1-	1 can (10$^{1}/_{2}$ ounces)
inch pieces	consommé
$^{1}/_{4}$ pound mushrooms,	2 tablespoons cream
sliced	sherry
$^{1}/_{2}$ cup orange juice	Salt and pepper to
	taste
	1 orange for garnish

Brown pheasant pieces in melted butter and place to one
side of skillet. Lightly fry celery and mushrooms. Transfer
these vegetables to crockpot, placing pheasant on top. Add
remaining ingredients. Begin cooking on HIGH and after
$^{1}/_{2}$ hour turn to LOW and continue cooking for 7 to 8
hours. Garnish with orange sections.

(Serves 3)

Baked Pheasant or Grouse with Apples

Especially with pheasant, apples always add a pleasant flavor and enable you to keep your birds moist during preparation.

1 pheasant, quartered or 2 grouse, halved	1 teaspoon sugar
4 tablespoons butter, divided	3 tablespoons cream or half and half
4 medium-sized cooking apples, peeled and chopped	Salt and pepper to taste

Melt 3 tablespoons butter in a skillet and place pheasant pieces skin side down first; brown on all sides. Remove pheasant and add 1 tablespoon more butter to drippings in skillet. Sauté chopped apples in skillet and add 1 teaspoon of sugar. When apples are a little softened, place them in bottom of a casserole. Put pheasant pieces on top of apples with juices from pan. Pour cream over the pheasant and add salt and pepper. Cover casserole and bake in a 350° oven for 1 to 1½ hours or until meat is fork tender.

(Serves 3)

Stir-Fried Sweet and Sour Pheasant

Sometimes the gang drops in unexpectedly. That's when you will appreciate this first-rate stir-fry recipe. Of course you can substitute two grouse or partridges, but it's really made to order for quickly prepared pheasant.

1 whole pheasant, boned, skinned and cut diagonally in bite-size pieces	1 can (8³/₄ ounces) pineapple chunks in heavy syrup
2 tablespoons cooking oil	¹/₂ cup chicken broth
²/₃ cup diagonally sliced celery	¹/₄ cup sugar
	1 tablespoon cornstarch
¹/₂ cup sliced green onions	¹/₂ teaspoon powdered ginger
1 can (8¹/₂ ounces) water chestnuts, sliced	2 tablespoons vinegar
1 package (6 ounces) frozen Chinese or snow pea pods	2 tablespoons soy sauce

In wok (or electric skillet or frypan on stove top), heat oil on high setting. Add pheasant and stir fry for 5 minutes. Add celery, onions and water chestnuts and stir fry 2 minutes more. Then add pea pods, pineapple chunks with syrup, and broth; stir fry 2 more minutes. In small bowl, mix together sugar, cornstarch, ginger, vinegar and soy sauce; pour over pheasant and vegetables. Reduce heat, stir and simmer until thickened, about 2 minutes. Serve over rice or Chinese noodles.

(Serves 4)

Note: Don't overcook; vegetables should be bright green and slightly crunchy.

Pheasant or Grouse Pie

My family is especially fond of pot pies. They can be prepared ahead and then placed in your oven—a convection
oven works well—to brown and heat through just before
serving.

1 pheasant or 2 grouse, ruffed or sharptailed	3 tablespoons butter
1 onion, quartered	3 tablespoons flour
4 whole carrots, peeled	3/4 cup stock
1 bay leaf	1/2 cup milk
1 teaspoon salt	3 tablespoons Madeira or cream sherry (dry sherry lacks flavor)
1 package (10 ounces) frozen peas, cooked	Salt
	1 pie crust

Skin and quarter pheasant or grouse, place in a deep kettle
and cover with water. Add onion, carrots, bay leaf and salt.
Simmer, covered, for 1 hour or until meat is fork tender.
Strain stock and reserve for use in sauce. Remove meat
from bones and cut into bite-size pieces. Slice cooked carrots and place meat and carrots in a 2-quart casserole.
Cook peas until just tender and add to casserole. For
sauce, melt butter and blend in flour. Slowly stir in stock
and milk. Add Madeira or sherry and salt to taste. Pour
this sauce over the casserole. Make your favorite pie crust
or use a frozen pie shell and cover the casserole, securing
crust to the rim of the dish. Slit crust and bake in a 425°
oven 25 to 30 minutes until crust is a golden brown and
sauce bubbles.

(Serves 4)

Wild Turkey

Now it's time to discuss the one upland bird we've left out. So let's talk turkey! Wild turkey should be cleaned immediately after shooting. Upon returning home, pluck bird, wash out cavity well, and remove oil sacs at the base of the back near the tail. Remove any badly shot areas.

Wild turkey can be cooked the same as a domestic one. The meat will be leaner than a turkey you would buy. Therefore, it should be roasted either covered with aluminum foil or in an oven cooking bag to keep the meat from being too dry. Just follow the turkey roasting instructions that come with the heavy duty foil or with the turkey-size oven cooking bags.

One difference between domestic and wild turkeys, of course, is in the size. An average wild turkey will weigh from 8 to 18 pounds and provide more leftovers than you've seen in a long while. Here's a great recipe to take care of this money-saving situation.

Wild Turkey Pie

Filling

2 cups cooked wild
turkey, chopped
1 package (10 ounces)
frozen mixed
vegetables, cooked and
drained

$^1/_2$ teaspoon salt
$^1/_8$ teaspoon pepper
1 can (10$^3/_4$ ounces)
condensed cream of
chicken soup

Pastry

1$^1/_2$ cups all-purpose flour
1 teaspoon salt
$^1/_2$ cup shortening

$^3/_4$ cup quick or old
fashioned oats,
uncooked
8 to 9 tablespoons cold
water

Preheat oven to 375°. Combine filling ingredients and set
aside. To make crust, sift together flour and salt. Cut in
shortening until mixture resembles coarse crumbs. Add
oats and mix lightly. Add water, a tablespoon at a time,
stirring until pastry forms a ball. Divide dough in half. Roll
out half of the dough on lightly floured board or canvas to
form a 13-inch circle. Fit loosely into a 9-inch pie plate. Fill
with turkey filling. Roll out other half of dough to form a
12-inch circle. Cut slits for steam to escape and place over
filling. Trim, turn under edges and flute. Bake about 40
minutes or until top crust is golden brown.

(Serves 4)

31

Upland Bird Dinner for Oven Menu

BARBARA'S HOT CHEESE DIP/DIPPING CHIPS

ANY UPLAND BIRD RECIPE FOR OVEN

SHERRIED RICE

VEGETABLE MEDLEY

PORT CRANBERRY SAUCE

SWEET POTATO MUFFINS

ICE CREAM WITH CHESTNUT SAUCE

LEMON COOKIES

Note: By preparing the rice and vegetable in the oven along with the game dish, you'll be saving energy.

See Accompaniment Section for recipes.

Waterfowl Cookery

When it comes to cooking, wild waterfowl are quite different from domestic ducks and geese. The difference is that any bird that flies thousands of miles each year is going to be tougher and far less fatty than one that is penned and never exercises its wings.

Ducks, and geese too, fly at almost unbelievable speeds. That is why they are such a challenge to us earthbound creatures who go forth in freezing rain or subzero cold hoping to secure a wild duck dinner, often without success. On one of our typical duck hunts, we arose long before dawn, saw plenty of waterfowl passing overhead while setting out decoys before legal shooting hours, and then nothing the rest of the day except God's blue heaven. Our best success has always been with the cold rain soaking through my storm suit, or when it is so cold and windy my hands threaten to drop off. Ducks and geese never get cold or wet, since they're insulated by the warmest substance known, downy feathers.

As with all game birds, waterfowl should be opened and cleaned out as soon as possible. Always bring a cooler with ice and a plastic bag for holding the delicious hearts and livers, which are wonderful sautéed or in a paté.

Plucking is a chore no matter how you do it. There are now some excellent machines on the market. We've hunted with Bob Mayo of Richmond, Virginia, who owns one,

33

and it was a treat to pluck a duck in less time than it takes to tell about it. The easiest way for most of us to pluck birds is to cut off the wings and then either hang the dressed waterfowl in a cool place or keep them refrigerated for a day or so. This makes plucking less difficult. Some people melt paraffin in boiling water, plunge the duck, and then rip feathers off after the wax congeals. If you have the hands and arms of a wrestler or gymnast, this is the quickest way of all.

After you've struggled through the plucking process, clean out the body cavity again and run cool water through it, washing out all blood and residue. Smaller ducks, such as widgeon, can be cut up the backbone with kitchen shears to simplify cleaning.

To prepare waterfowl for freezing, place them in two heavy duty plastic freezer bags. Or you can double wrap them in freezer paper with all seams taped. Because of their size, you'll have to use freezer paper with geese.

The worst mistake with wild waterfowl is to open roast them. As already mentioned, they have very little fat, so roasting makes them tough and dry, unless you use oven cooking bags or aluminum foil. You can also cook waterfowl in your crockpot or cut them up for braising in a skillet or heavy pot.

Scoters, coots and other sea ducks *must* be cooked in a crockpot. It is the only way to eliminate their strong taste. But don't throw these ducks away! They won't need plucking, since you can simply cut off and skin the breasts before discarding the carcass. All the meat is on the breasts. With a crockpot, you can turn the breasts of "skunk heads" and other supposedly inedible ducks into excellent, well-flavored table fare. I personally draw the line at mergansers. Maybe I'll try one someday and see what happens. Meanwhile, I feel scoters, coots, buffleheads and so forth are enough.

For large ducks and geese, I prefer an oven cooking bag. It helps you brown these birds nicely without drying them out, and you get an ample bonus in gravy.

Wild Duck

Orange Brandied Wild Duck

2 medium or large ducks	½ cup frozen orange
Salt	juice concentrate,
1 large orange,	thawed
quartered	¼ cup brandy
2 small onions	2 tablespoons brandy
1 tablespoon flour	

Salt ducks inside and out. Place 2 orange quarters and 1 onion in each cavity. If ducks are fatty, prick skin with a sharp fork. Place a large, (14″ × 20″), oven cooking bag in a 2-inch deep roasting pan. Add flour to bag along with orange juice concentrate and brandy. Stir mixture with a plastic or wooden spoon. Place ducks in bag, close with twist tie and make 6 ½-inch slits on top of bag. Place in a 375° oven for 1¼ to 1½ hours, or until tender. Skim off any fat and add 2 tablespoons brandy to gravy. Heat but do not boil. Cut ducks in half and garnish platter with thin slices of orange and a teaspoon of currant jelly in center of each slice.

(Serves 4)

Roasted Duck in Foil

Another more traditional method is to roast your ducks in foil, and then open and brown them just before serving.

1 mallard or similar type duck	¼ cup orange juice
1 teaspoon salt	1 tablespoon lemon juice
1 teaspoon ginger	1 teaspoon orange peel
1 teaspoon ground basil	⅛ teaspoon dry mustard
½ cup honey	⅛ teaspoon salt
2 tablespoons butter	1 orange, quartered
	Cornstarch

Combine 1 teaspoon salt, ginger and basil; rub half of mixture on inside of duck. Mix honey, butter, orange juice, lemon juice, orange peel, mustard and ⅛ teaspoon salt together and heat until butter melts. Place orange quarters in duck cavity. Pour half of honey mixture in duck cavity. Rub remaining seasoning mixture on outside. Place bird on a large piece of heavy duty aluminum foil and pour remaining honey mixture over duck. Bring foil around duck and seal edges with double fold. Roast in a 425° oven for 1 to 1½ hours or until tender. Unwrap, baste with drippings and bake 10 to 15 minutes longer or until brown. Place duck on a hot platter to keep warm. For gravy, pour drippings into a small saucepan, skim off any grease and thicken with cornstarch dissolved in small amount of water.

(Serves 2)

Braised Duck

With utility bills at record highs nearly everywhere, all of us want to save energy and dollars. Here's an excellent way to prepare wild ducks by braising them in a heavy skillet or electric frypan.

2 wild ducks, halved	1 teaspoon instant
1 cup red or rosé table	parsley flakes
wine	1/4 teaspoon marjoram
1/4 cup brandy	leaves
1 bay leaf	1/2 teaspoon thyme leaves
1 teaspoon instant	1/4 teaspoon ground
minced onion	allspice
1/2 teaspoon salt	2 tablespoons fat or
	cooking oil

Place duck halves in an oblong glass or ceramic dish. Combine next 9 ingredients and pour over duck. Cover with a piece of plastic wrap and marinate in the refrigerator for at least 5 hours. Put fat in a heavy skillet or electric frypan. When hot, add pieces of duck and brown well on all sides. Remove bay leaf from marinade and pour over duck in skillet. Cover and simmer for about 1 1/2 hours or until tender. Add more liquid, chicken broth or wine, during cooking if needed. To serve, remove duck to a hot platter. Thicken sauce slightly and pour over meat.

(Serves 4)

Duck a la Terry

My neighbor, Terry Carter, is a lovely person whose husband spends much time supplying her with wild ducks and geese. She's developed a wonderful way of preparing ducks with her pressure cooker.

2 ducks, 1 to 2 pounds each	1/2 cup Burgundy
1 apple, halved	2 tablespoons chopped onion
1 onion, halved	1 small bay leaf
1 cup water	Salt and pepper to taste
2 tablespoons butter	1 can (4 ounces) mushrooms, drained
2 tablespoons flour	
1 cup chicken broth	

Place halves of apple and onion in the cavity of each duck. Place ducks in pressure cooker, add water and cook under 15 pounds pressure for 15 minutes or until tender. Cool cooker at once. Discard apple and onion. Cut large ducks in quarters and smaller ones in half. In a skillet, melt butter and brown duck pieces. Transfer browned pieces to a baking dish. Blend flour into butter in skillet; add chicken broth, Burgundy, chopped onion, bay leaf, salt and pepper. Cook, stirring constantly, till bubbly. Add mushrooms and pour over ducks. Cover and bake in a 350° oven for 15 minutes or until thoroughly heated.

(Allow 1/2 duck per serving)

Wild Goose

When 12 years old and a Boy Scout, Artie asked me for a
pheasant to take along on an overnight hike. He didn't
want to cook the regular fare of hamburgers, hot dogs and
baked beans. We compromised on a Cornish game hen,
and what do you suppose happened? The scoutmaster, a
retired cavalry colonel, appointed our son as his personal
cook! With that beginning, it's not surprising that today
Art is a successful chef with great recipes for everything,
including wild goose.

Art's Roasted Goose

1 wild goose	1 cup white table wine
1 apple, quartered	1 bay leaf
1 onion, quartered	5 peppercorns
1/4 cup flour	Cornstarch
1 cup natural apple juice	
or cider	

Place apple and onion quarters in cavity of goose. Add flour to a large (14″ × 20″) oven cooking bag and shake. Place bag in a 2-inch deep roasting pan. Add juice and wine to bag along with bay leaf and peppercorns. Stir contents of bag with a wooden or plastic spoon until well blended. Place goose in bag and close with tie. Make 6 1/2-inch slits in top of bag. Roast in a 375° oven for 2 to 2 1/2 hours or until tender. If goose needs more browning, then split bag up the middle and expose breast of bird. Strain gravy and remove grease. To thicken gravy, add cornstarch dissolved in small amount of water. Season with salt to taste. If a sweeter gravy is desired, then add some currant jelly and a little ground cloves. Gravy can also be darkened by using Kitchen Bouquet.

Note: Two large ducks can be substituted for a goose in this recipe. Roast ducks for 1 1/2 to 2 hours.

(Serves 4 to 6 depending on size of goose)

Terry's Tough Old Goose

Some wild geese are "wilder" than others! This is especially true with Canada geese, which can live to be more than 70 years old and become tougher with each passing season. You can tell an older goose because it is much easier to pluck, and, when the outer feathers are removed, there's very little down and no pinfeathers. Terry Carter and her pressure cooker united to discover a good way to prepare these birds.

1 old wild goose, 4 to 5
  pounds
  Apple, onion, and
  celery for cavity

1 can (10³/₄ ounces)
  golden mushroom
  soup
¹/₂ cup white table wine

Stuff goose cavity with apple, onion and celery. Place goose in cooker and add the amount of water needed for your pressure cooker. Cook under 15 pounds pressure for 30 minutes or until tender. Reduce pressure at once. Remove goose from cooker and, when cooled, pull meat gently away from thigh and legs. Remove both portions of breast trying to keep them intact. Slice breast meat diagonally and place all meat in a casserole. Combine soup and wine and pour over meat. Cover and place in a 350° oven until thoroughly heated.

(Serves 4 to 6 depending on size of goose)

Goose Soup

Do not throw away your geese carcasses, as they make superb soup. It will resemble turkey soup and be a meal in itself. If you have only one carcass, then just cut this recipe in half.

2 geese carcasses
2 tablespoons salt
12 cups water
4 stalks celery, cut in ½-inch pieces
6 carrots, sliced
1 large onion, sliced
1 can (1 pound) tomatoes with liquid, cut up
1 can (8 ounces) tomato sauce
1 cup brown rice
Leftover gravy, up to 1 cup

Put carcasses and any leftover meat into a large, heavy pot or in a deep electric one. Add salt and water. Cover and bring to a boil; reduce heat and simmer for 1½ to 2 hours or until meat falls off carcass. Remove any meat left on bones and return to soup pot. Add rest of ingredients and continue cooking until rice and vegetables are tender.

(Serves 10 to 12)

Sea Duck

And now we reach scoters and the other sea ducks mentioned earlier. There's a long season, a large bag limit, and far too much waste of these wildfowl. They are not brightly colored or pretty but are fine eating if done in the crockpot. Don't believe those tales about throwing the duck away and eating the pot! Try them this way, and use the same recipe for any very lean wild ducks. Remember with scoters and coot you use only the breasts. Lean wild ducks of other species can be split in half.

Scoter in Crockpot

4 to 6 skinned scoter breasts	1 tablespoon soy sauce
Salt	1 teaspoon grated orange rind
¹/₂ cup orange juice	¹/₂ teaspoon ginger
¹/₄ cup port wine	¹/₄ cup honey

Soak skinned scoter breasts in salt water for an hour unless you plan on freezing them—then *do not* soak in salt water. Place breasts upright inside crockpot. Mix all ingredients together in a small bowl and pour over duck breasts. Cover and cook in your crockpot on low heat for 8 to 9 hours. Don't be alarmed if you notice an odd odor during the cooking process. This means that by the time the breasts are cooked, the strong, natural flavor of these ducks will have escaped during the slow cooking, leaving the scoters delicious.

(Allow 1 breast per serving)

Holiday Game Dinner Menu

HARVEST SOUP

PHEASANT, DUCK OR GOOSE

BANANA SWEET POTATOES

SPINACH WITH PECANS

CRANBERRY MOUSSE

HERBED CHEESE MUFFINS

BRANDIED APPLE CAKE

See Accompaniment Section for recipes.

Small Game Recipes

When I was a child, my parents gave me an archery set. It came complete with target and rubber tipped arrows and gave me visions of becoming another William Tell or Robin Hood. After all, why couldn't a girl do what they did?

Lacking a Greenwood Forest filled with deer and other exciting game, and knowing no one who would pose for me with apple on head, I stalked robins and starlings in the yard. The Audubon Society would approve of my results. I couldn't hit anything! It finally dawned on me that shooting birds with bow and arrow is very difficult.

Our native Indian tribes had known this fact for centuries. That's why they ate so much small game. Rabbits, raccoons, beavers, squirrels and woodchucks cannot spread their wings and fly away. Nonmigratory, they could always be depended on to provide a meal.

All our native small fur bearers are tasty morsels. Beaver is especially delicious. Maybe you've read of mountain men sitting about gnawing on beaver tails. If so, let me tell you that there is nothing to a beaver tail but bone and gristle, but the animal itself tastes much like tender beefsteak. If a practical joker recommends beaver tail, let him try it!

Woodchucks, called ground hogs in many areas, are

closely related to squirrels, and the younger ones are quite good. Granted, few animals are homelier, yet they are cleaner than a chicken, and it's a shame to see them wasted. As for squirrels, they are wonderful. Because they're tough, they need to be cooked by a moist method.

All these animals, including rabbits and squirrels, should be field dressed at once. Otherwise, you risk developing a strong gamy flavor. Skin them when you arrive home, being sure to wear gloves if you are skinning rabbits. Gloves protect you against tularemia, or rabbit fever, and against bites from fleas, which many rabbits harbor year round.

Split your squirrels and rabbits up the breast bone with kitchen shears and save rabbit hearts, livers and kidneys to prepare just like chicken livers and hearts. Then wash these animals out with cool water and cut away any badly bruised areas before wiping dry with paper toweling. For the right size portions, cut squirrels in half and rabbits in quarters.

Freezer burn can be avoided by double wrapping with good freezer paper, sealing all seams, or using both an inner and an outer plastic freezer bag to insure against puncturing by sharp bones.

If you like everything fried, you can fry squirrels and rabbits too. Because they are tough, you'll first need to parboil them or braise them in a skillet after browning. *Never* broil or dry roast squirrels or rabbits. It will remove all moisture and leave them terribly tough.

Squirrel and Rabbit

Lee Carter, a high school boy who lives nearby, is a dedicated squirrel hunter who brings me all he shoots—cleaned, skinned and ready for the freezer. He loves to come over and help us eat the squirrels that his skill provided. That's when I take out my crockpot. It's excellent for small, tough animals like these.

Squirrel or Rabbit in Crockpot

3 to 6 squirrels, cut in half, or 1 to 2 rabbits, cut into serving pieces
1/4 cup firmly packed brown sugar
1/4 cup soy sauce
3 tablespoons lemon or lime juice
1/4 cup water
1/4 teaspoon garlic powder
1/4 teaspoon ground ginger

Place squirrel halves or rabbit pieces in crockpot. Mix all ingredients in a small bowl and pour over meat. Cover and cook on low heat for 7 to 8 hours. To thicken gravy, use either flour or cornstarch mixed with water. Cook on high until thickened.

Slow-Baked Squirrel

Another way to enjoy squirrels is to bake them very slowly in your oven with this recipe.

4 to 6 squirrels, cut in half
Flour
Beef or vegetable fat for browning
1 bay leaf

$^1/_2$ package onion soup mix
1 can (10$^3/_4$ ounces) golden mushroom soup
$^1/_2$ soup can milk

Roll squirrel pieces in flour and then brown in hot fat in skillet. After browning, remove pieces from skillet and place in a deep oven casserole with cover. In a small bowl, mix rest of ingredients and pour mixture over squirrels. Cover and cook in a 325° oven for 1$^1/_2$ to 2 hours or until tender.

(Allow 1 squirrel per serving)

Squirrel Pot Pie

My husband says that Squirrel Pot Pie is probably his favorite meal. He loves to tell friends that it's chicken pot pie and then get them all annoyed when he points out they've been enjoying squirrel. It is very good, and you can cook your squirrels a day ahead in your pressure cooker. This makes it easy to separate bones and meat. If you prefer, they can be stewed until fork tender before boning.

6 squirrels, cut in half
1 onion, quartered
  A few celery tops
1 bay leaf
4 tablespoons butter or margarine
4 tablespoons flour
1 cup squirrel stock
1 cup milk

3 tablespoons Madeira or cream sherry
  Salt to taste
1 can (1 pound) whole carrots
1 can (1 pound) whole potatoes
1 pie crust

Place onion, celery tops and bay leaf in bottom of pressure cooker. Place squirrel pieces on top of vegetables and add 1 cup of water. Cook under 15 pounds of pressure for 20 minutes. Cool cooker immediately. Strain stock and reserve for use in sauce. Remove meat from bones and leave in bite-size pieces. For sauce, melt butter in a medium saucepan and blend in flour. Slowly stir in stock and milk. Add Madeira or sherry and salt to taste. Place squirrel meat, carrots and potatoes in a casserole and pour sauce over ingredients. Make your favorite pie crust or use a frozen pie shell to cover casserole. Be sure that the crust is secured to rim of casserole. Make slits in crust and bake in a preheated 425° oven for 25 to 30 minutes or until crust is brown and sauce bubbles.

(Serves 4 to 6)

Squirrel Brunswich Stew

Brunswick Stew is a traditional squirrel dish throughout the South. As with the pot pie, squirrels should be pre-cooked and all bones removed before preparing this excellent dish.

4 to 6 squirrels, cut in half
2 teaspoons salt
2 cups water
1 onion, quartered
1 bay leaf
2 tablespoons dehydrated soup greens
1 can (10³/₄ ounces) condensed tomato soup

3 medium potatoes, sliced thin
1 tablespoon sugar
Favorite seasonings to taste
1 can (8 ounces) whole kernel corn
1 can (8 ounces) lima beans
2 tablespoons butter

Place squirrel pieces in pressure cooker and sprinkle with salt. Add water, onion, bay leaf and dehydrated soup greens. Cover and cook under 15 pounds pressure for 20 minutes. Reduce pressure instantly and let squirrel pieces cool. Remove meat from bones and leave in bite-size pieces. Place meat and stock in a large, deep pot and add soup, potatoes and sugar and cook until potatoes are tender. Then add corn, lima beans and butter. Cook 5 minutes or until hot.

(Serves 4 to 6)

Squirrel Barbecue in Pressure Cooker

When properly prepared, squirrel closely resembles turkey or chicken, and this barbecue-type recipe will let you make the most of its delicious flavor.

4 squirrels, cut in half
1 teaspoon dry mustard
1 teaspoon chili powder
1/2 cup water
1/4 cup catsup
3 tablespoons chopped onion

2 tablespoons light molasses
2 tablespoons lemon juice
1/4 teaspoon oregano
1/2 teaspoon salt

Combine dry mustard and chili powder and sprinkle over squirrel pieces. Place squirrel halves in cooker. Combine remaining ingredients and pour over squirrel. Close cover securely and cook under 15 pounds pressure for 20 minutes or 10 minutes if squirrels are very young and small. Cool cooker at once. Thicken liquid in cooker and serve over squirrels.

(Allow 1 squirrel per serving)

Gingersnap Rabbit for Pressure Cooker

Here's one of my favorite recipes for rabbit.

1 rabbit, cut into serving
  pieces
Flour
1 teaspoon salt
3 tablespoons fat
1 cup water
¼ cup vinegar

1 onion, sliced
1 bay leaf
1 cup (8 ounce carton)
  dairy sour cream
5 to 8 gingersnaps,
  crumbled

Dredge rabbit pieces in flour to which salt has been added. Brown rabbit in hot fat in cooker. Add water, vinegar, onion and bay leaf. Close cover securely and cook under 15 pounds pressure for 20 minutes or until tender. Reduce pressure instantly. Add sour cream and 5 crumbled gingersnaps. Cook until thick and smooth, stirring constantly. If sauce is not thick enough, add rest of crumbled gingersnaps.

(Serves 3)

Apple Cider Rabbit in Crockpot

This crockpot method is a fine way to prepare rabbits. It can also be used with muskrats, which are smaller and only require 6 or 7 hours of cooking on low heat.

1 rabbit, cut into serving pieces
Salt and pepper
2 to 3 tablespoons beef fat or lard
1 large onion, sliced
1 tablespoon flour
1 cup apple cider
1/4 cup raisins

Dry rabbit pieces thoroughly and season with salt and pepper. Heat fat in a skillet and fry onion until lightly browned. Transfer to crockpot. Brown rabbit pieces on all sides and add to crockpot. Drain all but 1 tablespoon of fat in skillet; stir in flour and cook for a minute. Add cider and raisins and bring to a boil, stirring constantly. Then pour sauce over rabbit, cover and cook on low heat for 8 to 9 hours.

(Serves 3)

Rabbit Pie

I mentioned Squirrel Pot Pie. Here's a slightly different version for rabbit. It gives you a complete, wholesome meal.

1 rabbit, cut into serving pieces	4 carrots, peeled and diced
Flour	3 potatoes, peeled and diced
Salt and pepper	
3 tablespoons butter	Rich biscuit dough crust
1 onion, sliced	

Dredge rabbit pieces in flour to which salt and pepper have been added. Melt butter in a deep skillet or an electric frypan and brown pieces of meat. Cover with water and simmer, covered, for 1 to 1 1/2 hours or until rabbit is tender. Add onion, carrots and potatoes to skillet and cook until vegetables are done. Stew gravy should now be thick enough, but if not, thicken with a flour and water paste. Pour stew in a greased, 2-quart baking dish and cover with a rich biscuit dough. Be sure dough is secured to rim of dish and then make several slits in crust. Bake in a 400° oven for 25 to 30 minutes or until crust is brown and gravy bubbles.

(Serves 3)

Sweet and Sour Rabbit for Pressure Cooker

Whenever we have Sweet and Sour Rabbit, there are no leftovers. This same recipe works well with beaver, raccoon or woodchuck.

1 rabbit, cut into servings pieces	2 tablespoons sugar
2 tablespoons beef fat or shortening	1 teaspoon salt
1 onion, thinly sliced	2 tablespoons chopped parsley
1 teaspoon ginger	2 tablespoons soy sauce
2 teaspoons dry mustard	2 tablespoons vinegar
	$^1/_2$ cup water

Heat cooker, add fat and sauté onion lightly. Remove onion. Brown rabbit pieces on all sides. Combine remaining ingredients and pour over rabbit; add onion. Close cover securely and cook under 15 pounds pressure for 20 minutes or until tender. Cool cooker at once. Serve liquid in cooker over rabbit. This gravy can be thickened if desired.

(Serves 3)

Raccoon, Beaver and Woodchuck

On the Eastern Shore and other rural areas, you can buy skinned, dressed raccoons at general stores and filling stations. Or you may have a coon hunter in your family. I've tried it, but running through the woods after dark is a sport I can easily do without. All my night time coon hunts were fiascos. Being scratched by briars, frozen in subarctic temperatures and finding yourself across the river from where hounds are baying with no way to reach them except wading in water running too fast to freeze, is enjoyable only in retrospect.

Our Brittany, Diane, had better luck. She treed a coon while hunting pheasant in Nebraska after the coon hounds had drawn a blank the night before. Of course I was proud of her. How many bird dogs can produce a raccoon along with plenty of quail and pheasant?

After shooting or trapping, raccoons must be opened and cleaned immediately. Skin them, split up the breast bone and remove blood and scent glands. Cut away all bruised or damaged areas and remove as much surface fat as you can. Be sure to double wrap raccoons when freezing them. Quarter them first.

If you have never dined on a small or medium size raccoon, you have a treat in store. You'll find the flavor reminiscent of pork but with a firmer texture. Besides, raccoons and beavers aren't as active as rabbits or squirrels and are therefore tender enough for oven roasting. The following oven cooking bag recipe is excellent with both raccoon and beaver.

Roast Oriental Raccoon

1 medium to large raccoon, quartered with rib area removed
1 tablespoon flour
$1/4$ cup lemon juice
$1/4$ cup soy sauce
$1/2$ cup cream sherry
2 tablespoons catsup
$1/4$ teaspoon garlic salt
1 tablespoon sugar
$1/2$ teaspoon ground ginger

Shake 1 tablespoon flour into a large (14″ × 20″) oven cooking bag and place bag in a 2-inch deep roasting pan. Trim all surface fat from raccoon and place pieces of meat in bag. Combine remaining ingredients and pour into bag. Close bag with twist tie and gently turn several times to coat meat. Refrigerate 3 to 4 hours or overnight. Remove from refrigerator and make 6 $1/2$-inch slits in top of bag. Cook in a 350° oven for $1 1/2$ hours or until meat is tender and thermometer reads 170°.

(Serves 4)

Sherried Raccoon for Crockpot

Obviously, I'm a believer in the crockpot. It's a very good means of preparing raccoon, beaver and woodchuck. This recipe works with all three animals.

1 medium size raccoon, quartered with surface fat removed
$1/4$ cup honey
3 tablespoons vinegar
1 cup stock or chicken bouillon

3 tablespoons cream sherry
2 tablespoons soy sauce
$1/4$ teaspoon garlic salt

Place raccoon pieces in crockpot. In a small bowl mix rest of ingredients together and pour over raccoon pieces. Cover and cook on low heat for 7 to 8 hours. Remove any grease from liquid before thickening it for gravy. The raccoon will brown nicely during cooking, and the meat will be tender and delicious.

(Serves 4)

Raccoon Chasseur for Pressure Cooker

Pressure cooking saves time and energy. The following recipe will give you mouth watering raccoon, beaver or woodchuck.

1 medium size raccoon, quartered with surface fat removed

1 can (1 pound) tomatoes, drained and chopped

1 onion, chopped
Salt and pepper

1 can (10³/₄ ounces) golden mushroom soup

1 tablespoon prepared mustard

¹/₂ cup sliced sweet gherkin pickles

Brown raccoon pieces in cooker using fat if necessary. Remove raccoon pieces and sauté onion in fat until lightly browned. Pour off any fat and return meat to cooker. Add salt and pepper. Mix soup and mustard together; pour over raccoon. Add chopped tomatoes and sliced pickles to cooker. Close lid securely and cook under 15 pounds pressure for 20 minutes or until tender. Cool cooker at once. Thicken liquid in cooker for gravy. This is delicious served over rice.

(Serves 4)

Armadillo

It might surprise you, but an armadillo is edible and very tasty. These mammals, which weigh from 8 to 17 pounds, are found from central Kansas south to Florida.

You should skin and dress an armadillo as soon as possible. The easiest method is to skin from the underside by using a sharp knife to split the skin from just in front of the anal opening to the neck, taking care not to puncture the abdominal cavity. Peel the animal out as you would a squirrel or rabbit. Remove all fat from under the front and back legs of the carcass and wash meat completely. Once cleaned, a 'dillo can be cut into quarters that resemble rabbit pieces, only larger.

Fried Armadillo

Place frying-size pieces of armadillo in a deep pot and cover with lightly salted water. Boil, gently, until meat is fork tender, about 20 to 30 minutes. Remove pieces from pot and let cool. Dust meat in seasoned flour. Melt enough butter or shortening to cover the bottom of heavy skillet or electric frypan. Brown meat on both sides; cover skillet and cook over medium heat for 20 to 40 minutes. If liquid is needed, add chicken stock or broth.

(Serves 6 to 8)

'Dillo Fricasse

Outdoor editor Don Mann of Miami, Florida always has armadillo in his freezer—lucky him! This is one of his favorite recipes for *Dasypus novemcinctus* (armadillo).

1 armadillo, cut into serving pieces
1/2 cup flour
Salt and pepper
1/2 cup butter or cooking oil
1 bay leaf
Pinch thyme
1/2 cup chopped celery
2 carrots, chopped
2 medium potatoes, sliced
2 medium onions, sliced

Place flour, salt and pepper in a brown paper bag and shake 'dillo pieces in bag until well coated. Melt butter in a Dutch oven; add 'dillo and brown on both sides. Add water, just to cover, and remaining ingredients. Cover pot and simmer over low heat until meat is tender, approximately 1 1/2 hours. Thicken liquid with a flour and water paste and adjust seasoning.

(Serves 6 to 8)

Small Game Dinner Menu

SHERRY CHEESE SPREAD/CRACKERS

ANY SMALL GAME RECIPE

BRANDY SWEET POTATOES

GREEN BEANS NAPOLI

SPINACH/MUSHROOM SALAD

BURGUNDY PEARS

CRANBERRY BREAD

See Accompaniment Section for recipes.

Small Game Dinner Menu

MEAT SPREAD/PARTY RYE

ANY SMALL GAME RECIPE

DUSTY POTATOES

CARROTS WITH WATER CHESTNUTS

MOLDED PINEAPPLE SALAD

PUMPKIN NUT CAKE

See Accompaniment Section for recipes.

How to Cook Big Game Animals

Deer, Moose and Elk

It was New Year's Day and raining very hard. I kept asking myself what I was doing here in the woods with ice water trickling down my back from a small leak in my rainsuit. After all, I could have stayed home this final day of deer season and had the ice tinkling in my glass.

Then, all of a sudden, two deer stepped out of the darkness. Taking careful aim at the larger one, I pulled the trigger. As I did so, thoughts of chops, roasts and steaks were already running through my mind. For deer and other American big game, cleanly killed and promptly dressed out, are absolutely delicious.

Deer, moose and elk all belong to the same family and can be prepared using the same cooking methods and recipes. In order to have prime meat, these animals should be field dressed and cooled down immediately. Otherwise a strong, gamy flavor can result. Remove and save the liver and heart. Place these in a plastic bag and keep iced in a cooler until you reach home.

The unsaturated fat in these animals breaks down quickly, and that is why fast cooling is essential so that the meat will not have a rancid taste. Unless you can hang the carcass at a temperature above freezing, but not over 40°, then take it to a meat locker plant for skinning and hanging. If this is impossible, skin the animal immediately. This is the first step for dropping the body temperature. Hang in a cool place by the hind legs until all blood has drained from the carcass and then butcher.

For the best flavor, all fat and bone should be removed from big game meat. Fat in the bone marrow does not freeze well. Double wrap and seal all edges to prevent freezer burn and mark cut, weight and date.

Never soak big game meat in anything. Soaking causes water to form ice crystals in the meat when frozen and become mushy upon defrosting. Just cut out any badly shot areas.

Venison is far healthier to eat than beef. It has ¹/₃ more protein and ¹/₃ fewer calories. This means that a half cup of deer meat has 120 calories compared to 323 calories for the same amount of beef. Since deer fat is unsaturated, it is low in cholesterol.

Deer is wonderful eating, and there are just two basic rules you need to remember for cooking it:

1. Deer roasts must be cooked slowly and by some steam method similar to those used in preparing beef rump roast. You can use aluminum foil, Dutch ovens, oven cooking bags, crockpots or pressure cookers.
2. Steaks, chops and liver should be cooked quickly and never past medium rare.

Venison Chops with Sauce

6 venison chops, ³/₄ to 1-inch thick
Butter
Salt and pepper

3 tablespoons red currant jelly
1 can (8 ounces) tomato sauce

Melt enough butter to cover bottom of a heavy skillet or electric frypan. Add chops and cook over medium-high heat about 5 minutes on each side or until meat is rare or medium rare. Remove chops to a warm platter; salt and pepper. Pour off any fat left in pan and then add currant jelly and mix until thoroughly melted. Pour in tomato sauce, mix well and boil for 1 minute. Serve sauce over chops.

(Makes 6 servings)

Rack and Saddle of Venison

This is a cookbook, and we're not about to waste valuable space on butchering big game. However, I do want to explain that the choicest parts of any big game animal are the rack, which includes the chops, and the saddle, which contains the tenderloin. Both these special cuts are the *only* ones which can be open roasted without toughness resulting. Yet even they must be done very quickly in a hot oven and are best served rare.

Trim both of these cuts well and remove chine bone. Rub outside of meat with peanut or olive oil and place in a roasting pan. Roast in a very hot oven, 400° to 425° until meat is rare (130° to 135°) on meat thermometer. Salt meat after removing from oven.

The tenderloin can be removed from the saddle and sliced as you would fillet mignon. The rack should be cut into chops for easy serving.

Serve with this sauce, if you wish.

Horseradish Sauce

¹/₂ cup heavy cream	3 tablespoons prepared
¹/₂ teaspoon salt	horseradish
Dash cayenne pepper	1 tablespoon vinegar

Beat cream until stiff. Fold in remaining ingredients.

(Makes about ³/₄ cup)

Venison Pot Roast

Big game roasts require moist cooking. Here's a great recipe using an oven cooking bag.

5 to 6 pound venison roast	1 can (12 ounces) beer
1 package onion soup mix	$1/2$ teaspoon salt
	3 peppercorns

Place large size (14″ × 20″) oven cooking bag in a 2-inch deep roasting pan. Combine onion soup mix, beer, salt and peppercorns in bag and stir with a wooden or plastic spoon to mix. Place roast in bag and close with tie. Marinate in refrigerator 3 to 5 hours or overnight; turn roast once. When ready to cook, make 6 $1/2$-inch slits in top of bag. Cook in a 350° oven for $2^1/2$ to 3 hours or until tender. Thicken juices for gravy.

Note: A 2 to 3 pound venison roast will require only $1^1/2$ hours of cooking time.

Sonny Brown's Venison Roast

For this delicious roast, use a Dutch oven or a cast iron covered pot atop your range. North Carolinian Sonny Brown developed this recipe.

6 strips bacon
1 medium to large venison roast
Several small slivers of garlic
Kitchen Bouquet
Salt and pepper
Flour

1 can (10³/₄ ounces) golden mushroom soup
¹/₂ can water
1 medium onion
1 can (4 ounces) mushrooms, drained

Cook bacon until crisp in large frying pan. Remove bacon, crush and set aside. Leave bacon fat in pan. Stick roast with knife and insert small slivers of garlic. Coat roast with Kitchen Bouquet, and salt and pepper it before lightly dusting with flour. Heat bacon fat and sear roast on all sides until thoroughly browned. Then set it aside for a moment. Meanwhile in Dutch oven or other deep cooking pot, mix your can of mushroom soup with ¹/₂ can of water. Remove enough rings from onion to cover roast, separate them and set aside. Dice remainder of onion and add to mushroom soup; heat and add salt and pepper to taste. Color this mixture slightly with Kitchen Bouquet. At this point place a rack in the bottom of your Dutch oven or other deep pot and place roast on the rack. Secure onion rings atop roast with wooden toothpicks. Sprinkle crushed bacon over top of roast and do the same with mushrooms. Finally, cover and cook very slowly for about 3 hours or until completely done.

Zesty Venison Roast

Now, let's turn to a roast that is similar but just enough different to be very interesting.

3 tablespoons butter
4 to 5 pound venison roast
$^1/_2$ cup water
$^1/_4$ cup soy sauce
$^1/_2$ envelope onion soup mix

$^1/_4$ cup sugar
1 cinnamon stick
1 teaspoon nutmeg
$^1/_4$ teaspoon anise seed (optional)
$^1/_2$ cup sherry

Melt butter in a large Dutch oven or in a similar electric or other deep cooking pot. At medium high heat (375° for electric pot) add meat and brown on all sides. In a small bowl, combine remaining ingredients and pour over meat. Cover, bring to boil, reduce heat to a simmer and cook 3 to 4 hours or until meat is fork tender. Gravy can be thickened with a flour and water paste.

Venison Barley Soup

Don't forget to save the bones from your big game roasts as they make marvelous soup which is enough for a hearty meal.

Leftover cooked venison bones with some meat left on them
1 can (16 ounces) tomato sauce
3 quarts water
3 carrots, sliced
3 stalks celery, cut into $1/2$-inch pieces
2 teaspoons instant minced onion
Favorite spices
$3/4$ cup pearled barley
Salt to taste

Place all ingredients in your crockpot. Cover and cook on low heat for 6 to 8 hours until barley is done and meat comes off the bones easily. Remove meat from bones and return to soup.

Spicy Venison Stew Under Pressure

When it comes both to saving energy and enjoying a pre-dictably tender big game stew, nothing beats the old-fash-ioned pressure cooker. Try this recipe, and you'll be convinced.

2 pounds venison stew meat, cut into 1-inch pieces
2 tablespoons oil
1 large onion, sliced
$^1/_2$ cup brown sugar
$^1/_2$ cup red or rosé table wine

$^1/_2$ cup water
$^1/_2$ teaspoon nutmeg
$^1/_2$ teaspoon cinnamon
$^1/_4$ teaspoon ginger
Salt to taste
2 bay leaves

Brown meat in oil in cooker. Remove meat and add onion; sauté until transparent. Then return your meat to cooker. In a small bowl dissolve brown sugar, wine, water and sea-sonings; add bay leaves. Pour mixture into cooker, close cover securely and cook under 15 pounds pressure for 20 minutes or until meat is tender. Serve over buttered noodles or rice.

(Serves 4 to 5)

Jim Heywood's Venison Stew

Many professional chefs both here and overseas enjoy cooking venison. This wonderful stew was developed by a chef at the Culinary Institute of America.

1 1/2 to 2 pounds lean venison stew meat, cut into 1-inch pieces
3 tablespoons cooking oil
1 medium onion, cut into small pieces
3 stalks celery, cut into 3/4-inch pieces
1 clove garlic
4 tablespoons flour
1 cup boiling water, stock or beef bouillon
1 can (1 pound) tomatoes, chopped, reserve juice

1 can (12 ounces) beer
1/2 teaspoon dried thyme
1 bay leaf
Salt and pepper to taste
1 teaspoon Worcestershire sauce
3 carrots, cut into 3/4-inch pieces
2 cups rutabaga, cut into 3/4-inch pieces
2 cups potatoes, cut into 3/4-inch pieces

Brown venison cubes in oil in a deep cast iron pot or other heavy Dutch oven type pot. Remove meat, leaving oil in pot. Add onions, celery and garlic to pot and cook until just tender; do not brown. Add flour to pot and stir in well. Now add boiling water, stock or beef bouillon and stir until thickened and smooth. Add tomatoes, reserved juice, beer, spices and browned venison. Stir until well mixed. Reduce heat and simmer, uncovered, for 1 hour and 15 minutes, stirring occasionally. Add carrots and rutabaga and cook an additional 30 minutes, covered. Add potatoes and cook until they're tender.

(Serves 6)

Note: you can easily double this recipe by using up to 5 pounds of venison stew meat, and the quantity of vegetables can be changed according to the number of people you're serving.

Venison Rutabaga Stew for Crockpot

Crockpots turn out tender game stews too. This one is especially fine.

1 medium onion, sliced 1/4-inch thick	1 1/2 pounds venison stew meat
1/2 small rutabaga, pared and cubed	1/4 cup snipped parsley
4 stalks celery, sliced diagonally	1/2 teaspoon basil
1 teaspoon salt	1 beef bouillon cube dissolved in 3/4 cup hot water

Place onion, rutabaga and celery in crockpot and sprinkle with salt. Add stew meat on top of vegetables; sprinkle parsley and basil over all. Pour beef bouillon over vegetables and meat. Cover and cook on low heat for 9 to 10 hours. Thicken liquid in pot for gravy.

(Serves 4)

California Venison Stew

Here's a very tasty stew you can prepare in a Dutch oven or in a deep cast iron pot.

2 tablespoons cooking oil
2 pounds venison stew meat, cut into 1-inch pieces
2 medium onions, quartered
1 teaspoon salt
3 whole allspice
1 bay leaf

$^1/_8$ teaspoon pepper
1 beef bouillon cube
$2^1/_2$ cups water
3 carrots, thinly sliced
1 pound zucchini, thinly sliced
1 cup dried apricots
$^1/_2$ teaspoon sugar
1 tablespoon flour

In Dutch oven or deep cast iron pot, heat oil; add venison and brown well on all sides. Add onions, seasonings, bouillon cube and $2^1/_2$ cups water; bring to a boil. Reduce heat, cover and simmer for $1^1/_2$ hours or until meat is tender. Add carrots to beef and cook 5 minutes. Then add zucchini, apricots and sugar; continue cooking 10 more minutes or until vegetables are tender. Remove bay leaf and discard. Blend four and $^1/_4$ cup water until smooth. Gradually stir this into stew liquid. Cook, stirring constantly, until sauce thickens and boils 1 minute. Serve over hot rice or noodles.

(Serves 6)

Venison Burgundy Pie

Meat pies have been a favorite with sportsmen for centuries. In medieval England the pastry for cooking game was called a "coffyn." American colonial housewives prepared "pastry coffins" of game to vary the winter fare. Whatever they are called, pies are a convenient one dish method for game.

1 ½ pounds venison stew meat, cut into 1-inch pieces
1 medium onion, sliced
1 tablespoon butter
1 cup Burgundy
2 cups hot water
1 ½ teaspoons salt
Pepper to taste

1 ½ cups sliced carrots
1 ½ cups diced, pared potatoes
1 cup diced celery
¼ cup chopped parsley
Flour
1 package pie crust sticks or mix

In a large skillet or electric frypan, brown venison and onion in melted butter. Add salt and pepper; stir in wine and hot water. Cover and simmer over low heat until meat is tender, about 1 ½ hours, adding more liquid if necessary. Stir in vegetables and parsley during last ½ hour of cooking. Make a paste of flour and water and stir into meat mixture. Cook, stirring constantly, until mixture thickens and boils.

Preheat oven to 450°. Prepare pastry for a one crust pie as directed on package. Roll dough into 10-inch square; cut slits in pastry. Place meat mixture in an 8″ × 8″ × 2″ baking dish. Place pastry over filling and secure to rim of dish. Bake until crust is brown and sauce bubbles.

(Serves 4 to 5)

Note: For a convection oven, bake at 375° until brown and hot through.

Venison Pie Supreme

What do you do with game leftovers? Try this easy venison pie.

3 to 4 cups cooked
   venison, cut into bite-
   size pieces
3 tablespoons butter
3 tablespoons flour
$1/2$ cup milk
$3/4$ to 1 cup beef broth
2 tablespoons Madeira
   or cream sherry
$1/4$ teaspoon Kitchen
   Bouquet

Salt to taste
1 package (10 ounces)
   frozen mixed
   vegetables, cooked and
   drained
Package instant
   mashed potatoes (for
   4)
$1/4$ cup grated Cheddar
   cheese

Melt butter in a large saucepan. Add flour to melted butter and stir well. Gradually add milk and beef broth until medium consistency is reached. Add wine, Kitchen Bouquet and salt to taste. Place cooked meat and vegetables into sauce; stir until well mixed and pour into a $1 1/2$-quart casserole.

Prepare mashed potatoes according to package directions. Top meat mixture evenly with mashed potatoes and sprinkle with cheese. Bake at 400° for 20 to 25 minutes until brown.

(Serves 4)

Venison Loaf Wellington

1 egg
1 pound ground venison
½ cup seasoned bread
   stuffing mix
3 tablespoons grated
   Parmesan cheese
   Salt and pepper to
   taste

Onion powder to taste
1 tablespoon chopped
   parsley
1 egg
1 tablespoon water
1 package (8)
   refrigerated crescent
   rolls

Preheat oven to 350°. Lightly beat 1 egg in medium size
mixing bowl. Add ground venison, stuffing mix, cheese,
seasonings and parsley; combine thoroughly. Form into a
loaf about 8″ × 4″ and place in a greased, oblong baking
dish. Beat remaining egg with water. Separate rolls and lay
over top and sides of loaf so that the loaf is completely
covered with rolls. Seal edges of rolls with egg-water glaze.
Brush with remaining glaze and bake 1 hour.

(Serves 4 to 5)

Venison Deep Dish Pizza

Venison pizza? You must think I'm putting you on! I'm not, and it's delicious. Teenagers will love it; if you don't tell them they are eating venison, they will never know!

1 package hot roll mix
1 cup very warm water (105°–115°)
1 can (15 ounces) tomato purée
1 teaspoon oregano
1/2 teaspoon salt
1/4 teaspoon pepper
1 cup (4 ounces) shredded Mozzarella cheese
1/2 pound ground venison, cooked and drained
1 can (4 ounces) sliced mushrooms, drained
1/4 cup grated Parmesan cheese
2 tablespoons chopped parsley

Preheat oven to 425°. (Move rack to lowest position.) In large bowl, dissolve yeast from hot roll mix in 1 cup water; add flour mixture from hot roll mix and blend well. Let dough stand for 5 minutes. Combine tomato purée, oregano, salt and pepper in small bowl. Grease with solid shortening one 13″ × 9″ oblong pan. With greased fingers, press dough into pan forming a rim around the edge. Sprinkle with Mozzarella cheese. Pour prepared sauce over cheese; top with cooked venison and mushrooms. Bake for 25 to 30 minutes or until crust is light golden brown. Top with Parmesan cheese and parsley. Serve very hot.

(Makes 8 to 12 servings)

Hunters' Delight

What do you take to a covered dish supper? This is one of my favorites. It is so good, there is never any of it left to bring home.

1 to 1½ pounds ground venison
1 can (8 ounces) tomato sauce
1 teaspoon salt
1 tablespoon instant minced onion
1 tablespoon sugar

1 tablespoon Worcestershire sauce
1 carton (8 ounces) dairy sour cream
1 package (3 ounces) cream cheese
1 package (8 ounces) egg noodles

Brown venison in a large skillet and drain. Add tomato sauce, salt, onion, sugar and Worcestershire sauce; simmer for 15 minutes. Blend sour cream with cream cheese. Cook noodles according to package directions and drain. Place a layer of noodles in a greased baking dish; cover with a layer of meat mixture and top with cream cheese mixture. Repeat process. Bake at 350° for 30 to 45 minutes or until thoroughly heated.

(Serves 6 to 8)

Venison Cabbage Rolls for Crockpot

The high cost of food is reaching all of us. Here is an economical tasty meal that's impossible to beat.

6 to 8 large cabbage
  leaves
1 egg, beaten
1/4 cup milk
1 tablespoon instant
  minced onion
1 teaspoon salt
1 pound ground venison

1/2 cup minute rice,
  uncooked
1 can (8 ounces) tomato
  sauce
1 tablespoon brown
  sugar
1 tablespoon lemon juice
1 teaspoon
  Worcestershire sauce

Place cabbage leaves in a large pot of boiling water, being sure leaves are immersed. Boil for a few minutes or until leaves are limp; drain. Combine egg, milk, onion, salt, venison and uncooked rice. Place 1/4 cup of meat mixture in center of each cabbage leaf. Fold sides in toward meat and roll ends over meat. Place rolls in crockpot. Combine next 4 ingredients and pour over rolls. Cover and cook on low heat for 7 to 8 hours.

(Serves 3 to 4)

Ground Venison in Wok

If you enjoy wok cookery, then try using your ground venison in this delicious, easy dish.

1 pound ground venison	1 tablespoon salad oil
1/3 cup slivered almonds	1/2 pound green beans,
4 eggs	cut into 1-inch lengths
1 tablespoon soy sauce	2 tablespoons water
1 teaspoon ground	1 medium onion,
ginger	chopped
1/2 teaspoon dry mustard	

Spread almonds in a shallow baking pan. Toast in a 325° oven until lightly browned (about 10 minutes); set aside. Beat together eggs, soy sauce, ginger and mustard; set aside. Place wok on high heat and when hot, add oil. When oil is hot, add beans and stir-fry 1 minute. Add water, cover and cook until beans are tender but crisp (about 2 minutes); set aside. Crumble ground venison into wok and stir-fry until no longer pink. Add onion and stir-fry until limp. Return beans to wok and add egg mixture, turning until eggs are set. Sprinkle nuts over top.

(Serves 4)

Ground Venison Quiche

1 pound ground venison
1 9-inch, deep-dish pie
shell
2 teaspoons instant
minced onion
1/2 teaspoon salt
1/8 teaspoon pepper

1/8 teaspoon garlic
powder
3/4 cup sliced fresh
mushrooms
1 cup grated Cheddar
cheese
2 eggs
1 can (5.33 ounces)
evaporated milk

Defrost pie shell and then prick bottom and sides of crust
with fork. Bake in a 425° oven until crust begins to brown;
let cool. Brown venison with minced onion in a heavy skillet or electric frypan. Drain off any excess fat. Add seasonings and spoon meat mixture into pie shell. Sprinkle
mushrooms and cheese evenly over top. Beat eggs and
milk until well blended and then pour over pie. Bake at
425° until set, about 20 minutes, then reduce oven temperature to 350° and continue baking until top is golden,
about 25 minutes. Let stand 10 minutes before cutting.

(Serves 4 to 5)

Venison Mincemeat

There is no point in buying mincemeat if you have venison. Just cook some stew meat ahead, and you can quickly make mincemeat economically. A pressure cooker will save both time and energy.

1 pound venison stew meat	1/2 cup vinegar
1/2 pound suet	2 cups apple cider
6 cups pared, chopped apples	2 cups sugar
2 cups raisins	1 teaspoon salt
1 box (11 ounces) currants	1 teaspoon cinnamon
	1 teaspoon cloves
	1/4 teaspoon ginger
	1 teaspoon nutmeg

Cook venison stew meat and grind with suet. Combine all ingredients and simmer for 1/2 hour. Cool and freeze in usable quantities.

Miniature Venison Balls

Use your imagination! Then you'll agree that miniature venisonburgers will make marvelous hors d'oeuvres. Here's how to do it.

1½	pounds ground venison	⅛	teaspoon pepper
¾	cup dry breadcrumbs	¼	teaspoon allspice
1	egg, beaten	¼	teaspoon nutmeg
1	teaspoon salt	⅛	teaspoon cloves
1	teaspoon brown sugar	⅛	teaspoon ginger
		4	tablespoons butter

Combine first 10 ingredients, mixing well. Shape into 1-inch balls. Melt butter in a large skillet or electric frypan and brown venison balls well, stirring occasionally. Cover and cook on low heat for 15 minutes.

(Makes about 4 dozen)

Note: You can use this recipe for an interesting entrée by making larger meat patties.

Deer Heart in Crockpot

Some people do not like the idea of eating deer heart, or chicken hearts for that matter. A shame, for deer hearts are delicious if properly cooked. Oven roasting will ruin these hearts, but braising makes them tender. Try this recipe with deer, moose or elk hearts and see for yourself.

2 deer hearts or 1 moose or elk heart	1 cup water
1 medium onion, sliced	1/2 cup brown rice, uncooked
1 cup thinly sliced carrots	1 teaspoon salt
1 can (1 pound) tomatoes, undrained and cut up	1/4 teaspoon pepper

Wash hearts and remove hard parts, if necessary. Slice hearts across grain and place in crockpot. Add remaining ingredients to crockpot. Cover and cook on low heat for 8 to 9 hours.

(Serves 4 to 5)

Braised Deer Heart

1 deer heart, diced in
small pieces
1/2 teaspoon salt
1/4 cup flour
3 tablespoons butter
1 can (8 ounces)
mushrooms

1 can (10³/4 ounces)
chicken broth
1 teaspoon instant
minced onion
1 teaspoon parsley flakes

Add salt to flour and place in a bag. Shake deer heart pieces in bag until well coated with flour. Melt butter in a heavy skillet or electric frypan and brown heart pieces. Add mushrooms and juice, broth, onion and parsley. Cover skillet and simmer on low heat for 1 hour. Serve over hot rice or cooked noodles.

(Serves 3)

Deer Heart Andalouse

1 deer heart, diced in small pieces
1 cup water
$1/2$ teaspoon salt
1 can ($10^1/2$ ounces) condensed tomato soup
1 tablespoon Worcestershire sauce
1 can (16 ounces) peas
$1/4$ cup flour
$1/2$ cup milk
$1/4$ pound Cheddar cheese, grated

Place pieces of heart in a deep, heavy skillet or electric fry-pan. Add water and salt. Cover tightly and cook slowly for 1 hour or until tender, adding more water if necessary. Then add tomato soup, Worcestershire sauce and peas. Make a paste of flour and milk and thicken heart mixture, stirring constantly. Add cheese and continue cooking until cheese is melted. Serve over rice.

(Serves 4)

Venison Liver Loaf

In addition to the heart, big game liver can be made into tasty dishes. Both are exceptional sources of essential food nutrients. A 3½-ounce serving of either heart or liver provides over half your daily requirement of protein, iron and riboflavin. For a change from fried liver, try this liver loaf. I know you'll enjoy it.

1 pound big game liver, sliced	¼ cup pork sausage
1 tablespoon cooking fat	1 egg, slightly beaten
2 teaspoons instant minced onion	½ cup milk
	1 cup soft bread crumbs
	½ teaspoon salt

Cook liver in fat until lightly browned on each side—about 5 minutes. Grind liver or put it in a processor. Soak instant minced onion in milk for a few minutes. Combine ground liver with rest of ingredients. Place in a greased 9″ × 5″ loaf pan and bake in a slow oven, 300° for 1 hour.

(Serves 4 to 5)

Venison Jerky

You probably would like to make your own jerky for camping, boating or hiking. A convection oven is an excellent, energy-efficient way of making a food first invented by Indians and explorers.

1 to 2 pounds venison steak	$^1/_2$ cup soy sauce
	Garlic salt

Slice steak with grain into pieces no larger than $^1/_4$-inch wide and $^1/_2$-inch thick. These strips can be 3 to 4 inches long. Dip them in soy sauce and place upon a rack in a 2-inch deep oven pan. Sprinkle generously with garlic salt. Place in a 150° oven or convection oven for 10 to 12 hours. Halfway through cooking time, turn jerky slices over. Your jerky, if kept dry, will last indefinitely, and no refrigeration is needed.

Wild Boar

Our daughter, Alison, has always been a traditionally feminine child. She thought it was rather dreadful of me to go hunting and, even worse, to pick her up at school in my boots and canvas jacket. Sometimes, she tried to pretend I was not her mother. For me to appear in such clothes before her friends was positively degrading.

So, now a young single, Alison has a boyfriend whose prime interest in life is hunting. His place is overflowing with guns, and a huge wild boar's head dominates his dining room. When Alison asked last Christmas for hunting boots, I nearly fainted!

Wild boar can mean more than one thing. Originally, there were none in this country, unless you include the peccary, which is not a true pig. Boars were imported from Europe to Tennessee and North Carolina by millionnaire sportsmen with large, fenced estates. They escaped, multiplied and have flourished ever since.

Domestic hogs turned loose throughout Dixie to fatten up on acorns have turned wild and become like their savage, lean ancestors. In many areas, they are also called wild boar.

Whether you are cooking a true boar or a wild razorback hog makes no difference. The meat on both is much leaner and firmer than domestic pork. All cuts should be braised, stewed or barbecued, since wild boar is too tough and dry for open roasting or broiling.

Another important point is to make sure cooked boar meat reaches a temperature of at least 170°, so that the organism that causes trichinosis is killed. You are actually more apt to get trichinosis from supermarket pork than from a wild animal, but why take a chance?

I don't have to take a chance in the woods facing a wild boar. Gary Crispens, Alison's boyfriend, does it for me! This is how I cooked a nice leg roast from his most recent boar.

Wild Boar Roast in Crockpot

1 (3 to 4 pounds) wild boar ham
2 cups water
1 teaspoon salt
1 teaspoon thyme
1 teaspoon rubbed sage
1 teaspoon grated lemon peel
1 tablespoon lemon juice
1/4 teaspoon garlic powder
1 package (7/8 ounces) gravy mix for pork

Pour water in a large glass or ceramic bowl and add remaining ingredients except for gravy mix. Place boar roast in bowl with marinade. Cover and refrigerate overnight, turning meat several times. Transfer meat and marinade to crockpot. Cover and cook on low heat for 10 to 12 hours. Turn meat once halfway through cooking. Drain and slice meat. Follow package directions for making gravy and serve over sliced boar. (Serves 6 to 8)

Boar Ribs

There are many other good recipes for boar. These are excellent, and Gary is responsible for them.

2 to 3 pounds boar ribs
1 1/2 cups water
1 can (12 ounces) beer
Barbecue sauce

Place ribs in a pan and cover with water and beer. Cover and boil for 45 minutes to 1 hour or until ribs are fork tender. Drain ribs and place in a 2-inch deep roasting pan. Add enough barbecue sauce to cover ribs. Cover pan with foil and bake in a 350° oven for 35 minutes or until thoroughly hot. (Serves 2 to 3)

Boar Chili

2 pounds lean, diced boar meat
2 tablespoons vegetable oil
1 medium onion, chopped
4 cans (1 pound each) chili beans, undrained
1 tablespoon cumin
$1/2$ teaspoon garlic salt
$1/2$ teaspoon cayenne pepper
1 tablespoon soy sauce
1 cup grated Cheddar cheese
Sour cream

Heat oil in a heavy skillet and brown meat and onion. Transfer these to a crockpot and then add rest of ingredients except for cheese and sour cream. Cover and cook on low heat for 6 to 8 hours. Place 2 tablespoons of grated cheese over each serving of chili and top with a tablespoonful of sour cream.

(Serves 8)

Boar Barbecue

2 pounds boar meat, cut into small pieces
2 tablespoons brown sugar

1 bottle (18 ounces) barbecue sauce
Dash cayenne pepper

Place all ingredients in a crockpot and mix together. Cover and cook on low heat for 6 to 8 hours. Serve on buns or over cooked rice.

(Serves 4 to 6)

Big Game Dinner Menu

BRANDIED BEEF SOUP

ANY BIG GAME RECIPE

BARLEY WITH MUSHROOMS

CURRIED PEAS

CHERRY MOLD

CHEESE BISCUITS

PECAN PIE

See Accompaniment Section for recipes.

Big Game Dinner for Oven Menu

GUACAMOLE DIP/FRESH VEGETABLES

ANY BIG GAME RECIPE FOR OVEN

CHEESY GRITS

YELLOW SQUASH CASSEROLE

SHERRIED FRUIT

FRANCES' COCONUT CAKE

Note: By preparing the grits, squash and fruit in the oven along with the game dish, you'll be saving energy.

See Accompaniment Section for recipes.

Care, Freezing and Selection of Fish

Before you cook fish, make sure it is fresh. If it is not, serious illness can result. You know fish is fresh if you catch it and keep it on ice. Fish left hanging on a stringer in warm water can spoil.

If you buy your fish at a dockside fish market, check whether the gills are red, the eyes are bright, shiny and not sunken and the flesh springs back when poked. Fresh fish does *not* smell fishy. There may be a slight, rather pleasant odor.

Salt water fish should always be cleaned at the earliest possible moment and then skinned or scaled. With fresh water fish, especially trout, immediate cleaning is not as important, although recommended—at least by me. When cleaning fish or preparing them for your freezer, *never* soak in water. You should rinse your cleaned fish to remove any blood remaining along the backbone. After rinsing, let them drain. Soaked fish absorb water readily, which interferes with proper cooking and forms destructive ice crystals upon freezing.

The last time we were in England, we gave a dinner party at a private club in London featuring trout we had caught. One guest admitted in advance to not caring much for trout, yet cleaned her plate and asked for more. She'd never eaten such delicious fish. The reason was that we had cleaned them promptly. Her husband left his trout in the car overnight or in the kitchen until the next morning!

If you're away from home and either catch or buy fish, you can easily keep them fresh for up to a week. All you basically need is a cooler and plenty of ice and salt. Rock salt (not the kind used on roads) can be used, or use regular table salt or Kosher salt.

With a good insulated ice chest, ice and salt you can do something called "superchilling." The salt makes the ice start melting, and this absorbs heat from the fish, cooling them. The better the insulation in your cooler, the longer the fish will stay fresh.

Begin by lining the bottom of your ice chest with three to four inches of crushed ice or ice cubes. You may want to place a rack or tray on the chest bottom to make certain your fish are not lying in water as the ice melts.

Next, add salt and mix with the ice. Finally, add a layer of fish. You can keep adding alternate layers of fish and ice with salt until the cooler is filled, using one pound of salt for each twenty pounds of ice.

Whole fish can be layered unwrapped. Dressed fish, steaks or fillets should be protected by wrapping in plastic film or placed in a large plastic bag before putting them in the chest.

When the cooler is filled, top it off with a generous layer of ice and close the lid. Then keep the ice chest cool and in the shade. If you're traveling for several days, drain off melted water at overnight stops and add more ice. Do not take out the fish until you've reached home.

On arriving home, unpack your fish and rinse in fresh cold water. Either drain and package them for your freezer, or prepare to cook a fish dinner.

There is a secret for freezing fish. By using it you can keep frozen fish at least a year. It involves a protective dip made of lemon juice and gelatin.

Here's how to prepare this protective dip or glaze:

96

1 envelope	¼ cup fresh or
(1 tablespoon)	reconstituted lemon
unflavored gelatin	juice
	1¾ cups water

Stir gelatin into cold water-lemon mixture. Heat over low heat, stirring constantly until gelatin is dissolved and mixture is almost clear. Cool to room temperature.

Fish can be whole, in steaks or fillets. Dip the fish into this lemon glaze and drain for several seconds before wrapping individually in a heavy duty plastic film. Then place within heavy duty plastic feezer bags for double protection, marking the date and other details, such as exact contents, on bag. The best size packages to freeze are those which represent a meal for your family.

This protective dip works because the gelatin provides an airtight glaze holding the lemon juice in contact with the fish. The lemon juice serves as an antioxidant, odor inhibitor and color stabilizer.

Many of us buy frozen fish at our supermarket. In this case, we probably wouldn't worry about a protective dip. However, we should look for solid freezing with no discoloration or freezer burn, which gives a white cottony appearance. Frozen fish should not smell fishy, and it should be wrapped tightly in a moisture and vapor proof wrapper with little or no air space. The package must be undamaged and labeled clearly.

One must be careful when buying fish, fresh or frozen. When first married, I went to the fish market for some beautiful smelts, brought them home, cooked them and then discovered they had never been cleaned! My husband thought it was very funny—except that he would rather have eaten the smelts.

Here are the market forms of fish that you need to know:

Whole or round is fish just as it comes from the water. Before cooking it must be scaled or skinned and eviscerated.

Drawn or pan dressed fish is the same as whole or round, except the scales or skin, insides and usually head, tail and fins have been removed.

Steaks are vertical, cross-section cuts of large, dressed fish and are ready to cook.

Fillets are lengthwise cuts of fish, usually skinned, and ready to cook.

Butterfly fillets are two single fillets from opposite sides of a fish connected by a small piece of skin.

When buying fish you need:

Whole fish: $3/4$ pound per person
Drawn or pan dressed: $1/2$ pound per person
Steaks or fillets: $1/3$ pound per person

After bringing fresh fish home, immediately place it in the refrigerator in its original leakproof wrapper. It should be stored in the coldest part of your refrigerator at about 35°. Even then, do not keep fish in the refrigerator more than a day or two after purchase. If you cannot cook it within two days, freeze it.

Commercially packaged frozen fish should be dated and placed in your freezer at once. Since it's not apt to have a protective glaze, storage time will be less than for fish you have prepared for freezing at home. Very oily fish, such as shad and bluefish, will keep up to 3 months when bought frozen. Moderately oily fish, such as catfish, will keep up to 6 months, and lean fish, such as cod, haddock and sea trout, may be kept for a year.

Proper thawing of frozen fish is as important as correct freezing. You should thaw fish in your refrigerator, allowing 18 to 24 hours to defrost each pound. For quicker thawing, place the package under cold running water. Or you can use the lowest cycle on a microwave oven for thawing, but then I feel the fish should be cooked immediately.

Never thaw fish at room temperature or in warm water. This will cause loss of moisture and flavor and encourage bacteria to become active. Once thawed, fish should *never* be refrozen. If you have uncooked, thawed fish remaining, use it within a day or discard.

Instead of thawing your frozen fish, consider cooking it straight from the freezer, allowing some additional time. But enough of this discussion. Now that you've caught or bought fish, you want to enjoy some delicious seafood meals. Let's get on to cooking.

Small Whole Fish

If your family goes fishing, most of your catch probably consists of fish weighing less than a pound. So let's begin with recipes for small whole fish. By small whole fish I mean perch, catfish, sunfish, porgies, spot, trout and all their relatives. They are easy to prepare for cooking: just scale and clean out. Some species, especially bass, fresh water perch and catfish, are better skinned than scaled.

To skin any of these species, cut skin all the way around behind pectoral fins. These are the paired fins just behind the head. Also cut to and around dorsal fin, which is the large fin on the fish's back, and around the anal fin, which is located near the tail on the underside of the fish. Then, using head and pectoral fin spines as handle in one hand, use pliers to pull off skin.

To fillet a fish, except for flatfish such as flounder, take a very sharp knife and lay fish on its side. Cut behind gills and pectoral fin to backbone and follow backbone to tail, staying as close to backbone as possible without cutting it.

With a flounder or similar fish, lay it white side down. Take a sharp knife and cut behind head to pectoral fin and then cut directly down middle of spine to tail. Next, work with knife along spine on each side of first cut, all the way to the fringe fin, which runs along each edge, and cut free. Turn over and repeat on bottom side.

101

To skin any fillet, place it skin side down on a hard surface and, using a very sharp knife, work it between skin and flesh, pressing downwards. An electric carving knife does an excellent job.

This is your basic recipe for pan-fried whole fish. An advantage of this recipe is that it provides a nice crust which seals in the moisture.

Crusty Pan-Fried Fish

6 whole small fish, about	$^1/_8$ teaspoon pepper
$^1/_2$ pound each	$^1/_2$ cup cornmeal
1 egg, beaten	$^1/_2$ cup flour
2 tablespoons milk	Cooking oil for frying
1 teaspoon salt	Lemon wedges

Thaw fish, if frozen, and dry. Combine egg, milk, salt and pepper. Mix cornmeal and flour together. Dip fish into egg mixture and roll in cornmeal mixture. Place a single layer of fish in hot oil in a large, heavy skillet or electric frypan. Fry at moderate heat, 350°, approximately 4 to 5 minutes. Turn carefully and cook 4 to 5 minutes longer or until brown and fish flakes easily when tested with a fork. Drain on absorbent paper and serve with lemon wedges.

Beer Batter Fish

Batter-fried whole fish are a family favorite with us. This method works particularly well with small bass, catfish and other fish that are skinned before cooking.

6 whole small fish, about	½ teaspoon salt
½ pound each	1 egg
4 tablespoons butter	½ cup beer
1 cup biscuit baking mix	

Melt butter in a heavy skillet or electric frypan. Combine biscuit mix, salt, egg and beer; mix until smooth. Dip fish into batter, letting excess drip into bowl. Fry at moderate heat, 350°, until golden brown on both sides and fish flakes easily when tested with a fork.

Broiled Whole Fish

Broiling is a popular method for preparing whole fish.
The oilier fish, such as members of the mackerel family,
are excellent broiled. However, in warm weather, the oven
will overheat your kitchen. So broiling is best reserved for
cooler months, unless you can use a convection oven or
counter top broiler, which are more economical and far
cooler.

6	whole small fish, about	Lemon/pepper
	1/2 pound each	seasoning
1/4	cup melted butter	Paprika
	Salt	

Thaw fish, if frozen, and dry. Place fish in single layer in
foil-lined shallow baking pan. Brush liberally with butter
and sprinkle lightly with seasonings. Broil 4 inches from
source of heat, 5 to 8 minutes. Turn, baste and season as
above. Broil 5 to 8 minutes more or until fish is browned
and flakes easily when tested with a fork. Be careful not to
overcook.

Basic Baked Fish

Of course you can bake small whole fish in any type of oven. Since the oven door is closed, you're not leaking heat into an August kitchen. This simple recipe is easy to use with your favorite seasoning.

6 whole small fish, about
$\frac{1}{2}$ pound each
$\frac{1}{4}$ cup melted butter

$\frac{1}{2}$ teaspoon salt
$\frac{1}{4}$ teaspoon your favorite seasoning

Thaw fish, if frozen, and dry. Place fish in single layer in foil-lined shallow pan. Mix rest of ingredients together and pour over fish in pan. Bake at 350° for 25 to 30 minutes or until fish flakes easily when tested with a fork.

Note: for variation, thinly sliced onion, toasted almonds or mushroom caps may be added when fish is almost done. Pour pan drippings over fish when serving.

Poached Fish with Elegant Sauce

Now, let's turn to a superb recipe that is more sophisticated. I recently used it on a television show, and a gentleman in the audience took one taste and insisted on taking home all the leftover sauce in a plastic coffee cup!

Fresh water trout and bass are excellent this way, as are small walleyes, white perch, surfperch and croakers. You will need a pressure cooker, either the conventional model or an electric one. If you have no pressure cooker, you can prepare this recipe in a skillet.

2 to 4 whole small bass, trout, catfish or similar fish	2 tablespoons butter
	2 tablespoons flour
	1/4 cup sliced almonds
1 cup water	2 ounces mushrooms, sliced
1 bay leaf	
1 teaspoon instant minced onion	2 tablespoons white table wine
1 tablespoon lemon juice	2 tablespoons half and half cream
1/2 teaspoon salt	

Place fish, water, bay leaf, onion, lemon juice and salt in pressure cooker. Close cover securely and cook under 15 pounds pressure for 3 minutes. Reduce pressure immediately. Remove poached fish and place on a platter, covering with foil to keep warm. Remove bay leaf. For sauce, add butter and flour to liquid in cooker and whisk well with wire whisk. Heat gently, whisking all the time until a smooth, thickened sauce. Add mushrooms and almonds and simmer 2 to 3 minutes. Stir in wine and cream. Pour some sauce over fish and serve rest in a gravy dish.

Alternate Method: Place fish, water, bay leaf, onion, lemon juice and salt in a deep skillet or electric frypan. Cover and simmer for 10 to 15 minutes or until fish flakes easily when tested with a fork. Remove fish from skillet and follow directions for sauce.

106

Large Whole Fish

What do you do when you are faced with a large fish weighing three to five pounds or more? If it's not too big, you can cook it whole by any of three methods: baking uncovered, baking in an oven cooking bag or baking with aluminum foil. If you want to use your outdoor grill, you can turn to the appropriate chapter in this book.

Here, we're going to stay with baking, because it is sensible, simple and lets you provide a regal repast for family and friends.

Some fish should not be stuffed. This is especially true of shad, bluefish and other oily varieties. The reason is that the stuffing will absorb fish oil and lose its real flavor. If you want to stuff a large fish, consider sea trout, bass of any kind, rockfish, halibut, codfish and the like.

Beginning with open baking, here's a recipe which I use regularly for shad, large bluefish, king mackerel and other large oily fish.

Open Baked Fish

1 (3 to 4 pound) whole,	Salt
dressed American	Lemon slices
shad or other oily fish	Paprika

Line a 2-inch deep roasting pan with aluminum foil. Place fish in pan and salt cavity and both sides. With a sharp knife, make slits part way through one side of fish. The slits allow oil to seep out during baking and can also be used after cooking for cutting the fish into serving-size pieces. Place a thin slice of lemon in each slit and sprinkle top of fish with paprika or other seasoning. Bake fish in a 350° oven for 45 to 60 minutes or until fish flakes easily when tested with a fork.

(Serves 4)

Baked Whole Fish with Tomatoes

When fresh tomatoes are in season, they work very well in this recipe for whole striped bass, northern pike, large walleyes, muskies, pollock and similar non-oily fish.

1 (3 to 5 pound) whole, dressed fish Salt and pepper 1 medium onion, thinly sliced	2 medium tomatoes, cut into small pieces $1/2$ teaspoon basil

Line a 2-inch deep roasting pan with aluminum foil. Place fish in pan; salt and pepper cavity and both sides. Place onion slices and tomato pieces on top of fish and sprinkle with basil. Bake, uncovered, in a 350° oven for 45 to 60 minutes or until fish flakes easily when tested with a fork. During cooking, baste several times with juices from pan to keep the fish moist.

(Serves 4 or 5)

Baked Stuffed Fish

When stuffing, be sure you are cooking a pike, bass or cold water ocean fish, none of which (except mackerel) is oily. It is not a good idea to use a fancy stuffing for fish, since it would overpower the delicate flavor of the fish. For that reason, I like this recipe which has a simple corn bread stuffing.

1 (3 to 5 pound) whole, dressed fish
Salt and pepper
3 cups corn bread, crumbled
$^1/_4$ cup onion, finely chopped
$^1/_4$ cup celery, finely chopped
1 teaspoon salt
1 egg, beaten
$^1/_2$ cup butter, melted (divided)

Sprinkle cavity of fish lightly with salt and pepper. For stuffing, combine remaining ingredients using $^1/_4$ cup melted butter and toss lightly. Fill cavity of fish with stuffing; bind with string to close. Brush outside of fish with remaining butter and sprinkle lightly with salt and pepper. Place fish in a 2-inch deep roasting pan lined with foil and bake in a 350° oven for 1 hour or until fish flakes easily when tested with a fork.

(Serves 4 or 5)

Stuffed Fish in Oven Cooking Bag

There's nothing better for a rather dry fish than oven cooking bags. These bags have many advantages, including eliminating oven cleaning and cutting down on cooking odors. Leaving you with a clean oven saves energy.

1 tablespoon flour
1 (3 to 5 pound) whole, dressed fish
1/4 cup butter, melted (divided)
Salt and pepper
1 small onion, sliced
1/4 cup celery, chopped

1 cup herb seasoned stuffing mix
2 tablespoons snipped parsley
2 tablespoons grated Parmesan cheese
2 tablespoons lemon juice

Shake flour in a large size (14″ × 20″) oven cooking bag and place in a 2-inch deep roasting pan. Brush fish with half of melted butter; season inside and out with salt and pepper. Chop sufficient onion to measure 2 tablespoons and then place remaining onion slices in bag. To prepare stuffing, sauté chopped onion, celery and remaining 2 tablespoons butter in a medium size skillet until tender. Add stuffing mix; toss. Stir in parsley, Parmesan cheese and lemon juice. Place stuffing in fish cavity and bind with string to close. Place fish on top of onion in bag and close with twist tie; make 6 1/2-inch slits on top of bag. Place in a 350° oven for 1 to 1 1/4 hours or until fish flakes easily when tested with a fork.

(Serves 4 or 5)

Baked Whole Salmon in Foil

Aluminum foil is an old standby in fish cookery. It's as good today as ever, especially for salmon, lake trout and other dry fish.

1 (7 to 10 pound) whole, dressed salmon or similar fish
Salt
Butter

1 lemon, cut into thin slices
$1/4$ teaspoon thyme
$1/2$ teaspoon basil

Tear off a piece of heavy duty aluminum foil slightly longer than your fish and place this in a 2-inch deep roasting pan. Salt fish lightly and dot with butter. Place lemon slices atop fish and sprinkle herbs over all. Bring foil up over fish and close all edges with a double fold. Bake in a 375° oven allowing 12 to 15 minutes per pound. Fish is done when the flesh flakes easily when tested with a fork.

(Serves 8)

Fresh Tuna

Maybe you have your own boat and enjoy blue water fishing. Or perhaps you have friends who do or who will join you in renting a charter boat for offshore action. If you go, you may come back with tuna, which can range anywhere from 15 to 900 pounds each. What do you do then? There's not a single cookbook that explains. Whatever you do, don't pay attention to the boat captains who tell you to fry tuna steaks. They're good but *very* indigestible. There is only one first-rate way to handle bluefin, blackfin and yellowfin, or Allison tuna, and I'll tell you about it in a moment.

First let me say that I would never have seen whales if it were not for tuna. We were off Montauk Point, and there was a pod of whales, all of them blowing steam just as if they'd been reading *Moby Dick*. The tuna were there too, and it was the best day of fishing of the entire summer.

Returning to the dock, the captain tried to give me all the skipjack and keep all the tuna for himself. As you can imagine, I didn't let that happen!

Small tuna should be filleted and then skinned so you can remove all dark meat or "liver," as the insiders call it. Larger fish can be cut into steaks if more convenient, but skin and "liver" should be removed. You'll be surprised to see that tuna looks more like beef than fish, and it takes a long time to cook. You can have fresh tuna professionally smoked, and it is superb eating.

To enjoy your own tuna, get your skinned, "de-livered" tuna home on ice, cut it into chunks that will fit your pressure cooker or a large pot and cook for 2 hours under 10 pounds pressure. Or you could boil the meat until it flakes when tested with a fork. If your pressure cooker offers only a 15 pound option, try cooking an hour and a quarter.

You may want to wrap your tuna chunks in cheesecloth so they won't flake apart, and you will certainly want to dip or drain off the oil released in cooking.

When you freeze your own tuna, pack the cooked fish chunks in freezer cartons or bags and seal very tightly. It will keep several months.

Incidentally, if you're freezing, you should not add salt or sugar to your tuna while cooking. Wait and add whatever seasoning you want when you're preparing it as a meal. Your home-cooked tuna will have a better flavor than any canned tuna in the market.

Fish Steaks

As a young bride, I quickly became involved in surfcasting. It was fun, good excercise, and there were plenty of fish. One morning, I reached the beach to find an elderly gentleman in my favorite spot. He'd been there for hours. We chatted amiably, and I moved a few yards away, cast out and was rewarded by a hard strike. A few minutes later, I had a striped bass nearly four feet long on the shore. The elderly gentleman suggested it would make wonderful steaks. He was correct!

Fish steaks, unlike fillets, are cut across the fish and are usually $5/8$ to 1-inch in thickness. Salmon, swordfish, halibut, striped bass, king mackerel, dolphin (the fish of course), wahoo, muskellunge, large catfish and pike make excellent steaks.

Of course, your basic cooking methods are going to be frying, broiling, baking and poaching. Steaks from relatively dry fish should be served with a sauce, as in this recipe.

Sweet and Sour Fish Steaks

2 pounds fish steaks
$^1/_3$ cup flour
1 teaspoon salt
Fat for frying
$^3/_4$ cup vinegar
$^3/_4$ cup brown sugar
$^1/_2$ cup water
2 teaspoons soy sauce
$^1/_2$ teaspoon salt

2 tablespoons cornstarch
$^1/_4$ cup water
$^1/_2$ cup green pepper strips
$^1/_4$ cup chopped green onions
2 medium tomatoes, cut into sixths

Thaw fish, if frozen, and dry. Combine flour and salt and roll fish in mixture. Place fish in a heavy skillet or electric frypan which contains about $^1/_8$ inch of fat. Fry at moderate heat, 350°, until fish is brown on one side. Turn carefully and continue cooking until fish is brown and flakes easily when tested with a fork. Drain on absorbent paper. In a 2-quart saucepan, combine vinegar, sugar, $^1/_2$ cup water, soy sauce and salt. Bring to a boil. Combine cornstarch and $^1/_4$ cup water; add gradually to vinegar mixture and cook until thick and clear, stirring constantly. Add green pepper and onion and continue cooking for 3 minutes. Stir in tomatoes and heat. Serve over fish steaks.

(Serves 6)

Crispy Broiled Fish Steaks

Here is a special recipe that gives your fish steaks a browned topping, which helps to keep them moist.

2 pounds fish steaks	1 cup crushed potato
¹/₂ cup butter, melted	chips
¹/₄ cup lemon juice	¹/₂ cup crushed saltines
1 teaspoon salt	Lemon wedges
Dash paprika	

Thaw steaks if frozen. Place fish in a baking dish. Combine butter, lemon juice, salt and paprika. Pour sauce over fish and marinate for 30 minutes, turning once. Combine crushed potato chips and saltines. Remove fish, reserving sauce. Roll fish in crumb mixture. Place fish on a well-greased broiler pan. Drizzle sauce evenly over fish. Broil about 5 inches from source of heat for 5 to 7 minutes or until brown. Turn carefully and broil 5 to 7 minutes longer or until brown and fish flakes easily when tested with a fork. Serve with lemon wedges.

(Serves 6)

Barbecued Broiled Fish Steaks

Steaks from large codfish, grouper and red snapper need a tasty sauce. Try brushing such fish steaks with this barbecue sauce and discover the wonderful difference.

2 pounds fish steaks
1 can (6 ounces) tomato paste
1/3 cup water
2 tablespoons lime juice
2 tablespoons Worcestershire sauce
1 tablespoon sugar
1 tablespoon cooking oil
1 teaspoon salt
1/8 teaspoon garlic powder

Thaw fish if frozen. Combine remaining ingredients in a small bowl. Place fish steaks on a well-greased broiler pan. Brush steaks generously with sauce. Broil 5 inches from source of heat for 5 to 7 minutes. Turn, brush with more sauce and continue broiling for 5 to 7 minutes or until fish flakes easily when tested with a fork.

(Serves 6)

Fish Steaks with Piquant Meringue

If you are ever in Bellevue, Washington, visit Johnston's Seafood Store for smoked salmon and Dungeness crabs. The owners will give you their file of customers' seafood recipes, some of which are excellent. Here's one of them, and it is especially delicious with halibut and similar fish steaks.

2 pounds fish steaks
Salt and pepper
$1/4$ cup melted butter
1 egg white
$1/2$ cup mayonnaise
$1/2$ teaspoon prepared mustard

1 teaspoon Worcestershire sauce
$1/2$ cup grated Cheddar cheese

Thaw fish if frozen. Sprinkle fish steaks with salt and pepper and then brush with melted butter. Place fish on a well-greased broiler pan and broil about 5 inches from source of heat for 5 to 7 minutes or until slightly brown. Turn, brush steaks again with butter and broil for 5 to 7 minutes. Meanwhile, beat egg white until stiff and gently fold in remaining ingredients. Place mixture on top of steaks and brown in broiler about 1 minute.

(Serves 6)

Fish Steak Surprise

Maybe your family or guests would like something quite different from the usual fish recipe. This unique combination of ingredients is enjoyed by everyone.

2 pounds fish steaks
$1/2$ cup clear French dressing
2 tablespoons lemon juice
$1/4$ teaspoon salt

1 can ($3 1/2$ ounces) French fried onions, crumbled
$1/4$ cup grated Parmesan cheese

Thaw fish if frozen. Place fish in a single layer in a shallow baking dish. Combine dressing, lemon juice and salt. Pour this sauce over fish and let stand 30 minutes, turning once. Remove fish from sauce and place in a single layer in a well-greased baking pan. Combine onion and cheese; sprinkle over fish. Bake in a 350° oven for 25 to 35 minutes or until fish flakes easily when tested with a fork.

(Serves 6)

Fish Steaks Florentine

You can also cook your fish steaks on a bed of spinach.
This recipe includes an oven cooking bag which naturally
insures moist, tasty fish.

2 packages (10 ounces each) frozen, chopped spinach, thawed	$^1/_2$ teaspoon nutmeg
	4 fish steaks (4 ounces each)
$^1/_2$ teaspoon instant minced onion	1 tablespoon lemon juice
$^1/_2$ teaspoon salt	$^1/_4$ cup butter

Place a large size (14" × 20") oven cooking bag in a 2-inch
deep roasting pan. Remove excess moisture from spinach.
Combine spinach, onion, salt and nutmeg; place in bag,
distributing evenly. Arrange fish steaks on spinach bed.
Sprinkle with lemon juice and dot with butter. Close bag
with twist tie and make 6 $^1/_2$-inch slits in top of bag. Place in
a 350° oven and bake for 35 to 40 minutes or until fish
flakes easily when tested with a fork.

(Serves 4)

Poached Fish Steaks

Along with everything already mentioned, you can poach fish steaks as well and serve them with Hollandaise, herb butter or other sauces. See how good this is by trying it.

2 pounds fish steaks	3 peppercorns
2 cups water	1 bay leaf
1/4 cup lemon juice	Hollandaise Sauce
1 teaspoon instant minced onion	Herb Butter
1 teaspoon salt	Paprika

Thaw fish if frozen. Remove skin from steaks. Combine water, lemon juice, onion, salt, peppercorns and bay leaf in a well-greased 10-inch skillet and bring to a boil. Reduce heat. Place fish in a single layer into hot liquid. Cover and simmer 8 to 10 minutes or until fish flakes easily when tested with a fork. Carefully remove fish to a hot platter. Serve with Hollandaise Sauce or Herb Butter and sprinkle with paprika.

(Serves 6)

Hollandaise Sauce

2 egg yolks
1 teaspoon flour
1/4 cup butter, melted

1 tablespoon lemon juice
1/2 cup boiling water
Pinch of salt

Beat egg yolks; add flour and butter. Then add lemon juice, water and salt. Cook, stirring constantly, in top of a double boiler over hot, but not boiling, water for 30 seconds. Serve hot over poached fish steaks or chill in refrigerator and serve over cold, poached fish.

Herb Butter

1/4 cup butter
3 tablespoons white table wine
Dash cayenne pepper
1 tablespoon minced parsley

1/2 teaspoon salt
2 tablespoons minced chives
1 teaspoon minced fresh dill or dill weed

In a small saucepan, melt butter and add rest of ingredients. Pour hot over poached fish steaks.

Cooking Fish Fillets

No matter where you live, you can usually buy fish fillets, either fresh or frozen. The seafood industry likes to give you fillets because they represent a huge saving in shipping costs. You, the consumer, should be pleased because they save room in your freezer or refrigerator, and there is no waste. In addition, because fillets are generally free from bones, skin and blood, they will freeze and taste better. Another bonus is that they take less energy to cook.

Most fish, including fresh water bass, taste better when filleted and skinned. Oily fish, including tuna, albacore and the mackerel family, should always be filleted and skinned. A possible exception would be Boston and Sierra mackerel, which simply are not large enough.

I never knew how good bluefish could be until I filleted and skinned them. I even prefer flounder fillets skinned, as skinning does away with any possible muddy flavor.

Fish that are to be skinned should not be scaled. Scaling them will only make removing the skin much more difficult. Also, there are fish that are better left unskinned, even as fillets. These include the trout and salmon families, weakfish and codfish, along with its many relatives.

What about your costs for filleted fish? You can pay nearly twice as much per pound for fillets as for whole fish and come out about the same. Bluefish fillets yield 41.04%

of the whole fish; flounder fillets yield 47.12% of the whole; and Spanish mackerel fillets yield 57.54% of the whole.

There is something else about fillets you should know. If you go out on a charter boat or your own craft and come back with bluefish, tuna, albacore and bonita, you'll notice very dark red meat under the skin. This dark meat, called "liver" by tuna fishermen, should be removed before freezing. Granted some people like its oily flavor, but because it is oily, it does not freeze well, and your fish will become strong tasting.

As with small fish and steaks, you have a wide choice of cooking methods with fillets. They can be fried, sautéed, broiled, baked and poached. So let's start cooking with that classic American tool—the frying pan.

Frying is easy, isn't it? All you do is put some grease in a pan, turn up the burner and toss in your fillets!

Actually, if you don't want clouds of blue smoke, it is best to fry in vegetable oil or a vegetable oil/butter mixture. Temperature is important too. Too hot frying will brown your fillets on the outside but leave the inside raw. Too cool means greasy, soggy fillets and indigestion.

Something else to keep in mind is not to dunk your fillets in flour or corn meal or anything else before you are ready to cook them. Coat them too early and your coating absorbs moisture from the fish and, when fried, will not come out brown and crisp.

Now that we have solved these problems, let's move ahead to a recipe that's different in that self-rising flour is used with self-rising cornmeal.

Lemon Dill Fried Fillets

2 pounds fish fillets
²/₃ cup lemon juice
³/₄ cup self-rising flour
³/₄ cup self-rising cornmeal

1 teaspoon dried dill
¹/₈ teaspoon pepper
Oil for frying
Lemon wedges

Thaw fish if frozen. Cut fillets into serving size portions and place in a shallow glass baking dish. Pour lemon juice over fillets and let stand about 1 hour in refrigerator, turning once. Mix together flour, cornmeal, dill and pepper. Just before frying, coat fish evenly with flour mixture. Place fillets in a heavy skillet or electric frypan that contains about ¹/₈ inch fat, hot but not smoking. Fry at moderate heat, 350°, for 5 to 7 minutes or until brown. Turn carefully and cook 5 to 7 minutes longer or until brown and fish flakes easily when tested with a fork. Serve with lemon wedges.

(Serves 6)

Note: If all-purpose flour is used, add 1 teaspoon salt.

Fish Fry Delight

There is nothing as delicious as fish fillets fried soon after being caught. We ate a lot of these years ago while fishing at Gananoque, Ontario. But, the best fillets of all got away. Our Artie, then about seven years old, was trolling with a spinner and hooked a beautiful smallmouth bass. Just as he worked it to the boat, it made one final leap and escaped. Artie broke into tears. "I'll never get another," he wailed. Luckily, over the years, his prediction has been proved wrong many times.

If Artie had landed his fish, we would have cooked it this way.

2 pounds fish fillets	1 tablespoon prepared
2 eggs	mustard
³/₄ cup cold water	Oil or fat for frying
1 envelope (3 ounces)	
potato pancake mix	

Thaw fish if frozen. Cut fish fillets into serving size portions. Combine eggs, water and potato pancake mix. Stir until well blended; let stand 10 minutes. Blend in mustard. Dip fish fillets in pancake batter and place in a heavy skillet or electric frypan that contains about ¹/₈ inch oil or fat, hot but not smoking. Fry at moderate heat, 350°, for 5 to 7 minutes or until brown. Turn carefully and cook 5 to 7 minutes longer or until brown and fish flakes easily when tested with a fork.

(Serves 6)

Super Fish Fillets with Chives

Some fillets, just like some human beings, are thicker than others. That doesn't mean they are not good; maybe they are even better! Here's a great way to prepare thick fillets from catfish, paddlefish, lake trout, grouper or other large fish.

1 pound thick fish fillets	$^1/_2$ teaspoon salt
1 cup sour cream	$^1/_8$ teaspoon pepper
4 tablespoons dehydrated chopped chives	$^1/_2$ cup biscuit mix Fat for frying Paprika

Thaw fish if frozen. Cut fish fillets into serving size portions. Combine sour cream, chives, salt and pepper. Let stand approximately 30 minutes. Reserve 3 tablespoons sour cream mixture for garnish. Dip fillets into sour cream mixture and then roll in biscuit mix. Place fish in a heavy skillet or electric frypan that contains about $^1/_8$ inch fat, hot but not smoking. Fry at moderate heat, 350°, for 5 to 7 minutes or until brown. Turn carefully and cook 5 to 7 minutes longer or until brown and fish flakes easily when tested with a fork. Drain on absorbent paper. Garnish each serving with 1 tablespoon sour cream mix; sprinkle with paprika.

(Serves 3)

Marinated Tangy Fillets

While fried fish is traditional, and many people have never eaten fillets cooked any other way, broiling is wonderful too. It is especially good with bluefish, Spanish mackerel and other rather oily fishes. This recipe uses the acid in tomatoes and lemonade to break down the fats and oils. You'll find this an excellent way to prepare coho salmon and steelhead.

2 pounds fish fillets	1 tablespoon prepared mustard
1/3 cup butter, melted	1/2 teaspoon salt
1/3 cup catsup	1/4 teaspoon garlic salt
1/3 cup frozen lemonade concentrate, thawed	1 bay leaf, crumbled

Thaw fish if frozen. Cut fish fillets into serving size portions. Place fish in a single layer in a baking dish. Combine remaining ingredients, mix well and pour over fish. Turn fish to coat evenly. Cover and marinate in refrigerator at least 30 minutes. Arrange fish on a well-greased broiler pan. Brush with sauce. Broil about 4 inches from source of heat for 4 to 5 minutes. Turn carefully and brush with sauce. Broil 4 to 5 minutes longer or until fish flakes easily when tested with a fork.

(Serves 6)

Fillets Amandine

While I usually prefer my fillets skinned, unless they are from trout or salmon, not all people do, so here is a way to cook them, skin and all, with a traditional amandine sauce.

2 pounds fish fillets, unskinned
1/2 cup flour
1 teaspoon salt
1 teaspoon paprika
2 tablespoons butter, melted
1/3 cup slivered almonds

2 tablespoons butter, melted
1 tablespoon lemon juice
1 tablespoon white table wine
1 tablespoon chopped parsley

Thaw fish, if frozen, and dry. Cut fillets into serving size portions. Combine flour, salt and paprika. Roll fish in flour mixture and place skin side down in a well-greased broiler pan. Drizzle 2 tablespoons melted butter over fish. Broil about 4 inches from source of heat for 8 to 10 minutes or until fish flakes easily when tested with a fork. While fish is broiling, cook almonds in remaining 2 tablespoons butter until golden brown, stirring constantly. Remove from heat and stir in lemon juice, wine and parsley. Pour sauce over fish and serve at once.

(Serves 6)

Zesty Fillets

Along with providing important nutrients, fish is good news for all of us who must watch our weight. All fish is low in calories and high in unsaturated fats, the kind that are supposed to be good for you. By cooking your fillets this way, you won't add unwanted calories.

1 pound fish fillets	1 tablespoon prepared
1/4 cup chili sauce	horseradish
1 tablespoon oil	1 teaspoon
1 tablespoon prepared	Worcestershire sauce
mustard	1/4 teaspoon salt

Thaw fish if frozen. Cut fish fillets into serving size portions. Place fish on a well-greased broiler pan. Combine remaining ingredients and spread sauce evenly over fish. Broil about 6 inches from source of heat for 5 to 8 minutes or until fish flakes easily when tested with a fork.

(Serves 3)

Sumptuous Fillets

If you want to lose weight, or at least not gain, you need not suffer gastronomically. Here's a great way to cook fillets with mushrooms and cheese that doesn't add many calories and is inexpensive to prepare.

1 pound fish fillets	1 can (4 ounces) mushroom stems and pieces, drained
2 tablespoons melted butter or oil	
1/2 teaspoon salt	1/2 cup Cheddar cheese, grated
Dash pepper	1 tablespoon chopped parsley

Thaw fish if frozen. Cut fish fillets into serving size portions. Combine butter, salt and pepper. Chop mushrooms and then combine with cheese and parsley. Place fish on a well-greased broiler pan and brush with butter. Broil about 4 inches from source of heat for 3 to 4 minutes. Turn carefully and brush with remaining butter. Broil 3 to 4 minutes longer or until fish flakes easily when tested with a fork. Spread mushroom mixture on fish and broil 2 to 3 minutes longer or until lightly brown.

(Serves 3)

Fillets with Sauce Doria

When a chef comes to dinner, what do you serve? One of my sons is a chef, and he came over one evening when I was broiling some bluefish fillets. Noticing some fresh cucumbers in the refrigerator, he asked if he could prepare a cucumber sauce for the fish. Naturally, I said "yes" and moved out of the way, wondering how much cleaning up I'd have to do. Chefs, in case you don't know, are not much on cleaning. They have helpers to do it for them. In this case, luckily, things worked out quite well, and here is the recipe.

2 pounds fish fillets	Salt
2 tablespoons butter, melted	Paprika
	Sauce Doria

Thaw fish if frozen. Cut fish fillets into serving size portions. Place fish in a single layer on a well-greased broiler pan. Pour melted butter over fish and sprinkle with salt and paprika. Broil about 4 inches from source of heat for 8 to 10 minutes or until fish flakes easily when tested with a fork. Remove fish to a warm platter and serve with Sauce Doria.

(Serves 6)

Sauce Doria

2 cucumbers, peeled, halved and seeded
2 tablespoons butter
1 tablespoon fresh dill, chopped or 1 1/2 teaspoons dried dill

1/2 cup white table wine
1 tablespoon cornstarch
1/4 cup water
Salt and white pepper to taste

Slice each cucumber half diagonally into 1/2-inch pieces. In a medium size skillet, melt butter and sauté cucumber pieces until transparent. Add dill and wine to skillet. Dissolve cornstarch in water and add to cucumber mixture. Simmer sauce, stirring constantly, until clear and bubbly. Add salt and pepper to taste.

Fish Puffs

You can bake fillets too, in a regular oven or a convection or counter top model, providing you place them in a greased baking dish and keep them moist and flavorful.

If your fillets are not skinned, try these Fish Puffs. They are delicious.

1 pound fish fillets	Few drops onion juice
Salt and pepper to taste	1/2 teaspoon Worcestershire sauce
1 egg white	Dash liquid hot pepper sauce
1/4 cup mayonnaise	

Thaw fish if frozen. Cut fish fillets into serving size portions. Place fillets in a single layer in a well-greased baking dish and season with salt and pepper. Beat egg white until stiff but not dry; fold in mayonnaise, onion juice, Worcestershire and hot pepper sauce. Spread mixture on fish fillets and bake in a 425° oven for 15 to 20 minutes or until fish flakes easily when tested with a fork and sauce is golden brown.

(Serves 3)

Baked Pinwheel Fillets

In many areas where fresh fish is hard to find, you can purchase frozen turbot. Since turbot comes in large fillets, you can stuff and roll them easily. Actually, you can use any fairly long fillets in this manner.

6 fish fillets (about 2 pounds)
2 cups fine, dry bread crumbs
1 cup (4 ounces) Cheddar cheese, shredded
1/2 cup grated Parmesan cheese
1/2 cup celery, chopped
1 teaspoon salt
1 teaspoon dried parsley flakes
3/4 teaspoon tarragon
2 eggs, beaten
1 cup milk
Salt and pepper to taste
3 tablespoons butter
1 lemon, thinly sliced

Thaw fish if frozen. Stir together bread crumbs, cheeses, celery, salt, parsley and tarragon. Combine eggs and milk; add to crumb mixture and toss to blend. Salt and pepper fish to taste. Pat about 1/3 cup crumb mixture over each fillet. Roll up jelly roll fashion; secure with a wooden toothpick. Place each roll on end in a well-greased baking dish. Dot with butter. Arrange lemon slices over fish. Bake in a 350° oven for 30 to 45 minutes or until done and fish flakes easily when tested with a fork. Meanwhile, divide remaining stuffing among 6 paper-lined muffin cups; bake with fish the last 20 minutes.

(Serves 6)

Baked Fillets in Wine Sauce

Now here's an easy, inexpensive formula that provides wonderfully delicious fillets when you have guests.

2 pounds fish fillets, skinned	2 tablespoons butter, melted
1 1/2 teaspoons salt Dash pepper	1/2 cup milk
3 tomatoes, sliced	1/3 cup white table wine
2 tablespoons flour	1/2 teaspoon crushed basil Chopped parsley

Thaw fish if frozen. Cut fish fillets into serving size portions. Sprinkle both sides of fillets with 1 teaspoon salt and pepper. Place fillets in a single layer in a well-greased baking dish. Arrange tomatoes on top of fillets and sprinkle with remaining 1/2 teaspoon salt. In a medium saucepan, blend flour into melted butter. Add milk gradually and cook until thick and smooth, stirring constantly. Remove from heat and stir in wine and basil. Pour sauce over top of tomatoes. Bake in a moderate 350° oven for 25 to 35 minutes or until fish flakes easily when tested with a fork. Sprinkle with parsley.

(Serves 6)

Baked Fillets with Clam Dressing

For those skinless thick fillets, here's a truly great baked fillet recipe.

1 pound fish fillets, skinned	1/4 cup chopped parsley or 1 tablespoon dried parsley flakes
1 tablespoon lemon juice	
1/2 teaspoon salt	1 egg, beaten
1 can (8 ounces) minced clams	2 tablespoons grated Parmesan cheese
2 slices white bread, crumbled	1/4 teaspoon oregano

Thaw fish if frozen. Cut skinned fillets into serving size portions. Place fillets in a single layer in a well-greased baking dish. Sprinkle fillets with lemon juice and salt. Drain clams, reserving 1/4 cup liquid. Combine clams, bread crumbs, parsley, egg, cheese and oregano. Spread clam mixture evenly over fillets and sprinkle with reserved clam liquid. Bake in a hot oven, 400°, for 20 to 25 minutes or until fish flakes easily when tested with a fork.

(Serves 3)

Marinated Fish Fillets

Later on, we'll discuss poaching as the first step in some unique methods of seafood preparation. Now, let's talk about poached fillets which can be used as tasty entrées. This first recipe, tried on my family, brought the response from my husband that he wished I would write a cookbook every year. You can use these as a first course or as a salad. It's best with flounder, turbot, pollock or other bland fish.

2 pounds fish fillets, skinned	1 small onion, sliced
1 cup water	1 teaspoon pickling spice
$^{1}/_{2}$ teaspoon salt	3 tablespoons sugar
$^{1}/_{4}$ cup lemon juice	$^{1}/_{4}$ cup white table wine

Thaw fish if frozen. Cut fish fillets into serving size portions. Heat water with salt in a 10-inch skillet. Add fish fillets, cover and simmer about 5 to 10 minutes or until fish flakes. Carefully remove cooked fillets and place in a single layer in a glass baking dish. Reserve $^{1}/_{2}$ cup liquid from the skillet and discard remainder. Return this reserved liquid to skillet and add lemon juice, onion, pickling spice, sugar and wine; bring to a boil. Pour liquid over fish. When room temperature, cover and refrigerate for 5 to 6 hours or overnight, turning fish occasionally. When ready to serve, drain and place on lettuce leaves with lemon slices.

(Serves 6)

Lemon Dill Fish with Noodles

With this recipe, you begin poaching and then add ingredients to complete a wonderful dish right in the skillet.

1 pound fish fillets, skinned	¹/₈ teaspoon pepper
¹/₄ cup water	1 teaspoon sugar
2 tablespoons lemon juice	6 ounces medium noodles
1 tablespoon grated lemon peel	2 teaspoons dried dill
1 teaspoon salt	1 cup (8 ounce carton) plain yogurt

Thaw fish if frozen. Cut fish fillets into serving size portions. In a 10-inch skillet, bring water, lemon juice, peel, salt, pepper and sugar to a boil. Add fish fillets to liquid and simmer for 5 to 10 minutes or until fish flakes easily when tested with a fork. Meanwhile, cook noodles in boiling salted water according to package directions. Drain noodles. Stir dill and yogurt into fish dish and heat thoroughly. Serve immediately over drained noodles.

(Serves 3)

Fish with Sauerkraut in Skillet

You have probably never considered cooking fish with sauerkraut. Here's an excellent recipe which needs only some hot biscuits to make a complete meal.

1½ pounds fish fillets, skinned
½ cup chopped onion
2 tablespoons melted butter or cooking oil
1 can (1 pound, 11 ounces) sauerkraut, well drained

½ cup water
½ teaspoon caraway seed
1 package (3 ounces) cream cheese, cut into ½-inch cubes
2 slices processed American cheese, cut into strips

Thaw fish if frozen. Cut fish fillets into 1-inch pieces. Cook onion in butter in a 10-inch heavy skillet or electric frypan until tender but not brown. Add sauerkraut, water and caraway seed. Cover and simmer about 30 minutes or until flavors are well blended. Stir cream cheese into sauerkraut. Top with fish pieces. Cover and simmer about 10 minutes or until fish flakes easily when tested with a fork. Top fish with strips of cheese; cover and allow cheese to melt.

(Serves 4)

Sesame Fillets

When my husband saw me preparing this recipe he said, "Wok do you know about that!" Maybe his puns are awful, but a wok is a first-rate utensil for fish dishes. With an electric wok, you can cook your meal right at the table.

1½ pounds fish fillets, skinned	½ cup fine, dry bread crumbs
Salt and pepper	3 tablespoons sesame seed
1 egg	
1 tablespoon milk	2 tablespoons each cooking oil and butter

Thaw fish if frozen. Cut fish fillets into serving size pieces. Sprinkle fish with salt and pepper. In a bowl, beat egg and milk together. In a flat dish or pan, mix bread crumbs with sesame seed. Dip fish into egg/milk mixture and then into crumb/seed mixture coating fish evenly on all sides. Have wok at medium high heat and then add oil and butter. After butter has melted, add a few pieces of fish at a time; gently turn fish to brown on both sides and cook until fish flakes easily when tested with a fork—about 2 minutes. Remove fish and keep warm. Repeat, using more oil and butter if necessary.

(Serves 4)

Kedgeree

A one dish meal saves both work and energy, making for a better natured cook and reduced utility bills. Here are some good ones, all of which begin with skinned fillets from pike, bass, walleyes, flounder, catfish or almost any other fish.

Let's start with a famous English breakfast dish that doubles very nicely as a hearty lunch or supper.

1 pound fish fillets, skinned
1 can (10³/₄ ounces) condensed chicken broth
1 soup can water
³/₄ cup raw regular rice
1 teaspoon salt
Dash pepper
2 hard-cooked eggs, chopped
2 tablespoons finely chopped parsley
Lemon/herb seasoning to taste

Thaw fish if frozen. Cut fillets into 1-inch pieces. In a large saucepan, combine broth, water, fish, rice, salt and pepper. Bring to a boil and then reduce heat. Cover and cook over low heat for 20 minutes or until liquid is absorbed. Stir occasionally. Remove from heat and stir in eggs, parsley and seasoning.

(Serves 4)

Fisherman's Stew

When first married, I came down with a terrible case of mumps. One of the worst parts of this affliction was that my husband took over the cooking, and when feeling better, I visited the kitchen and saw the mess he had made. I nearly collapsed! However, he did prepare some excellent fish stew using fillets as a main ingredient. This next recipe makes a great family meal in about 10 minutes.

1 pound fish fillets, skinned
1/2 cup chopped onion
2 tablespoons butter, melted or cooking oil
2 cans (10 3/4 ounces each) cream of potato soup
2 cups milk

1 can (1 pound) tomato wedges, undrained
1 package (10 ounces) frozen mixed vegetables, thawed
1 can (8 ounces) whole kernel corn, drained
1 teaspoon salt
1/8 teaspoon pepper
1 bay leaf

Thaw fish if frozen. Cut fillets into 1-inch chunks. In a large saucepan, cook onion in butter until tender but not brown. Add soup, milk, tomato wedges, vegetables, corn, salt, pepper and bay leaf; heat, stirring occasionally, until simmering. Add fish; simmer approximately 10 minutes or until fish flakes easily when tested with a fork.

(Serves 6)

Fish Pie with Biscuit Topping

Meat pies are probably the oldest kind of pie. Maybe fish pies are the most recent. I don't know, but here is proof that a good fish pie is inexpensive, delicious and another fine way of serving fish.

1 pound fish fillets, skinned

1 package (10 ounces) frozen mixed vegetables, broken apart

1 can (10^1/$_2$ ounces) cream of celery soup

^{1}/$_2$ cup milk

^{1}/$_2$ teaspoon onion salt

^{1}/$_2$ teaspoon salt

1^1/$_2$ cups prepared biscuit mix

^{3}/$_4$ cup shredded Cheddar cheese

^{1}/$_2$ cup milk

Thaw fish if frozen. Cut fillets into 1-inch pieces. In a 10-inch skillet, combine mixed vegetables, soup, ^{1}/$_2$ cup milk, onion salt and salt; mix well. Cover and cook over low heat about 5 minutes, stirring occasionally. Add fish and heat thoroughly. Pour mixture into a well-greased 1^1/$_2$-quart baking dish. In a 1-quart mixing bowl, combine biscuit mix, cheese and ^{1}/$_2$ cup milk; stir to make a smooth dough. Drop biscuit mixture by tablespoons onto hot fish mixture. Bake in a hot oven, 400°, for 18 to 20 minutes or until biscuits are done and brown.

(Serves 4)

Recipes Using Cooked, Flaked Fish

It's Murphy's Law that says, "Whatever can go wrong will go wrong." Because so many things can and do go wrong on a fishing trip, the cook, instead of being challenged by large, easy-to-prepare testimonials to the piscatorial success of family members, must make do with small, bony, undersized fish.

Small, bony fish aren't much fun fried or broiled. Dissecting them is not a job for children who might choke on fishbones. It's these little sunnies, bluegills, bullheads, Norfolk spot, opaleye and the like that give fish dishes a bad name.

Yet there is an answer, a very easy one. All you do with fish too small to have left their mother is poach them gently, slide off the skin and bones and then use the cooked, flaked meat in a variety of exciting dishes. Just remember that four cups of flaked, boneless, skinned, poached fish is equivalent to a pound of fish fillets.

Let's begin all these recipes by explaining the easiest way of poaching these small fish.

147

Poached Small Fish

4 to 6 small pan fish
2 tablespoons lemon
  juice

2 tablespoons water
¼ teaspoon salt

Place an inch of water in a deep skillet and bring to a
gentle boil. Arrange your fish on a piece of heavy duty
aluminum foil and turn up edges of wrap. Add lemon
juice, water and salt and then place in skillet. Cover and
cook gently for 5 to 10 minutes or until fish flakes easily
when tested with a fork. Then remove skin and bones and
flake fish.

Note: Flaked fish can be frozen in an airtight container
and kept up to three months.

Fish Toasties

What about hors d'oeuvres or canapes from your cooked
flaked fish? They hit the spot at cocktail time but are not
too heavy to spoil your appetite for a delicious main
course.

1 cup cooked, flaked fish
3 egg whites, stiffly
  beaten
2 tablespoons
  mayonnaise

⅛ teaspoon salt
1 teaspoon paprika
1 tablespoon onion juice

Gently fold all ingredients into beaten egg whites. Spread
mixture on small, lightly salted crackers and place under
the broiler until slightly browned and puffy.

148

Easy Fish Casserole

Most fish you would poach, especially bass, sunfish, catfish and their salt water equivalents, have firm meat. This means you can use it in casseroles because your flaked fish will not change shape with additional heating. Here's a casserole your family and guests will enjoy. It's inexpensive too!

2 cups cooked, flaked, firm fish
1/2 cup chopped onion
4 tablespoons butter
2 tablespoons flour
1/2 cup milk
1/2 cup tomato sauce
1/2 teaspoon salt
Dash pepper
1/4 cup grated Cheddar cheese
1/2 cup soft bread crumbs

Cook onion in butter until tender. Blend in flour; add milk gradually and cook until thick, stirring constantly. Add tomato sauce, salt, pepper and flaked fish. Place in a well-greased 1 1/2-quart casserole dish. Combine cheese and crumbs; sprinkle over casserole. Bake in a moderate oven, 350°, for 20 to 25 minutes or until brown and thoroughly hot.

(Serves 4)

Codfish Cakes

New England codfish cakes are famous and salty. You can make better ones, without all the salt of dried codfish, by substituting other fish. Cod relatives such as haddock, pollock, whiting, hake and ling work especially well.

4	cups cooked, flaked cod or similar fish	$1\frac{1}{2}$	teaspoons poultry seasoning
3	cups hot, seasoned mashed potatoes	$\frac{1}{2}$	teaspoon salt Flour
1	egg, beaten		Shortening
1	tablespoon instant minced onion		

Combine flaked fish with mashed potatoes, egg, onion, poultry seasoning and salt. Chill until mixture can be shaped into patties. Form into 12 patties, $\frac{1}{2}$-inch thick. Coat patties with flour and place in a heavy skillet or electric frypan containing about $\frac{1}{8}$ inch shortening, hot but not smoking. Cook over moderate heat, 350°, until brown. Turn carefully and cook 5 to 6 minutes or until brown and thoroughly hot.

(Makes 12 patties)

Blue Ribbon Fish Loaf

In these days of high prices, there is a lot of meat loaf eaten and enjoyed. Here's a fish loaf, and it is so good that many folks who claim not to be fish eaters will come back for seconds.

2 cups cooked, flaked fish
1 egg, beaten
1/4 cup half and half cream
3/4 cup dry bread crumbs
1/2 teaspoon salt
1/4 teaspoon paprika

1 tablespoon lemon juice
1 tablespoon melted butter
2 tablespoons minced parsley
1 teaspoon instant minced onion

Combine egg and cream; add to flaked fish. Add remaining ingredients and mix together with a fork. Pat the fish mixture into a greased loaf pan and bake in a hot oven, 400°, for 30 minutes.

(Serves 4)

Croquettes with Chicken-Rice Sauce

When it comes to croquettes, most of us automatically think of chicken. Yet, in the immortal words of George Gershwin, "It ain't necessarily so." This recipe works as well with fish leftovers as it does with the poached, smaller fish we've been working with.

1½ cups cooked, flaked fish	1 tablespoon lemon juice
1½ cups soft bread crumbs	½ teaspoon salt
2 eggs	⅛ teaspoon pepper
½ teaspoon onion juice	Fat for frying
⅓ cup finely chopped celery	Chicken-Rice Sauce

Combine fish, bread crumbs, eggs, onion juice, celery, lemon juice, salt and pepper; mix well. Chill. Shape mixture into balls, using about 1 tablespoon mixture per ball. Place croquettes in a 10-inch heavy skillet or electric frypan containing about ⅛ inch fat, hot but not smoking. Cook over moderate heat, 350°, about 8 to 10 minutes, turning carefully to brown on all sides. Drain on absorbent paper. Serve with Chicken-Rice Sauce. (Serves 4)

Chicken-Rice Sauce

1 tablespoon melted butter	1 can (10½ ounces) chicken and rice soup
1 tablespoon flour	

In a 1-quart saucepan, combine melted butter and flour. Gradually add undiluted soup and cook until thick, stirring constantly. (Makes about 1 cup)

152

Crescents

Getting back again to the oilier fish, salmon, mackerel, tuna, albacore and bluefish, this recipe is outstanding.

3 cups cooked, flaked bluefish, salmon or similar fish
1 tablespoon instant minced onion or $1/4$ cup chopped onion
$1/2$ cup chopped celery
1 tablespoon butter
1 cup (2 slices) finely torn bread
$1/2$ teaspoon salt

1 can ($10^3/4$ ounces) cream of celery soup
1 can (8 ounces) refrigerated crescent dinner rolls
1 tablespoon butter, melted
$1/4$ cup milk
Paprika
Lemon slices

Preheat oven to 375°. In a small skillet, cook onion and celery in butter until tender. In a large bowl, combine cooked onion and celery, fish, bread, salt and $1/3$ can of soup (reserve remaining soup for sauce). Separate dough into 8 triangles. Press or roll to enlarge. Spread about $1/3$ cup fish mixture on each triangle. Roll up starting at the shortest side of triangle and roll to opposite point. Place rolls, point side down, 2 inches apart in ungreased oblong jelly roll pan. Brush rolls with melted butter. Bake in a 375° oven for 20 to 30 minutes or until golden brown. In small bowl, blend remaining soup and milk. Spoon evenly over baked rolls and sprinkle with paprika. Return to oven and bake 2 to 4 minutes or until sauce is heated. Garnish with lemon slices.

(Serves 4 to 5)

Fish Pizzas

In these days when a hamburger costs a dollar or more, children are turning to pizzas. This fish pizza will be avidly eaten by children who drearily chant, "I hate fish." You don't even have to tell them there is fish in their pizza until after they have eaten it. You can use almost any kind of poached, flaked fish.

2 cups cooked, flaked fish
1 cup catsup
$1/2$ teaspoon onion powder
$1^1/2$ teaspoons oregano
8 individual small pizza crusts
$1^1/2$ cups grated Mozzarella cheese

Combine catsup, onion powder and oregano. Add fish and mix well with a fork. Place several tablespoons of fish mixture on each pizza crust. Sprinkle about 2 tablespoons of cheese on each small pizza and place on a cookie sheet. Heat in a 350° oven for about 20 minutes or until hot and cheese melts.

(Makes 8 pizzas)

Sausage Patties

Fish is a very good source of protein. So why not use it to make sausages? These sausages do not resemble fish in taste and are delicious served in split, hot biscuits.

1 cup cooked, flaked fish	$^1/_2$ teaspoon black pepper
1 cup pork sausage meat	$^1/_4$ teaspoon red pepper
1 teaspoon salt	$^1/_2$ teaspoon sage

Mix all ingredients thoroughly using your hands. Form into small patties and place these in a cold frying pan. Add 2 to 3 tablespoons of water, cover pan and cook over low to medium heat until water is evaporated. Remove lid and continue cooking until patties are cooked through and brown on both sides. A little butter may be needed during the browning process depending on the fat in the pork sausage meat. Serve patties hot.

(Makes 15 to 20 small patties)

Savory Quiche

I like crabmeat, shrimp and lobster as well as anyone. Yet
I've found you can get an almost identical flavor with firm,
flaked poached fish in a recipe like this.

2 cups cooked, flaked
   fish
3 eggs
1 can (10³/₄ ounces)
   cream of onion soup
1 can (2 ounces)
   mushroom stems and
   pieces, drained and
   chopped

³/₄ teaspoon lemon-
   pepper seasoning
1 cup shredded Swiss
   cheese
1 unbaked, deep 9-inch
   pie shell
¹/₂ cup shredded Swiss
   cheese
   Paprika

Combine eggs and soup; beat well. Stir in flaked fish,
mushrooms and lemon-pepper seasoning. Sprinkle pie
shell with 1 cup shredded Swiss cheese. Pour fish mixture
over cheese. Sprinkle with remaining ¹/₂ cup cheese and
paprika. Bake in a moderate oven, 375°, on lowest oven
shelf for 35 to 40 minutes or until golden brown and knife
inserted in center of quiche comes out clean. Let stand 10
minutes before serving.

(Makes 6 servings)

Fish Salad

All of us can make fish salads from canned tuna and
salmon. Yet if you haven't tried a fish salad made from
your own cooked, flaked fish, you're missing a lot. Oily
fish, such as bluefish and albacore, are extra good. Or if
you have leftover Great Lakes salmon, use it too. Be sure
always to remove the dark oily "liver" before making your
salad.

2 cups cooked, flaked bluefish, albacore or similar fish	½ cup diced celery
	2 tablespoons sweet pickle relish
½ cup mayonnaise or salad dressing	½ cup cooked peas

Combine all ingredients, being careful not to break the
fish flakes too small. Serve in lettuce cups and garnish with
quarters of tomatoes and sliced eggs. If using this recipe
for a sandwich spread, finely chop the fish and omit peas.

(Serves 4)

Molded Fish Salad

You can also make a molded salad with cooked, flaked fish that is economical and tasty.

2 cups cooked, flaked fish

1 package (3 ounces) lime gelatin

½ teaspoon salt

1 cup boiling water

2 teaspoons vinegar

¾ cup cold water

2 hard-cooked eggs, sliced

½ cup chopped dill pickle

¼ cup diced celery

Dissolve gelatin and salt in boiling water. Add vinegar and cold water. Chill until thickened. Fold in remaining ingredients. Pour into a 1-quart mold or loaf pan and chill. Unmold and garnish as desired.

(Serves 4)

Fish Mousse

Believe it or not, there really was a Fanny Farmer. My
mother, a home economist, was one of her students at
Columbia University. Mother, in her late eighties, is still
cooking and sends me recipes from time to time. She ate
this mousse at a friend's house and liked it. You will too.
The original recipe called for canned salmon, but I find
bluefish, with dark meat removed, is as good or even better. Or you can try wahoo, king mackerel or any other
mackerel.

2 cups cooked, flaked
  bluefish or similar fish,
  finely chopped
1 envelope
  (1 tablespoon)
  unflavored gelatin
$^{1}/_{4}$ cup cold water
$^{1}/_{2}$ cup boiling water
$^{1}/_{2}$ cup mayonnaise
1 tablespoon lemon juice

1 tablespoon grated
  onion or $^{1}/_{2}$ teaspoon
  onion powder
$^{1}/_{2}$ teaspoon hot pepper
  sauce
$^{1}/_{4}$ teaspoon paprika
1 teaspoon salt
1 tablespoon chopped
  capers
$^{1}/_{2}$ cup heavy cream

Soften gelatin in cold water; add boiling water and stir until gelatin has dissolved. Cool. Add mayonnaise, lemon
juice, onion, hot pepper sauce, paprika and salt; mix well.
Chill to the consistency of unbeaten egg whites. Add fish
and capers and beat well. Whip cream and fold into the
fish mixture. Turn into an oiled 4-cup mold and chill until
set. Unmold on a serving platter and garnish.

(Serves 4 to 6)

Note: For a 6-cup mold, use a recipe and a half.

Fish Dinner Menu

PEANUT BUTTER SOUP

ANY FISH RECIPE

CARROT-RICE BAKE

COMB OF THE ROOSTER SALAD

RICH BISCUITS

MOTHER'S CARAMEL CUSTARD

See Accompaniment Section for recipes.

Fish Dinner for Warm Weather Menu

CHUTNEY CHEESE SPREAD/CRACKERS

ANY FISH RECIPE

POTATO SALAD

MARINATED BROCCOLI

BLUEBERRY MUFFINS

MOTHER'S ANGEL BERRY PIE

See Accompaniment Section for recipes.

Shellfish

Purchasing and Freezing

One taste of crabmeat or lobster, a single bucket of steamed clams or maybe a dish of Oysters Rockefeller are among the many ways of getting hooked on shellfish. They're good to eat and good for you too, low in calories, easy to digest, and some characters will even tell you that shrimp and oysters make for better loving!

Yet both main types of shellfish, crustaceans such as shrimp, crabs and lobsters, and mollusks, which include oysters, clams, mussels and conches, spoil easily and have often caused fatal poisoning to unwary diners.

You are safe enough when you catch them yourself and know they're alive and fresh. If you cannot do so, the advantage of commercially landed shellfish is that all of it comes from safe waters. But this does not mean it will be safe to eat by the time it reaches you.

Never buy a crab or lobster that is not alive. This applies to soft-shelled crabs too, unless they have been frozen. If they do not move but lie limp, they spell ptomaine! Frozen crabmeat, soft-shelled crabs and lobster meat should be sealed tight and have no cottony signs of freezer burn or any dark areas.

163

When you buy shrimp be sure the flesh is free from black spots and there is no disagreeable odor. Raw shrimp should be firm, with a translucent appearance. Cooked shrimp should appear pink but *never* red. Soft, red shrimp usually have a sickening aroma. If you can stand it, they do make wonderful bait for large catfish and snapping turtles. But do not eat them yourself.

Buying clams and oysters in the shell is easy and safe enough. Just be sure they are alive. Live mollusks have tightly shut shells. If they gape open and do not snap shut when touched, the animal has died.

You can buy oysters shucked and packed in jars or in tins with a clear top. Look to see that they are normally plump and the liquid in which they are packed is clear. When opened, they should smell fresh and mild.

You can tread or dig for clams, tong for oysters, catch crabs with a pot or line and trap lobsters with a pot. Yet scallops are only caught commercially.

Mussels, the type we eat, are the large blue ones which cling tightly to rocks and pilings in the ocean and some inshore tidal areas. There are several species of ribbed mussels, known as horse mussels, in salt water marshlands, but they are not edible. Stick with the smooth-shelled blue, sometimes nearly black mussels, and give them the same test as other mollusks, being sure they are tightly closed.

Canned shellfish must be in undamaged cans and look and smell fresh when opened. Frozen shellfish should be dated and kept at 0° or colder in your freezer, where they can be kept for four to six months if packaged properly.

Let's turn now to the clams, crabs and other shellfish you catch yourself. Keep them cool! Be sure they are alive, and if you keep them on ice, make certain no fresh water can reach and kill them.

When it comes to defrosting frozen shellfish, either your own or storebought packages, let them thaw in your refrigerator and then cook them immediately. *Never* refreeze frozen shellfish. If you do, you are asking for trouble.

Crab

The blue crab found from Massachusetts to Mexico is my favorite seafood. Always hungry, it is caught by the millions each summer by people with droplines on wharves and in rowboats, or even standing in the water. Others dip them with crabnets, or use long lines with dozens of separate baits or crabpots and traps made of chicken wire.

While all crabs must shed to grow, only blue crabs are available in the soft-shell stage. You can seine them over sandy bottom, especially in stands of eelgrass, or buy them commercially from crabbers who catch huge quantities of hard crabs and put them in holding pens to molt. With sharp eyes, you can spot a peeler or shedder that is about to get rid of its shell by very slight changes in color, such as a red line on the tiny paddle of the swimming legs. These shedders are then sorted out and either sold as bait— there's nothing better for most inshore fish—or "shed out" and sold to restaurants or wholesalers.

We keep a crabpot under our boat not a mile from home, so I can pick crabmeat from May to September. It's a tedious, time consuming job, but the result is worth the effort. We can have crabmeat, frozen of course, for Christmas.

If you buy crabmeat in eastern markets, it's available as lump or backfin, the most expensive; special, small pieces of white meat; and claw meat, which is brownish and sweet. You can also buy live hard crabs, steamed hard crabs or live and frozen soft-shelled crabs.

On the West coast there are Dungeness crabs in the northwest states and of course king crabs, really a type of spider crab, in Alaska. Maybe I should mention that spider crabs, though horrible looking, are very good to eat and are a delicacy in Europe. But almost no one along our Atlantic coast is willing to try them. Oddly, with Atlantic spider crabs, all meat is in the body, and with the Alaskan variety, it's all in the legs!

165

Another crab worth mentioning is the stone crab, which lives far offshore in deep water. It's all edible, but in Florida, where there is a big fishery, only claws, cooked right on board the boat, or immediately after landing, are available. A law requires that the body of the crab be returned to the sea to grow new claws.

Getting down to cooking, the first step with live crabs is always to boil or steam them, which we will discuss shortly. Then you can either eat them hot or cold or take out the meat and use it in any number of ways.

If, like me, you freeze your own crabmeat, it won't last much over three months before it loses both taste and moisture. On the other hand, store-bought crabmeat has been pasteurized and will keep longer without change in taste or texture. Just remember that once you thaw and open crabmeat in a container, it must be used within a day or so and kept well iced in the interim.

Here's the easiest, least costly method for boiling live blue crabs.

Boiled Blue Crab

12 live, hard-shelled blue crabs	3 quarts boiling water
	2 tablespoons salt

Place live crabs in boiling salted water. Cover and return to the boiling point. Reduce heat and boil gently for 5 to 7 minutes. Drain. Rinse in cold water. Serve hot or cold with Cocktail Sauce (see Index), or remove meat from body and claws for use in crabmeat dishes.

Batter Fried Soft-Shelled Crabs

When we were first married and living in Red Bank, New Jersey, you could buy soft-shelled crabs any summer morning from elderly gentlemen who set up sidewalk stands in front of the town's largest bank. The price was $3 a dozen or less, and the crabs were nicely packed with sea-weed and carried home in an old shoe carton.

Soft-shelled crabs like these are very perishable and must be alive before cleaning and cooking. The only other problem they present is their wetness, for as crabs shed in order to grow, they soak up salt water and expand in size before their new shell hardens. That's why I find that dipping soft-shelled crabs in a batter before sautéeing them is the best method of preparation.

12 soft-shelled crabs, cleaned	2 eggs
1 cup flour	1/2 cup milk
1/2 teaspoon salt	4 tablespoons butter
1/2 teaspoon baking powder	Lemon wedges

In a medium size bowl, combine flour, salt and baking powder. In a small bowl, beat eggs and add milk. Then add liquid to flour mixture and stir until smooth. In a large, heavy skillet or electric frypan melt butter. Just before placing crabs into skillet, dip them into the batter, letting excess drip back into bowl. Place crabs, top side down, in hot butter and sauté about 3 minutes at moderate heat, 350°, until brown. Turn and sauté on opposite side for 3 minutes or until brown. Garnish with lemon wedges.

(Serves 6)

Eastern Shore Crabcakes

You will hardly believe that I discovered the best crabcake recipe hundreds of miles from salt water, while at college in Pittsburgh. One of my classmates gave me an Eastern Shore recipe that's so good I never order crabcakes in a restaurant because they are always a disappointment. After trying these, you'll probably feel the same way.

1 pound blue crabmeat, fresh or pasteurized	1 teaspoon Worcestershire sauce
1 egg, slightly beaten	2 tablespoons mayonnaise
1 teaspoon salt	1 egg for dipping
1 teaspoon dry mustard	Dry bread crumbs
1 teaspoon chopped parsley	2 to 3 tablespoons butter

Remove any pieces of shell or cartilage from crabmeat. Place meat in a medium bowl. Add egg, seasonings and mayonnaise, mixing lightly with a fork. If mixture does not hold together, add a small amount of flour. Form into cakes. Dip cakes into beaten egg and then coat with bread crumbs. Melt butter in a heavy skillet or electric frypan. Place cakes in hot butter and brown about 5 minutes on each side.

(Makes 4 or 5 cakes)

Zucchini Crabmeat Casserole

Suppose you have to prepare a luncheon or covered dish supper and want a delicious dish that is easy. This recipe could be the perfect answer. It's one of my favorites, and I've never known anyone who did not complain that there just was not enough!

12 ounces blue crabmeat, fresh or pasteurized

4 cups (3 to 5 medium) ¼-inch slices zucchini

1½ cups biscuit baking mix

1½ cups shredded Cheddar cheese

2 teaspoons instant minced onion

½ cup vegetable oil

3 eggs

1 teaspoon oregano

1 teaspoon salt

¼ teaspoon pepper

Preheat oven to 400°. Remove any pieces of shell or cartilage from crabmeat. Mix all ingredients together and spread in a 12″ × 7¼″ × 2″ greased baking dish. Bake uncovered until golden brown and knife inserted in center comes out clean, 25 to 30 minutes.

(Serves 6)

Crabmeat Supreme

Here's something else you can do with crabmeat. I think the dish is far better than anything you'll find in most restaurants.

1 pound blue crabmeat, fresh or pasteurized
1 package (6 ounces) chicken flavored stuffing mix
1 cup mushrooms, sliced
2 teaspoons Worcestershire sauce
1 teaspoon salt
2 eggs, slightly beaten
$^1/_2$ teaspoon paprika
1 can (8$^1/_2$ ounces) water chestnuts, drained and sliced
2 cups diced celery
1 package (2$^1/_4$ ounces) slivered almonds
2 cups shredded Cheddar cheese

Remove any pieces of shell or cartilage from crabmeat. Prepare stuffing mix according to package directions. Spread stuffing mixture in a 12″ × 7$^1/_4$″ × 2″ baking dish. Combine rest of ingredients except for 1 cup cheese and almonds. Layer seafood mixture over stuffing mix. Combine reserved cheese and almonds; place on top of casserole. Cover with foil and bake in a 375° oven for 30 to 45 minutes or until thoroughly heated. Remove foil for the last 10 minutes of baking.

(Serves 8)

Crabmeat Soufflé

Crabmeat is so delicate and finely textured that is can be used in many varied ways, as in this soufflé.

1 pound blue crabmeat, fresh or pasteurized	$^1/_4$ teaspoon paprika
3 tablespoons butter	$1^1/_2$ cups milk
3 tablespoons flour	$^1/_2$ cup ripe olives, cut up
$^3/_4$ teaspoon salt	3 eggs, separated

Remove any pieces of shell or cartilage from crabmeat. In a large saucepan melt butter and then add flour, salt and paprika; stir. Add milk and cook until mixture thickens, stirring constantly. Cool. Add crabmeat, olives and well-beaten egg yolks; mix gently. Fold in stiffly beaten egg whites and pour into a well-greased baking dish. Place baking dish in a pan of hot water and bake in a 350° oven for 1 hour or until a knife inserted in soufflé comes out clean. Serves at once.

(Serves 4)

King Crab in Skillet

King crabmeat from Alaska is available frozen from coast to coast. Because the meat is firmer than that of blue crab, king crabmeat is especially well suited to this skillet dish.

1 pound king crabmeat, fresh or frozen	2 tablespoons cornstarch
1 can (8¾ ounces) crushed pineapple	2 cups chicken broth
3 tablespoons butter	½ cup toasted, blanched, slivered almonds
½ cup thinly sliced celery	1 tablespoon lemon juice
	1 can (5 ounces) chow mein noodles

Thaw frozen crabmeat and drain. Remove any pieces of shell or cartilage. Drain pineapple, reserving liquid. Melt butter in a 10-inch heavy skillet or electric frypan. Add celery, pineapple and crabmeat. Cook over low heat for 5 minutes, stirring frequently. Dissolve cornstarch in pineapple juice and then stir into crab mixture. Add chicken broth gradually and cook until thick, stirring constantly. Add almonds and lemon juice. Serve over noodles.

(Serves 4)

Crabmeat in Wok

If you own a wok, use it with crabmeat, because it's really a time saver. Since crabmeat has already been cooked, it only needs a few minutes of heating time.

½ pound blue crabmeat,
   fresh or pasteurized
4 tablespoons vegetable
   oil
¼ cup thinly sliced onion
½ cup diced celery

1 package (10 ounces)
   frozen mixed
   vegetables, unthawed
3 cups cooked rice
¼ cup dry-roasted salted
   peanuts
   Soy sauce

Remove any pieces of shell or cartilage from crabmeat. Put oil in wok and let reach a medium heat (350°). Add onion and stir-fry 1 minute; push up the side. Add celery and stir-fry 1 minute; push up the side. Then add mixed vegetables and stir-fry these for 5 minutes; push up the side. Add rice and stir-fry 5 minutes. Lastly, add crabmeat and peanuts, let heat, and then stir all foods in wok until evenly mixed. Serve immediately with soy sauce.

(Serves 4)

Crabmeat Bisque

Seafood bisques are always delicious, and this one, made with West Coast crabmeat if you prefer, is easy to put together.

2 cups king or Dungeness crabmeat, fresh or frozen
4 tablespoons butter
¼ cup finely chopped celery
¼ cup finely chopped onion
2 tablespoons flour
1 teaspoon salt
¼ teaspoon paprika
Dash white pepper
4 cups milk, or 2 cups milk and 2 cups half and half cream

Thaw crabmeat if frozen. Remove any pieces of shell or cartilage from crabmeat. Melt butter in a large saucepan and cook celery and onion until tender. Stir in flour and seasonings. Add milk gradually and cook until thick, stirring constantly. Fold in crabmeat and heat thoroughly. Serve at once.

(Serves 6)

Easy Crab Chowder

Something else you might enjoy is a wonderful crab chowder. This one is quick to make, saving you time, energy and money.

12 ounces blue crabmeat, fresh or pasteurized
2 tablespoons butter
1 teaspoon instant minced onion
1 teaspoon celery seed
2 cups milk
1 can (10³/₄ ounces) cream of potato soup

1 can (8 ounces) cream style corn
1 bay leaf
¹/₄ teaspoon thyme
¹/₄ teaspoon salt
¹/₄ cup cream sherry
2 tablespoons dried parsley flakes (for garnish)

Remove any pieces of shell or cartilage from crabmeat. Melt butter in a large saucepan and add minced onion and celery seed; cook 1 minute. Add milk, soup, corn, bay leaf, thyme and salt. Continue cooking until heated through, stirring frequently. Add crabmeat and sherry and heat for an additional few minutes until hot. Discard bay leaf and garnish each serving with parsley.

(Serves 4)

Crab-Flounder Newburg

If we don't pick our own crabmeat, it's apt to be very expensive. That is why so many recipes call for extending it with all kinds of things, including mashed potatoes. Most of the extenders spoil the special delicious flavor that only pure crabmeat can give. Here is one extender that works much better than the rest. It's easy too. Just use equal amounts of crab and cooked, flaked flounder, sea trout or other white, delicate fish and mix, as in this recipe.

$\frac{1}{2}$ pound blue crabmeat, fresh or pasteurized
$\frac{1}{2}$ pound cooked, flaked flounder
$\frac{1}{3}$ cup butter
3 tablespoons flour
$\frac{1}{2}$ teaspoon salt
$\frac{1}{2}$ teaspoon paprika

Dash cayenne pepper
$1\frac{1}{2}$ cups milk or half and half cream
3 egg yolks, beaten
2 tablespoons cream sherry
Toast points

Remove any pieces of shell or cartilage from crabmeat. In a medium size saucepan, melt butter and blend in flour and seasonings. Add milk gradually; cook until thick and smooth, stirring constantly. Stir a little of the hot sauce into egg yolks; then add to remaining sauce, stirring constantly. Add crab-flounder meat and heat. Remove from heat and slowly stir in sherry. Serve immediately on toast points.

(Serves 4)

176

Shrimp

Did you ever meet anyone who did not enjoy shrimp? All of us seem to be able to eat as many as our hostess provides. I remember one enormously overweight fellow who used to elbow his way to every bowl of shrimp and devour it all!

South of Chesapeake Bay, you may be able to catch your own shrimp with throw nets. Yet most of us eat the various commercial varieties—white, brown and pink. Although they are separate species, the flavors are indistinguishable, and you can mix them in any shrimp recipe.

Oddly enough, all raw shrimp in the shell are called "green" shrimp. When cooked, the translucent shells take a pinkish cast, and the meat will be white with a reddish covering.

If not already cleaned, fresh shrimp should be beheaded at once. Then you can either keep the shrimp a day or so in the refrigerator or freeze them. If you buy shrimp that are cleaned but not shelled, you can freeze them as they are. They will last longer than frozen cooked shrimp. You can keep raw shrimp frozen about six months, but once cooked, they lose quality after about a month in the freezer.

For all your recipes, figure that two pounds of "green," headless shrimp will yield you one pound of cooked, peeled, deveined shrimp.

Something else to realize is that you should never boil shrimp. Just simmer them gently, for overcooking makes them tough and dry. As soon as they become opaque and white, they are done.

You can peel shrimp either before or after cooking. I find it easier to do it first to save both salt and cooking time.

No matter how you serve them, you'll generally want to simmer your shrimp first.

How to Cook Shrimp

To Cook *Before* Peeling:

1½ pounds raw, headless shrimp, fresh or frozen	1 quart water
	¼ cup salt

Thaw shrimp if frozen. In a 4-quart saucepan, bring water and salt to a boil. Add shrimp. Cover and return to boil. Reduce heat and simmer for 3 to 4 minutes or until shrimp are opaque in the center when tested by cutting in half. Drain. Rinse shrimp under cold running water. Remove shell and sand vein from shrimp. Rinse and refrigerate.

(Yields ¾ pound cooked shrimp)

To Cook *After* Peeling:

1½ pounds raw, headless shrimp, fresh or frozen	1 quart water
	2 tablespoons salt

Thaw shrimp if frozen. Remove shell and sand vein. Rinse. In a 4-quart saucepan, bring water and salt to a boil. Add shrimp. Cover and return to boil. Reduce heat and simmer for 2 to 3 minutes or until shrimp is opaque in the center when tested by cutting in half. Drain. Rinse under cold running water. Chill.

(Yields ¾ pound cooked shrimp)

Note: Cooking time will vary according to the size and species used.

Shrimp in Electric Frypan

Instead of simmering them, you might like to prepare raw shrimp in your electric frypan, as in this recipe.

2 pounds raw, headless shrimp, fresh or frozen	¼ teaspoon white pepper
	¼ cup dry vermouth
	2 tablespoons lime or lemon juice
¼ cup salad or olive oil	
2 teaspoons salt	

Thaw shrimp if frozen. Peel shrimp leaving the tail section of the shell on. Remove sand vein and rinse. Preheat electric frypan to 320°. Add oil, salt, pepper and shrimp. Cook for 8 to 10 minutes or until shrimp are pink and tender, stirring frequently. Increase temperature to 420°. Add vermouth and lime juice. Cook one minute longer, stirring constantly. Drain. Serve hot or cold as an appetizer or entrée.

(Serves 4 to 6)

Pickled Shrimp

For great nibbles with beer, try these unusual shrimp.
They won't last long!

2 pounds peeled,
deveined, raw shrimp,
fresh or frozen
2 cans (12 ounces each)
light beer
1/2 cup lime juice
1 tablespoon capers
(optional)
1/2 teaspoon salt
1/2 teaspoon whole
allspice

1/4 teaspoon whole black
peppercorns
2 whole bay leaves
2 tablespoons oil
1/4 teaspoon liquid hot
pepper sauce
1 clove garlic, halved
Parsley (garnish)

Thaw shrimp if frozen. Cook shrimp in 1 can beer until
pink and firm, about 2 to 3 minutes. Drain. Mix 1 can beer
with remaining ingredients except parsley. Pour over
shrimp and marinate in refrigerator overnight. Add parsley sprigs and serve with toothpicks.

(Makes about 50 shrimp)

Phyllis' Italian Broiled Shrimp

Phyllis Smith, a friend and neighbor in Williamsburg, teaches bridge, plays much duplicate and is a fine cook who developed this tasty shrimp dish.

2 pounds raw, large shrimp, shelled and deveined	1/4 cup olive oil
	4 tablespoons butter
	Drawn Butter Sauce
1/4 cup flour	

Place shrimp and flour in a paper bag and shake well. Place oil and butter in a flat broiling pan or dish and melt under broiler. Then arrange shrimp on top of melted fat and broil at low broiling heat about 4 inches from source of heat for 8 minutes or until pink and tender. Cover with Drawn Butter Sauce and broil under high heat for 3 minutes.

(Serves 4 to 6)

Drawn Butter Sauce

2 tablespoons butter
2 tablespoons flour
$^1/_2$ teaspoon white pepper
1 teaspoon garlic
  powder
1 cup hot water

2 tablespoons butter
Juice from 1 small
lemon
4 tablespoons chopped
  fresh parsley

In a small saucepan, melt 2 tablespoons butter and then stir in flour and seasonings. Gradually add hot water, stirring constantly. Boil 5 minutes, stirring occasionally. Add 2 tablespoons butter, lemon juice and parsley. Pour sauce over shrimp for last 3 minutes of broiling.

Curried Shrimp

My husband is a curry freak. He likes anything as long as it has curry sauce and some chutney on the side. After he devoured this version, he said we must try squirrel curry!

$^3/_4$ pound cooked, peeled, deveined shrimp ($1^1/_2$ pounds raw shrimp)
3 tablespoons butter
$^1/_2$ cup chopped onion
3 tablespoons flour
1 teaspoon salt
Dash pepper
1 can ($10^3/_4$ ounces) chicken broth
1 teaspoon curry powder
$^1/_2$ cup applesauce
Curry Accompaniments

In a heavy, medium size saucepan, melt butter; add onion and cook until tender. Blend in flour, salt and pepper. Add broth gradually and cook until thick, stirring constantly. Add curry powder, applesauce and shrimp; heat. Serve over rice with any of the following Curry Accompaniments.

(Serves 4 to 5)

Curry Accompaniments

Chopped hard-cooked egg whites
Sieved hard-cooked egg yolks
Chopped salted peanuts
Chopped tomatoes
Chutney or grated coconut

Shrimp Pilau

Shrimp Pilau (you pronounce it pee-lō) is an Oriental dish. The shrimp are cooked by conduction and steam produced by the hot rice.

1 pound raw, peeled, deveined shrimp, fresh or frozen	1 can (1 pound) whole tomatoes, undrained
3 slices bacon, cut into small pieces	³/₄ cup water
	³/₄ cup uncooked rice
1 cup chopped celery	1 teaspoon salt
¹/₄ cup chopped onion	¹/₈ teaspoon pepper
	¹/₈ teaspoon thyme

Thaw shrimp if frozen. Cut large shrimp in half. In a 2-quart saucepan, cook bacon until crisp. Remove bacon. Cook celery and onion in bacon fat until tender. Break tomatoes into small pieces, removing tough centers. Add tomatoes and liquid along with water and bring to a boil. Stir in rice and seasonings. Reduce heat. Cover and cook rice mixture over low heat for 18 to 20 minutes. Mix in shrimp, cover and continue cooking for 10 to 12 minutes or until shrimp are tender. Garnish with bacon.

(Serves 4)

Shrimp in Wok

Seafood as delicate as shrimp must never be overcooked.
This makes them perfect for your wok. You'll be amazed
at how quickly the result vanishes.

1 pound raw, peeled and
deveined shrimp,
fresh or frozen
1 teaspoon cornstarch
$1/4$ teaspoon ginger
$1/8$ teaspoon garlic
powder
2 tablespoons cream
sherry
2 tablespoons soy sauce

$1/2$ cup chicken bouillon
2 tablespoons vegetable
oil
1 package (6 ounces)
Chinese pea pods,
thawed
$1/2$ can ($8^1/2$ ounces) water
chestnuts, drained and
thinly sliced

Combine cornstarch, ginger and garlic powder; then
blend in sherry, soy sauce and bouillon; set aside. Place
wok on high heat and when hot, add oil. When oil is hot,
add shrimp and stir-fry about 1 minute. Add peas and stir-
fry 2 minutes. Then stir in water chestnuts. Add cornstarch mixture and stir until it boils and thickens.

(Serves 3)

Shrimp Mousse

A shrimp mousse is a terrific dish with high potential. You can use it as an hors d'oeuvre for a crowd, as a salad or a buffet entrée. It also makes a marvelous luncheon.

1½ pounds cooked, peeled and deveined shrimp. fresh or frozen (3 pounds raw shrimp)

1 can (10¾ ounces) condensed tomato soup

1 package (8 ounces) cream cheese

2 tablespoons unflavored gelatin

1 cup mayonnaise or salad dressing

¾ cup finely chopped celery

1 teaspoon onion juice

1 teaspoon Worcestershire sauce

1 teaspoon lemon juice

Thaw shrimp if frozen. Chop. Heat tomato soup and cream cheese in the top of double boiler until cream cheese melts. Cool slightly. Stir in gelatin and mix well. Add shrimp, mayonnaise, celery, onion juice, Worcestershire sauce and lemon juice; mix well. Pour into a well-greased 1½-quart mold. Cover and refrigerate at least 8 hours. Serve with crackers or as an entrée.

(Makes approximately 5 cups)

Shrimp with Fruit

Sure, you've eaten shrimp salad, some of it wonderful, but too often with very little shrimp and lots of mayonnaise and celery. Here are two really great shrimp salads, so take your pick.

1 pound cooked, peeled and deveined shrimp, fresh or frozen (2 pounds raw)
2 cups diced, unpared fresh pears
2 cups diced, unpared red apples
1 cup thinly sliced celery
½ cup mayonnaise or salad dressing
2 tablespoons milk
1 tablespoon cider vinegar
1 teaspoon salt
Salad greens
Paprika

Thaw shrimp if frozen. Cut large shrimp in half. Combine shrimp, pears, apples and celery. Combine mayonnaise, milk, vinegar and salt; mix well. Pour dressing over shrimp mixture and toss lightly. Serve on salad greens and sprinkle with paprika.

(Serves 4 to 6)

Shrimp with Caper Sauce

This recipe is special because it gives you a shrimp cocktail with only 100 calories.

3/4 pound cooked, peeled and deveined shrimp, fresh or frozen (1 1/2 pounds raw)

Lettuce
Caper Sauce
Lemon or lime wedges

Arrange lettuce in seafood cocktail glasses. Place shrimp on lettuce; cover with Caper Sauce. Garnish with lemon or lime wedges.

(Serves 6)

Caper Sauce

1 cup yogurt
2 tablespoons chopped capers
2 tablespoons lemon or lime juice

2 teaspoons instant minced onion
1 tablespoon chopped parsley
1 teaspoon grated lemon or lime rind

Combine all ingredients and mix thoroughly. Chill. Makes approximately 1 1/4 cups of sauce.

Lobster

Technically speaking, there's only one species of lobster here in North America. But why get technical? The spiny or rock lobster, lacking large pincers, are just as delicious as the real American lobster found in the North Atlantic in 40° water. The lobster tails you'll find at your food store are always the spiny or rock lobster variety. The spiny lobster head, having no claws, is discarded at the packing plant, and this usually means it winds up in livestock feed.

You can figure one pound of raw, "green," whole lobster, spiny or American, per person. However, you can mix your one pound of lobster meat with other ingredients to serve six. A one pound, uncooked lobster will yield only about one-third as much cooked meat.

For best results, freeze green lobsters live, and they will keep well up to four months. Frozen, cooked lobster in the shell is better if used within two months. Cooked lobster should be eaten within two of three days. When you cook lobster, remember to keep it just below the boiling point. Overcooking will toughen lobster just as it does shrimp.

There are three basic ways to cook lobster. You can poach, broil or bake them. The best I've ever eaten was poached in sea water by Stacey Osborn, a licensed Maine guide. We bought them right on the shore of Penobscot Bay and cooked them immediately. Stacey pointed out the best lobsters are those that have shed recently and are slightly soft. These don't ship well, and that explains why lobster bought far from the sea are always as hard-shelled as bullets.

Let's begin with the simplest method.

Cooked Lobster

2 live or frozen whole, green lobster (1 pound each)	3 quarts boiling water 3 tablespoons salt Melted butter

Thaw lobster if frozen. In a 6-quart saucepan, bring water and salt to a boil. Plunge live or thawed lobster head first into boiling salted water. Cover and return to the boiling point. Reduce heat and simmer for 12 to 15 minutes. (Larger lobster will require a little longer cooking time.) Drain. Rinse with cold water. Split and clean lobster and serve with melted butter.

(Serves 2)

Note: Frozen spiny lobster tails (5 to 8 ounces each) can be cooked by the above method. Reduce cooking time to 5 to 10 minutes depending on size. Drain. Rinse in cold water and then cut in half lengthwise and serve with melted butter.

Broiled Live Whole Lobsters

Broiled lobster is a gourmet dish, and it's easy too. Just read this over and try it with your very next lobsters.

2 live lobsters (1 pound each)
1 tablespoon butter melted
1/4 teaspoon salt
Dash white pepper
Dash paprika
1/4 cup butter, melted
1 tablespoon lemon juice

It is difficult to split a live lobster. Placing it in the freezer for 20 to 30 minutes will make it easier to handle and clean without harming the quality of the meat.

Place lobster on its back; insert a sharp knife between body shell and tail segment, cutting down to sever the spinal cord. Cut shell in half lengthwise. Remove the stomach, which is just back of the head, and the intestinal vein, which runs from the stomach to the tip of the tail. Do not remove the green liver and coral roe, as they are delicious. Crack claws. Lay lobsters open as flat as possible on a broiler pan. Brush lobster meat with butter. Sprinkle with salt, pepper and paprika. Broil about 4 inches from source of heat for 5 to 10 mintues or until lightly browned. Combine butter and lemon juice and serve with lobsters.

(Serves 2)

Broiled Spiny Lobster Tails

6 frozen spiny lobster tails (5 to 8 ounces each)
1/3 cup butter, melted
1/2 teaspoon salt
Dash white pepper
Dash paprika
3/4 cup butter, melted
3 tablespoons lemon juice

Thaw lobster tails. Cut in half lengthwise. Lay lobster tails open as flat as possible on a broiler pan. Brush lobster meat with butter. Sprinkle with salt, pepper and paprika. Broil about 4 inches from source of heat for 5 to 10 minutes, depending on size of lobster tails. Combine butter and lemon juice and serve with tails.

(Serves 6)

Baked Stuffed Lobster

After graduating from high school in West Virginia, I was invited by an uncle to spend three glorious weeks in Nantucket. The baked lobster at the Grey Gull was outstanding, and I can still remember it.

2 live or frozen whole
  green lobsters
  (1 pound each)
1 1/2 cups soft bread crumbs
1/2 cup grated Cheddar
  cheese

2 tablespoons melted
  butter
1 tablespoon grated
  onion
  Paprika

Thaw lobster if frozen. Cut lobster in half lengthwise and remove stomach and intestinal vein. Rinse and clean body cavity thoroughly. Combine bread crumbs, cheese, butter and onion. Place stuffing in body cavity and spread over surface of the tail meat. Sprinkle with paprika. Place on a baking pan and bake in a hot oven, 400°, for 15 to 20 minutes or until lightly browned.

(Serves 2)

Easy Lobster in Skillet

A small amount of cooked lobster meat can go a very long way if you serve it like this.

1 pound cooked lobster
   meat, fresh or frozen
1 can (4 ounces)
   mushroom stems and
   pieces, drained
1 small onion, finely
   chopped
¼ cup butter

1 cup sour cream
2 tablespoons chopped
   parsley
¼ teaspoon salt
   Dash cayenne pepper
   Toast points or patty
   shells

Thaw lobster if frozen. Cut lobster meat into bite size pieces. Melt butter in a heavy skillet or electric frypan and cook mushrooms and onion until tender but not brown. Add lobster, sour cream, parsley, salt and pepper. Heat thoroughly, not allowing mixture to boil. Serve on toast points or in patty shells.

(Serves 4 to 6)

Lobster Salad

You may never have any lobster meat leftovers. Yet it can happen, and it happened to us one fall when we hunted woodcock with Wilmot "Wiggie" Robinson in Northern Maine. Wiggie met us at the airport with a crate of lobsters, and Joyce Robinson, great host that she is, made us lobster sandwiches to eat while hunting! You too, can make outstanding salad and sandwiches with cooked lobster meat.

³/₄	pound cooked lobster meat, fresh or frozen	¹/₂	cup sliced pitted ripe olives
6	cups lettuce, torn into small pieces	¹/₂	cup prepared cream Caesar salad dressing
2	medium tomatoes, cut into bite size pieces		Whole pitted ripe olives (garnish)
1	cup grated Cheddar cheese		

Thaw lobster if frozen. Remove lobster from shells. Cut lobster into ¹/₂-inch pieces. Combine lobster, lettuce, tomatoes, cheese and olives. Add dressing and toss lightly. Garnish with whole ripe olives. Serve immediately.

(Makes 6 servings)

Oysters

Oysters have been around a very long time. People ate them as soon as they discovered a way to open the shells, which was probably by roasting them over a fire. Our North American Indians left huge piles of oyster shells behind, and our ancestors, late in the nineteenth century, would go on amazing oyster binges at special oyster bars. Diamond Jim Brady is reputed to have eaten six dozen oysters as an appetizer.

Then growing pollution, oyster diseases and over-harvesting took their toll, and today oysters, though plentiful in some areas, are more costly than ever before.

Oysters are farmed just like a field crop, except of course they are raised underwater. Most of our oysters come from these farms, for only a handful of people have the time, temperament, location and equipment to tong their own or pick them, as can be done in a few places, from tree roots and rocks at low tide.

Commercial oysters are marketed in the shell alive, fresh shucked and frozen shucked, frozen breaded and canned. Live oysters in their shells will remain alive in your refrigerator for about a week at 35° to 40°.

Without an oyster knife and a heavy glove, you'll have a difficult time opening oysters. Clams are simple by comparison. Therefore, unless you want to eat the oysters raw on the half shell, it is more sensible to buy shucked oysters. Do not try to freeze these yourself. You don't have the quick-freezing capability of a commercial operation, and your results will be too mushy for enjoyment.

If you do buy commercially frozen oysters, eat them fairly soon. They should be used within two months and sooner if possible. Whatever you do, never refreeze oysters. Additionally, watch out for any odd color (a change from the natural creamy color) or odor. A dead oyster spoils quickly.

The wonderful thing about oysters is that they are delicious in many types of recipes. However, they must not be overcooked, for then they become tough, dry and hard and lose their delicate flavor. Too many restaurants serve fried oysters that are virtually inedible.

Oyster Hors D'Oeuvres

Let's start off with a recipe for oyster canapes to serve before dinner. By the way, the oyster liquid is referred to as "liquor."

1 pint shucked oysters, fresh or frozen	24 to 30 round sesame crackers
8 ounces port wine cheese	

Thaw oysters if frozen. Drain oysters and remove any remaining shell particles. Place oysters in a single layer in a well-greased baking dish. Dot oysters with cheese. Bake in a moderate oven, 350°, for 15 to 20 minutes or until edges of oysters curl and cheese melts. Remove each cheese-topped oyster with a fork from the baking dish and place on a sesame cracker.

(Makes approximately 24 to 30 canapes)

Oyster Stew

One of New York City's most famous restaurants is the Oyster Bar in Grand Central Station. It's been there for generations and is noted for oyster stew like this.

1 pint shucked oysters, fresh or frozen
4 tablespoons butter
1 teaspoon Worcestershire sauce
1 teaspoon celery salt
1 quart milk
Salt and pepper to taste
Paprika

Thaw oysters if frozen. Drain oysters, reserving liquor. Remove any remaining shell particles. In a 2-quart saucepan, place butter, Worcestershire sauce and celery salt. Cook slowly for 1 to 2 minutes. Add oysters and liquor and cook gently until oyster edges start to curl. Add milk, salt and pepper to taste. Heat thoroughly but do not boil. Pour into bowls and garnish with paprika.

(Serves 4)

Oyster Fritters

Oyster fritters are great for a luncheon or light supper and are as easy to prepare as they are good.

1 pint shucked oysters, fresh or frozen
$^3/_4$ cup mixture of $^1/_2$ flour and $^1/_2$ corn meal
$^3/_4$ teaspoon baking powder
$^1/_4$ teaspoon salt
Dash cayenne pepper
1 egg
$^1/_2$ cup milk
Butter
Tartar Sauce

Thaw oysters if frozen. Drain oysters and remove any remaining shell particles. Combine flour/corn meal mixture, baking powder, salt and pepper in a medium size bowl. In a small bowl, beat egg and milk together and add to flour/corn meal mixture. Stir in oysters. In a large heavy skillet or an electric frypan, melt enough butter, over medium-high heat, to cover bottom. For each fritter, spoon 1 rounded tablespoon batter containing 1 oyster into hot butter. Cook until brown on both sides, about 3 minutes. Remove to a platter lined with paper towel and keep warm. Repeat with remaining batter. Serve with Tartar Sauce.

(Serves 4)

Tartar Sauce

1/2 cup mayonnaise or salad dressing
1/4 cup drained sweet pickle relish

2 teaspoons instant minced onion
2 tablespoons lemon juice

Combine all ingredients. Mix thoroughly. Chill for at least 30 minutes.

(Makes approximately 1 cup)

Scalloped Oysters

Scalloped oysters are an old favorite, and here is the basic and best way to fix them.

1 pint shucked oysters, fresh or frozen
2 cups cracker crumbs
1/2 teaspoon salt
1/8 teaspoon pepper

1/2 cup butter, melted
1/2 teaspoon Worcestershire sauce
1 cup milk

Thaw oysters if frozen. Drain oysters and remove any remaining shell particles. Combine cracker crumbs, salt, pepper and melted butter. Sprinkle 1/3 mixture in a greased casserole; cover with a layer of oysters. Repeat layer. Add Worcestershire sauce to milk and pour over contents in casserole. Sprinkle remaining crumbs over top. Bake in a moderate oven, 350°, for 30 minutes or until thoroughly hot and brown.

(Serves 4)

Oyster Pie

When I served this oyster pie, my husband commented that the recipe was too small for four of us, only big enough for two!

1 pint shucked oysters, fresh or frozen	4 hard-cooked eggs, sliced
Pastry for double crust 9-inch pie or 2 deep dish frozen crusts	2 tablespoons butter
	$1/4$ teaspoon celery salt
1 can (1 pound) sliced potatoes, drained	$1/8$ teaspoon lemon/pepper seasoning
	Oyster Sauce

Thaw oysters if frozen. Drain oysters, reserving liquor for sauce. Remove any remaining shell particles. Place bottom crust in a deep pie plate or pan and put in sliced potatoes. Place oysters over potatoes. Then put egg slices over oysters. Dot butter over top and sprinkle with seasonings. Place top crust on pie and cut slits to allow steam to escape. Bake at 400° for 10 minutes; lower heat and bake at 375° until crust is lightly browned, about 30 minutes. Let stand a few minutes before serving (drain off any excess liquid). Serve with Oyster Sauce. (Serves 4)

Oyster Sauce

2 tablespoons butter	$1/2$ cup reserved oyster liquor and water to make volume
2 tablespoons flour	
$3/4$ cup milk	

In a small saucepan, melt butter and mix in flour. Slowly add milk, then oyster liquor, stirring constantly to keep mixture smooth. Cook, stirring, until mixture comes to a boil and thickens. Add salt and pepper to taste. Serve hot.

Bouillabaisse

Bouillabaisse must contain a variety of fish and seafood. That is why, to make his, my chef son once made off with king mackerel and flounder fillets I'd been saving for a special dinner. Even worse, he didn't invite me to eat it with his friends.

1 pound thick fish fillets, fresh or frozen, cut in 1½-inch chunks	4 cups water
½ pint oysters, fresh or frozen	1 large can (1 pound, 12 ounces) tomatoes, undrained, cut up
½ pound shrimp, fresh or frozen, peeled and deveined	½ cup white table wine
2 tablespoons butter	2 tablespoons chopped parsley
2 tablespoons vegetable oil	1 tablespoon lemon juice
¼ cup flour	1 bay leaf
½ cup chopped onion	½ teaspoon salt
½ cup chopped celery	⅛ teaspoon garlic powder
	Cayenne pepper to taste

Thaw seafood if frozen. Drain oysters, reserving liquor. Remove any remaining shell particles. In a large boiler pot over medium heat, melt butter and add oil. Slowly blend in flour, stirring constantly until mixture is light brown. Add onion and celery and continue cooking until vegetables are tender. Gradually stir in water. Add remaining ingredients except seafood. Bring to a boil and then simmer for 10 minutes. Add fish chunks and simmer 10 minutes more. Add shrimp and oysters with liquor and cook 5 minutes more or until seafood is done.

(Serves 8)

Oyster Stuffing

Oyster stuffing is famous for everything from turkey to fish, and it only takes a few minutes to put together.

1/2 pint shucked oysters, fresh or frozen	4 slices day-old bread, cubed
4 tablespoons butter	1/2 teaspoon salt
1 small onion, finely chopped	2 dashes pepper
1 stalk celery, finely chopped	2 dashes mace
	2 dashes poultry seasoning
	1 teaspoon lemon juice

Thaw oysters if frozen. Drain oysters, reserving liquor. Remove any remaining shell particles. In a medium size saucepan, melt butter and add onion and celery; cook until almost tender. Add oysters with liquor and cook until edges begin to curl. Add remaining ingredients and mix lightly but thoroughly.

(Makes 2 cups stuffing, enough for a 4 pound fish)

Turkey-Oyster Casserole

Here's a very special recipe. It's for those days, maybe after Thanksgiving or Christmas, when you find yourself wishing you knew of some easy way of using turkey leftovers. This recipe, for cooking "day after" turkey with oysters, makes it even better than when originally carved.

1 pint shucked oysters, fresh or frozen	¼ teaspoon salt
1 cup cooked, diced turkey	1½ cups reserved oyster liquor and milk to make volume
4 tablespoons butter	½ cup bread cubes
4 tablespoons flour	½ cup grated Cheddar cheese
1 teaspoon celery salt	

Thaw oysters if frozen. Drain oysters, reserving liquor. Remove any remaining shell particles. Melt butter in a small saucepan over medium-high heat. Gradually stir in flour and seasonings. Stir until smooth and then slowly add milk with oyster liquor, stirring constantly until sauce is smooth and thickened. Arrange half of oysters in bottom of a greased baking dish. Sprinkle ¼ cup bread cubes over oysters. Then pour ⅓ of hot sauce over casserole. Add a layer of turkey meat. Pour ⅓ more of the hot sauce. Add rest of oysters in another layer, and then remaining bread cubes and sauce. Dot with grated cheese. Bake in a moderate oven, 300°–325°, for 10 to 15 minutes or until cheese is melted and bread cubes are lightly browned.

(Serves 4)

Scallops

There are many species of scallops found world-wide. I'm only sorry some of the huge scallop fossils found around the Chesapeake are gone forever. They had shells measuring more than a foot across, and one alone would have fed a couple of people.

Today, in most of the United States, bay and sea scallops are sold commercially and are interchangeable in recipes. They are different species however, and the bay scallops are smaller and more delicate in flavor.

What we call a "scallop" is really just the muscle that holds the shell together. The entire animal is edible, but most of it is very soft and could only be marketed in the shell.

Commercial fisherman shuck all scallops aboard boats, as they die soon after capture. Often, the scallops are frozen raw while still at sea. Others may be quick frozen after precooking.

When buying scallops, they should be creamy white, light tan or slightly pink and have a mild, rather sweet odor. In addition, there should be very little liquid.

It is best to eat scallops the day you buy them, but they will keep a day or so in the refrigerator. Frozen raw scallops can be kept up to 3 or 4 months. Those frozen after cooking are not as good and won't keep as well.

Scallops are expensive, yet there is absolutely no waste. One pound of scallops is a pound of edible meat.

Something else to consider is that scallops, like most seafood, should not be overcooked. To check, cut a large scallop in half. If it is opaque and white clear through, it is ready to eat.

You can broil scallops if you baste them occasionally to insure that they do not dry out.

Broiled Scallops

1 pound scallops, fresh or frozen	Salt and pepper
¼ cup butter	Paprika
	Lemon wedges

Thaw scallops if frozen. Rinse scallops with cold water to remove any remaining shell particles. Drain. Place scallops in a single layer in a baking dish. Dot them with butter and sprinkle lightly with salt and pepper. Broil about 4 inches from source of heat for 2 minutes. Stir and baste scallops and broil 2 minutes longer or until delicately brown. Sprinkle with paprika and serve immediately with lemon wedges.

(Serves 3)

Scallops in Wine

Like other shellfish, scallops will save you energy in the kitchen, for they only take a few minutes of gas or electric heat. Here's a wonderful way to serve them with wine.

1 pound scallops, fresh or frozen	4 tablespoons butter
1/4 cup flour	3/4 cup white table wine
1/2 teaspoon salt	2 tablespoons chopped parsley
Dash pepper	

Thaw scallops if frozen. Rinse with cold water to remove any remaining shell particles. Drain. Dust scallops with flour to which salt and pepper have been added. Melt butter in a heavy skillet or electric frypan and add scallops. Sauté until lightly brown, shaking skillet to allow even browning. Add wine and simmer 3 minutes. Then add chopped parsley and serve with skillet juices over rice or toast points.

(Serves 3)

Chinese-Style Scallops

This Chinese-style recipe is a delicious way of serving scallops and takes only a few minutes to prepare.

2 pounds scallops, fresh or frozen
1 package (7 ounces) frozen Chinese pea pods
$^{1}/_{4}$ cup butter
2 tomatoes, cut into eighths

$^{1}/_{4}$ cup water
2 tablespoons cornstarch
1 tablespoon soy sauce
$^{1}/_{2}$ teaspoon salt
$^{1}/_{8}$ teaspoon pepper
Soy sauce

Thaw frozen scallops and pea pods. Rinse scallops with cold water to remove any remaining shell particles. Drain. Cut large scallops in half crosswise. Drain pea pods. Melt butter in a 10-inch skillet. Add scallops and cook over low heat for 3 to 4 minutes, stirring frequently. Add pea pods and tomatoes. Combine water, cornstarch, soy sauce, salt and pepper. Add to scallop mixture and cook until thick, stirring constantly. Serve over hot rice with soy sauce.

(Serves 6)

Scallop Rarebit

Cheese rarebits have always been a favorite of mine. This rarebit is different and very tasty.

1 pound scallops, fresh or frozen	1 tablespoon prepared mustard
2 tablespoons butter	2 cups grated Cheddar cheese
2 tablespoons flour	
1 teaspoon salt	2 eggs, beaten
Dash pepper	1 tablespoon chopped parsley
2/3 cup water	
1/3 cup catsup	Toast points

Thaw scallops if frozen. Rinse with cold water to remove any remaining shell particles. Drain. Cut scallops into 1/2-inch pieces. Melt butter in a medium size saucepan. Add scallops to butter and cook for 3 to 4 minutes, stirring occasionally. Blend in flour, salt and pepper. Add water gradually and cook until thick, stirring constantly. Add catsup, mustard and cheese; heat until cheese melts. Stir a little of the hot sauce into beaten eggs; add them to remaining sauce, stirring constantly. Add parsley and serve immediately on toast points.

(Serves 4 to 5)

Scallops and Pineapple in Wok

Have your children flown the nest? Here's a great way of using your wok to cook scallops for just the two of you.

$^1/_2$ pound scallops, fresh or frozen
1 can (8 ounces) chunk pineapple in juice
1 tablespoon vegetable oil
1 medium zucchini, sliced
1 tablespoon butter

2 tablespoons white table wine
1 teaspoon lime juice
$^1/_2$ teaspoon marjoram
$^1/_4$ teaspoon grated lime peel
$^1/_4$ teaspoon salt
1 medium tomato, seeded and chopped

Thaw scallops if frozen. Rinse with cold water to remove any remaining shell particles. Drain. Drain pineapple reserving 2 tablespoons juice. Heat oil in wok over high heat. Sauté scallops and zucchini about 2 minutes. Scallops will be firm and zucchini will be tender-crisp. Remove from pan. Add butter, wine, reserved pineapple juice, lime juice, marjoram, lime peel and salt to wok. Boil rapidly until mixture is reduced by half and slightly thickened. Add scallops, zucchini, tomato and pineapple chunks to sauce mixture. Stir gently and heat through.

(Serves 2)

Clams

Even those who most enjoy arguing the merits of New England versus Manhattan clam chowder agree on one point: they like clams. Most Americans do. In Europe, mussels are more popular, but here in America fourteen species of clams are harvested commercially.

Besides, you can catch your own clams. Clamming is a big sport in New England and continues farther south until somewhere in the Carolinas. Amateur clamdiggers go for hard clams in relatively shallow water by poking into the sand with their toes. When they feel something hard, it's either a pebble or a clam. Soft clams must be dug, usually with a garden fork, on mud flats at low tide. These clams are familiarly known as "steamers," because that's probably the best way to prepare them. Steamed clams are really tremendous.

The third main type of clam is the surf clam or skimmer, a large, rather flat clam found in the ocean, both along the beaches and way offshore in huge clambeds. Skimmers are the most important commercially, since they remain tender regardless of size. This attribute makes them the perfect clam for commercial chowder makers.

In some areas, you can pick up surf clams along the beach after a storm. Look for unbroken ones which are either tightly shut or snap shut when you touch them.

Another clam worth mentioning is the razor clam, so called because its shells are shaped like the handle of an old-fashioned straight razor. You can dig them with soft clams if you're fast enough. This is one clam that really does move and can burrow out of sight faster than most of us can shovel. Steamed with soft clams, they are absolutely delicious.

A cherrystone clam is a small hard clam (or quahog) that is tender enough to eat raw. The larger hard clams become tougher with age and size, except for the surf clams already mentioned.

211

If you do not have the time or geography to get your own clams, you can buy them fresh, fresh-shucked, frozen or canned—unless they are soft clams, which are only sold alive and in their shells. There are canned clams too, whole, minced and in chowder. If you buy live clams, they'll keep well for several days in your refrigerator. Even shucked clams, if kept cold, will stay fresh about a week.

The number of clams you need for any recipe will depend upon their size. A safe rule is to start with two dozen large, hard clams; three dozen clams if they're medium or small. Or you can substitute a quart of shucked clams.

As a child growing up in the Appalachians, I was delighted to visit my grandmother in New Jersey during summer vacations and buy soft clams for steaming. Now, my husband digs them for me. However you get them, here's what you should do after they've been well-scrubbed to remove sand and grit.

Steamed Clams

4 dozen small soft-   Melted butter
   shelled clams

Wash clams and place in a deep pot. Add a small amount of water, cover and bring to a boil. Reduce heat and steam 5 to 10 minutes or until shells open wide. Drain, reserving liquid. Serve clams hot with hot clam liquid and melted butter in separate bowls. Hold clams by neck, dip in broth and then in butter before eating. Do not eat necks.

(Serves 4 as an appetizer)

Fried Clams

Howard Johnson's is to me somewhat less glorious now than it was years ago when it opened as the first fast food and ice cream chain in all the land. Everyone looked for the bright orange roof and rushed in for an order of fried clams.

1 quart shucked clams	Dash pepper
1 egg, beaten	1 cup dry bread crumbs
1 tablespoon milk	or cracker crumbs
1 teaspoon salt	

Drain clams. Combine egg, milk and seasonings. Dip clams in egg mixture and roll in crumbs. Place clams in a heavy skillet or electric frypan that contains about $1/8$ inch of fat, hot but not smoking. Fry at moderate, 350°, heat. When clams are brown on one side, turn carefully and brown on the other side, about 5 to 8 minutes cooking time altogether. Drain on absorbent paper.

(Serves 6)

Clam Fritters

Clam fritters are another wonderful clam dish and are often served for breakfast in the South.

1 pint shucked clams, chopped (can use processor for 2 or 3 seconds)
3/4 cup flour
1/2 teaspoon salt
1 teaspoon baking powder
1 teaspoon instant minced onion
1 egg, beaten
Butter

Drain clams and chop. Combine flour, salt, baking powder and onion. Add just enough water to make a batter of medium consistency. Add beaten egg to batter and mix well. Stir in chopped clams. Melt enough butter to cover bottom of a 10-inch heavy skillet or electric frypan. Drop a tablespoonful of batter for each fritter. Brown fritters on both sides. Serve immediately.

(Makes 10 to 12 fritters)

Deviled Clams

If you are going to entertain at a seafood buffet or need a truly nice appetizer for special friends, you must try these.

1 pint shucked clams
4 tablespoons butter
1/2 cup chopped celery
2 tablespoons chopped onion
1 tablespoon chili sauce
1 tablespoon flour
1/2 teaspoon salt
1/4 teaspoon pepper
1/4 teaspoon thyme
1/8 teaspoon garlic powder
1/8 teaspoon liquid hot pepper sauce
1 egg, beaten
1/2 cup cracker meal
2 tablespoons chopped parsley
1/2 cup dry bread crumbs
2 tablespoons butter, melted

Drain and chop clams. Melt butter in a 10-inch heavy skillet or electric frypan. Cook celery and onion in butter until tender. Add clams and chili sauce and cook for 5 minutes. Blend in flour, salt, pepper, thyme, garlic powder and hot pepper sauce; cook until thick, stirring constantly. Stir a little of the hot clam sauce into egg and then add egg mixture to remaining sauce, stirring constantly. Add cracker meal and parsley; mix well. Place mixture in 6 well-greased individual baking shells or ramekins. Combine bread crumbs and 2 tablespoons butter. Sprinkle over top of clam mixture. Bake in a hot oven, 400°, for 10 minutes or until heated thoroughly and lightly browned.

(Makes 6 servings)

Manhattan Clam Chowder

Whenever I order clam chowder, I'm reminded of being a very pregnant young wife. Very conscious of my ever-growing tummy, I enjoyed going out after dark with my husband to the Long Branch Pier to fish for whiting and ling. Everyone else was so covered by multiple layers of clothes that my condition was totally unnoticed. Best of all, after fishing for a while in the cold, we would enter the pier restaurant and enjoy a bowl of truly wonderful, steaming hot chowder.

1 pint shucked clams, reserve liquor
$1/4$ cup chopped bacon
$1/2$ cup chopped onion
$1/2$ cup chopped green pepper
1 cup chopped celery
1 cup reserved clam liquor and water to make volume
1 cup diced potatoes
1 teaspoon salt
$1/4$ teaspoon thyme
Dash cayenne pepper
2 cups tomato juice

Drain clams and reserve liquor; chop. Fry bacon until lightly brown. Add onion, green pepper and celery; cook until tender. Add liquor, potatoes, seasonings and clams. Cook about 15 minutes or until potatoes are tender. Add tomato juice and heat.

(Serves 6)

New England Clam Chowder

New Englanders feel it is sacrilegious to place a tomato in clam chowder. Their form of chowder, sometimes called Quahog Chowder Down East, is delicious and very filling.

1 pint shucked clams, reserve liquor
1/4 cup chopped bacon
1/4 cup chopped onion
1 cup chopped celery
1 cup reserved clam liquor and water to make volume

1 cup diced potatoes
1/2 teaspoon salt
Dash pepper
2 cups milk
1 tablespoon chopped parsley

Drain clams and reserve liquor; chop. Fry bacon until lightly brown. Add onion and celery and cook until tender. Add liquor, potatoes, seasonings and clams. Cook about 15 minutes or until potatoes are tender. Add milk and heat. Garnish with chopped parsley.

(Serves 6)

Mussels

Mussels are found everywhere in salt water, and the dark blue or black variety are absolutely delicious. Europeans far prefer them to clams, and they are featured in French cookery.

You can buy them in some seafood markets or easily collect them from rocks and old wooden pilings. If you do get your own, be sure you are not collecting from polluted water.

Covered with a damp cloth, mussels will keep up to 24 hours in a cool place. As with clams and oysters, make sure all shells are tightly closed before you cook them. Discard any mussels which are open and lifeless.

Shucked mussels are very perishable, so the safest thing to do is steam and serve them in their shells.

Steamed Mussels

3 to 4 quarts live mussels in shell, scrubbed
2 tablespoons butter
1 small onion, chopped
1 cup white table wine
2 tablespoons chopped parsley

In a large kettle, melt butter. Add onion and cook until soft, stirring occasionally. Add wine and parsley; bring mixture to a boil. Add mussels, cover and simmer gently until mussels have opened, about 5 to 8 minutes. Discard any that do not open. With a slotted spoon, remove mussels from kettle and place in individual soup bowls. Pour cooking liquid evenly over servings.

(Serves 3 to 4)

Shellfish Dinner Menu

STRACCIATELLA SOUP

ANY SHELLFISH RECIPE

KAY'S TOMATO CASSEROLE

BARBARA'S CHINESE BEANS

SUPER YEAST ROLLS

BLUEBERRY DUMPLINGS

See Accompaniment Section for recipes.

Shellfish Dinner Menu

SESAME CHEESE STICKS

ANY SHELLFISH RECIPE

CORN MEAL FRITTERS

ASPARAGUS CASSEROLE

JIM'S ROQUEFORT CHEESE SALAD

BANANA SPLIT DESSERT

See Accompaniment Section for recipes.

Seldom Cooked Species

Conchs

Conchs, pronounced "konks" and sometimes known as
whelks, are familiar to all of us. Their empty shells, found
on the beaches everywhere, are taken home as souvenirs.
Put them to your ear, and you supposedly hear the sea.

Although not shaped precisely like snails, conchs are
similar to them and far more edible. Conchs are *very*
tough. The first time I saw one was when a party boat mate
was pounding it with a mallet, hoping to tenderize it
enough to be used as bait! Tenderized by modern cooking
methods, conchs, or whelks, are well-flavored, excellent
table fare. I have cooked the meat successfully in a pressure cooker and also ground it in my meat grinder.

The easiest way to acquire conchs is to go to a commercial fishery. Dragging for crabs in the winter and fish
in the summer brings up a large number of conchs. These
are extracted from their shells, split, cleaned and frozen
for sale.

If you get your own, the big problem is to remove the

221

animal from the shell. This is accomplished by hitting the small end of the shell with a hammer and using a narrow knife to cut the muscle that holds the conch to its stone-hard home. An alternative is to freeze the conchs in their shells for 24 hours and then thaw, after which you can remove the creature with a fork. Whichever method you use, scrub well under running water to remove all the black skin. Then cut off the light meat for cooking and discard what remains.

Conch has a delicious flavor and works very well in chowders and fritters. When preparing chowder, first use your pressure cooker. This takes only 30 minutes and results in tender meat. On the other hand, boiling conch can require $2^1/_2$ to 3 hours—hardly an energy saver.

My first experience with conch stew was in North Carolina. It was delicious and here's the recipe.

Conch Stew

1 quart conchs, fresh or
  frozen
3 cups water
4 slices bacon
3 medium potatoes,
  cubed
1 large onion, cut up

2 tablespoons flour
$^1/_2$ teaspoon thyme
2 tablespoons
  Worcestershire sauce
Salt and pepper to
  taste

Thaw conchs if frozen. Cut conch meat into $^1/_2$-inch pieces
and place in a pressure cooker with 3 cups water. Close
cover securely and cook under 15 pounds pressure for 30
minutes. Cool cooker and reduce pressure immediately.
While conch meat is cooking, fry bacon in a heavy skillet or
electric frypan. After bacon is crisp, remove from skillet,
crush and set aside. Add potatoes, onion, flour and thyme
to fat in skillet and sauté until potatoes are almost done.
After opening the pressure cooker, add potato mixture
to conch and liquid. Add Worcestershire sauce, salt and
pepper. Continue simmering until potatoes are done and
flavors blended. Sprinkle individual servings with crushed
bacon.

(Serves 4 to 6)

Conch Fritters

Another way to serve conch is in fritters. All you need to do is grind your conch meat, and no precooking is necessary.

1½ cups conch, fresh or
    frozen
1 cup flour
1 teaspoon baking
    powder
1 teaspoon salt
¼ teaspoon pepper
¼ teaspoon onion
    powder

1 egg
1 cup milk
1 teaspoon lemon juice
1 tablespoon chopped
    parsley
Vegetable oil for
    frying

Thaw conchs if frozen. Grind or chop conch meat finely. Mix flour, baking powder, salt, pepper and onion powder in a large bowl. Add egg and milk and gently whisk until smooth. Fold in meat, lemon juice and parsley and mix well. In a heavy skillet or electric frypan, heat oil to about 350°. Drop batter, about ¼ cup at a time, into hot oil and fry until well browned, about 7 to 8 minutes. Drain on absorbent paper.

(Serves 4)

Eel

The old cliche, "It's all a matter of taste," seems to apply to eels. You may not believe it, but there are eel wholesalers on the Atlantic seaboard who buy live eels for $1 a pound and more. Then, they ship them to Europe where the price is much higher. Maybe you've been missing out on something good?

First, let's get something straight. An eel is a fish, period. It has fins and scales, even though the scales are microscopic. Its life history is fantastic, for eels, just the opposite of shad and salmon, migrate to fresh water when tiny and then return to the Carribean to spawn, after which they die. Actually, only the female eels enter fresh water. The males hang around our salt water estuaries. In late summer, larger eels begin to mature. They turn lighter in color and are called silver eels.

Remember, we're discussing the common eel, dark above and light underneath. There are other species: conger eels, which are much like an ordinary eel but stay in the ocean; and moray eels, which you've seen in undersea pictures of coral reefs. All are excellent on the table. Generally speaking, you will only find the common or American eel on your hook or at the fish market. Eels are delicious sautéed, fried, baked or as an ingredient in soups, stew and casseroles.

Before cooking, eels must be dressed. If you catch an eel, use a sharp knife, cut the skin completely around behind the head, grab the head in one hand and use pliers to grab the skin with the other hand. All the skin will come off in a single piece. Then you clean it like any other fish and cut it crosswise into chunks about two inches long. This is the easiest way to cook them.

Sautéed Eel

Cut skinned, dressed eels into 1 to 2-inch crosswise pieces. Roll them in flour seasoned with salt and pepper. Sauté pieces in butter in a heavy skillet until golden brown and fork tender. Serve plain or with tartar sauce.

(Allow $\frac{1}{3}$ pound per person)

Did you know you could catch eels on bait without a fish-hook? It's called bobbing for eels, and all you do is wrap a large bunch of lively worms with fine silk thread. When you feel a bite, yank, and the eel's tiny teeth get caught in the thread. Then boat the eel and shake it loose over a sack or basket. If you've ever tried unhooking an eel, you will appreciate this method!

Eels in Beer

My husband enjoys both beer and eels, and he always looks forward to this recipe, which includes both.

1 pound eel, dressed, skinned and cut into 1 to 2-inch crosswise pieces

2 tablespoons butter
1 can (12 ounces) beer
Herbs: thyme, sage or tarragon

In a heavy skillet or electric frypan, lightly brown eel pieces in butter. Add beer, cover and cook for 10 minutes. Then add a pinch of one or more herbs and cook for 7 to 8 minutes longer or until eel is done and fork tender. If sauce is too thin, thicken with a small amount of flour or cornstarch. After eel has reached room temperature, re-frigerate and serve very cold. (Serves 3)

Fish Roe

Most fish have edible roe, or eggs. Of course some are better than others, and the best of all is shad roe, from either the American or hickory shad. You will find it served in springtime in fine restaurants everywhere. Herring roe is smaller, somewhat milder in flavor but almost as delicious. Like shad roe, it is available only in spring when the fish are migrating upstream from the ocean to spawn.

Lots of other fish, yellow perch, flounder and codfish, for example, have wonderful roe. Years ago, when my husband wrote a daily fishing column, he warned against eating blowfish roe (considered poisonous by scientists.) The phone proceeded to ring off the hook with loud razzberry comments of, "Hey, Art, must be I've been dead for years!" Frankly, I wouldn't eat blowfish roe, but people evidently do. Stick to roe from the usual fresh and saltwater food fish, and you needn't worry.

Cooking roe actually is cooking eggs, so you never have to parboil as some self-appointed experts suggest. Such overcooking makes eggs tough. Sautéing is the best way of preparing roe. Because some of the little eggs may pop, you should use a lid.

Sautéed Roe

In a heavy skillet or electric frypan, fry bacon, allowing 1 or 2 pieces per person. Leave just enough fat in skillet to cover the bottom. Dust roe lightly and gently with flour to which salt and pepper have been added. Place roe in hot bacon fat; cover loosely and brown well. Turn, using a spatula and brown on opposite side, allowing roe to cook until they appear done (dry and dull colored). Cooking time will depend on thickness of roe. Place cooked roe on platter with strips of bacon and serve with lemon wedges.

(Allow 1 small pair or $1/2$ large pair of shad roe per person. For small roe such as herring, allow $1/4$ pound roe per person.)

Frog Legs

As twilight fades on warm June evenings, you can hear the loud "heronk . . . heronk" of large bullfrogs as they sit croaking along marshy shores. Then, after dark, you can take a flashlight and a frog gig and go after them. You can even catch bullfrogs in the daytime on a fly rod. Just use a brightly colored fly, Scarlet Ibis or Yellow Sally, and dangle it before a bullfrog's nose. Suddenly, there'll be a snap of jaws, and you will have hooked your frog.

Some time ago, my husband, fishing with a bass maniac, had a solid hit on his Hula Popper and on reeling in, found he'd caught an enormous bullfrog. The frog, unhooked, leaped into the bass maniac's huge tackle box, made a horrendous mess of it and then blithely leaped overboard!

If you get your own frogs, remember you must cut off the legs and skin them, which is very easy to do. Then you have the most marvelous delicacy of all, providing you do not overcook it. In the Carribean, they have a frog so huge and delicious the natives call it "mountain chicken," but our own bullfrogs are smaller and even better. Try this with fresh frog legs or frozen ones from your food store.

Sautéed Frog Legs

6 to 8 pairs frog legs,
skinned
Milk
Salt and pepper
Flour
4 tablespoons butter

1 tablespoon chopped
parsley
$^{1}/_{2}$ cup white table wine
Juice from whole
lemon
2 shallots, chopped

Cut skinned frog legs in half. Soak in milk in the refrigerator for 6 to 8 hours prior to cooking. Before cooking, dry on paper toweling. Add salt and pepper to flour and roll frog legs in flour mixture. Sauté in hot butter until lightly browned and fork tender—about 5 to 7 minutes. Legs will not be too brown due to lack of skin. *Do not overcook!* Legs will become very tough with overcooking. While legs are sautéing, add chopped parsley. Remove legs to a warm platter and add wine, lemon juice and chopped shallots to butter drippings. Bring to a boil and pour over legs.

(Serves 3 to 4 as an appetizer)

Octopus and Squid

There I was in Spain, not hunting or fishing, but just touring with others. When the waiter at a sangria reception passed something that looked like fried onion rings, I tasted some. To my surprise, it was not onion rings at all but delicious octopus. Squid, a cousin to the octopus, is equally good, and millions of salt water fishermen who use squid for bait could do worse than eat the bait, if it's fresh, and forget about fishing!

One of nature's tricks is that both squid and octopus are mollusks and related to clams, snails and oysters. They do have a more highly developed nervous system, excellent eyesight and, in the case of some squid, can swim fast enough to take off and fly in the air. Their shells have become a transparent, penlike backbone or a harder, cuttle bone in some species.

These animals are important foods in the Orient and around the Mediterranean. There is almost no waste, so you get your money's worth. You can eat 60 to 80 percent of any squid, yet less than half of a fish and even less of most shellfish. As for nourishment, squid and octopus contain the same amount of protein as most fish, including all eight amino acids.

You are not apt to catch either squid or octopus yourself. Look for it where commercial fishing boats dock or in foodstores which cater to Italian and Japanese customers.

The basic difference between octopus and squid is that an octopus is much tougher and needs parboiling. Squid are far more tender, and your only problem is to keep from overcooking them.

Let's cook octopus first.

231

Boiled Octopus

After dressing octopus, cut the mantle and tentacles into bite size pieces and boil, in just enough water to cover, for 30 minutes. The cooked pieces can then be eaten. Melt butter and add garlic powder to taste. Dip each bite of octopus in the garlic butter before eating.

Octopus Pineapple Salad

You can also use octopus in a salad.

2 pounds octopus, fresh or frozen, cut into 1/2-inch pieces	1 tablespoon red hot chili sauce
Lettuce	1/2 teaspoon dill weed
1 cup chopped pineapple, drained	1 tablespoon chopped parsley
1/2 cup mayonnaise	Dash paprika
1/4 cup sour cream	Dash hot pepper sauce
	Salt and pepper to taste

Clean octopus and cut into 1/2-inch pieces. Cook in boiling water until tender, about 30 minutes. Drain. Place a bed of lettuce in a salad bowl. Place a layer of cooked octopus on top of lettuce; spoon on pineapple. Combine rest of ingredients and pour over salad. Chill and serve.

(Serves 6)

Do not try to eat the squid that's been frozen into packages for use as fishbait. Use only freshly caught squid or that frozen to be sold as food. Squid, like other mollusks, spoils quickly, and it doesn't pay to take chances.

If you buy fresh squid and it's uncleaned, just hold the body in one hand, twist off the head with the other, and all the insides will come out with the head. Then you pull out the backbone and remove the little wings near the tail, taking the skin with them. Finally, you can cut up the small legs or tentacles attached to the head into bite size pieces and use them too.

The body can then be sliced into rings or strips or stuffed whole. You'll find it an unusual and tasty treat.

Fried Squid

2 pounds whole squid, fresh or frozen	⅛ teaspoon white pepper
2 tablespoons lemon juice	1 egg, beaten
	2 tablespoons milk
1 teaspoon salt	1 cup flour
	Fat for frying

Clean squid. Cut large squid into several pieces and tentacles into 1-inch pieces. Sprinkle lemon juice, salt and pepper on squid. Combine milk and egg. Dip squid in mixture and roll in flour. Place squid in a single layer in hot fat in a 10-inch heavy skillet or electric frypan. Fry at a moderate heat, 350°, for 3 to 5 minutes. Turn carefully. Fry 3 to 5 minutes longer or until squid are lightly browned. Drain on absorbent paper. Serve with lemon wedges.

(Serves 3 to 4)

Sweet and Sour Squid

Because squid has such a mild flavor, it's easily seasoned for a meal like this.

2 pounds whole squid, fresh or frozen
1 cup chopped celery
¼ cup chopped onion
¼ cup cooking oil
¼ cup tomato paste
¼ cup cider vinegar
1 tablespoon sugar
Salt and pepper to taste

Clean squid. Cut into 1-inch pieces. Cook celery and onion in hot oil until tender. Add squid, cover and simmer for 5 minutes. Add remaining ingredients, cover and simmer for approximately 20 minutes or until squid is tender. Stir occasionally.

(Serves 3 to 4)

Squid Stew

2 pounds whole squid, fresh or frozen	1/4 cup chopped parsley
1 cup chopped onion	1 1/2 teaspoons salt
1/4 cup cooking oil	1/4 teaspoon pepper
1 quart water	3 cups cubed potatoes
1 can (6 ounces) tomato paste	2 packages (10 ounces each) frozen peas

Clean squid. Cut mantle into 1 1/2-inch strips and tentacles into 1-inch pieces. Cook onion in hot oil until tender. Add squid and cook for 5 minutes. Add water, tomato paste, parsley, salt and pepper; simmer for 10 minutes. Add potatoes and peas. Cover and simmer for 20 to 30 minutes or until potatoes are tender, stirring occasionally.

(Serves 5 to 6)

Squid Salad

You can make a salad from squid just like octopus.

2 pounds whole squid,
fresh or frozen
2 cups boiling water
2 teaspoons salt
$\frac{1}{2}$ cup salad oil
$\frac{1}{4}$ cup lemon juice
1 cup chopped celery

$\frac{1}{2}$ cup chopped red
onion
$\frac{1}{8}$ teaspoon garlic
powder
1 tablespoon chopped
parsley
1 teaspoon salt
$\frac{1}{4}$ teaspoon pepper
Lettuce cups

Clean squid. Cut mantle and tentacles into $\frac{1}{2}$-inch pieces.
Place squid in boiling salted water. Cover and simmer 5 to
10 minutes or until tender. Drain and rinse in cold water.
Combine oil, lemon juice, celery, onion, garlic powder,
parsley, salt, pepper and squid. Cover and refrigerate for
several hours. Serve in lettuce cups.

(Makes approximately 2 cups)

Rays and Skates

I'm a happy optimist. That's why I rush the season and
delight in agreeing with my husband that we must get out
and fish for flounder nearly a month too soon.

Of course the same scenario always takes place—all self-
respecting flatfish are too numb with cold to risk opening
their mouths. But I do get a hit! I've hooked a record
flounder! It tugs furiously, and my rod bows with the
strain. Finally I'm able to bring a two pound skate aboard
our boat, the Easy Game.

Still I'm delighted. Skates are not pretty, but when it
comes to the culinary arts, handsome is as handsome does!
The basic difference between rays and skates is that rays,
which are generally larger, bear live young whereas skates
lay eggs.

Skates and rays, including all the sting ray family, are
wonderful eating, and with today's boat fuel prices, wast-
ing them is like throwing away good money. The sting or
stings (some individuals will have a pair) are near the base
of the tail, not at its whiplike tip, and therefore easy to
avoid. Nevertheless, be careful. The barbed stinger is not
fatal, but it's no joke either.

What do you do with skates and rays? With the smaller
skates, it's easy. Just slice the wings off as near the body as
possible and ice down immediately. With the larger rays,
you may have to wait until the creature dies down somewhat. But you must get the wings off and on ice very quickly. Why the hurry? It's because, just like their shark
relatives, the skate/ray family is quick to spoil.

If the wings are a good size, slice them into one-inch
strips by cutting through skin, flesh and cartilage. Then
remove skin from both sides of each strip and peel the two
layers of flesh from the central cartilage. The result is two
long, thin fillets from each one-inch strip.

Small skates are more difficult to handle. So parboil the
wings in boiling water for about ten minutes. This makes it

easy to peel off the skin and shortens further cooking time.

For the larger rays you don't parboil, be sure to soak the skinned fillets in a brine solution of one half cup white vinegar or one cup salt to a gallon of water for an hour or so in your refrigerator. Always keep skate and ray meat on ice or refrigerated. Then, if you have used salt, rinse well or soak a few minutes in fresh water. There is a reason for this soaking. Just like sharks, rays have a high urea content which could give the meat a bitter flavor unless you get rid of it.

And now, let's get to cooking a fish which ranks at the very top in French cuisine and deserves a high place in America too. Here are my favorite ways to serve skates and rays.

Batter Fried Ray or Skate

	Fillets of ray or skate, cut into ¹/₂-inch pieces	1	teaspoon salt
1	cup flour	¹/₄	teaspoon pepper
2	teaspoons baking powder	1	egg, separated
		¹/₂	cup lukewarm water
		1	tablespoon melted fat

Combine flour, baking powder, salt and pepper in a bowl; drop in egg yolk. Add water and fat and mix well. Fold in beaten egg white. Dry fish pieces and dip in batter. Fry at 350° to 375° in a deep fryer for 4 to 6 minutes or until golden brown. Drain on absorbent paper.

(Allow ¹/₃ pound per serving)

Ray or Skate Casserole

1 pound ray or skate meat, cut into ¼-inch pieces
2 tablespoons butter
1 cup sliced mushrooms
3 stalks celery, diced
4 tablespoons grated onion
½ cup minced green pepper
⅛ teaspoon basil
4 tablespoons butter
4 tablespoons flour
½ teaspoon salt
¼ teaspoon pepper
Pinch nutmeg
2 cups milk
½ cup cracker crumbs
4 tablespoons grated Cheddar cheese

Melt butter in a large saucepan over medium heat. Add mushrooms, celery, onion, pepper and basil; simmer for 10 minutes or until celery is tender but not soft. Add ray meat, and extra butter if necessary, to mushroom mixture; stir well and let simmer for 5 minutes. While this is simmering, prepare the sauce: Melt 4 tablespoons butter in a saucepan and stir in flour and seasonings. Slowly add milk, stirring constantly until thick and smooth. Combine cream sauce and vegetable/ray mixture and pour into a casserole; cover with cracker crumbs and top with grated cheese. Bake in a 350° oven for 25 to 30 minutes or until golden brown. (Serves 6)

Pan Fried Ray or Skate

Cut meat into ½-inch pieces. Salt and pepper. Roll in flour until well covered. In a heavy skillet or electric frypan, fry ray pieces in oil at 350° to 375° until nicely browned and tender.

(Allow ⅓ pound per person)

Shark

For years sport fishermen have destroyed hundreds of thousands of dogfish and other small sharks. Yet shark meat contains more protein than either milk, eggs, oysters, salmon or mackerel. Besides, shark is boneless and offers such qualities as firm texture, leanness, mild flavor and cooking versatility.

A common and delicious shark is the bull or harbor shark. Unlike the dogfish, this species has teeth but appears to be harmless. It is found in saltwater rivers, harbors and small tidal creeks along Atlantic, Gulf and Pacific coasts. Other edible sharks are the mako, porbeagle, thresher, hammerhead and small dusky.

With all of these sharks, young fish are preferred to old. It is always best to eat shark under 200 pounds. In larger specimens the meat tends to become tough and have a coarser grain. Shark meat must be absolutely fresh, as it spoils faster than other kinds of fish. Always keep shark in a cool place and out of the sun. Do not clean shark until you are ready to refrigerate or freeze the meat, for it seems to keep better when intact. Once shark is butchered, the meat must be placed under refrigeration as soon as possible. If it is not to be eaten at once, or the next day at latest, it should be frozen.

As with bluefish, it is best to remove the dark meat in shark to eliminate any off flavor. Larger fish can be steaked; the smaller ones should be split and cut into fillets. Shark skin sticks and is difficult to remove, but after cooking it comes off easily. If you do skin shark, just be prepared to sharpen your knife often.

Shark meat can be broiled, baked, fried, poached, grilled or smoked. The cooked fish is also delicious flaked and then used in salads or spreads.

Baked Shark Fillets

2 pounds shark fillets,
  fresh or frozen
1 cup sliced celery
1/3 cup chopped onion
1/4 cup butter, melted
4 cups soft bread cubes
1/2 cup chopped pecans

1/4 cup orange juice
1 teaspoon grated
  orange rind
1/4 teaspoon salt
1/4 cup butter, melted
1 teaspoon salt

Thaw fish if frozen. Cut shark fillets into serving size
pieces. Cook celery and onions in 1/4 cup butter in a
10-inch skillet until tender. Stir in bread cubes, pecans, orange juice, orange rind and 1/4 teaspoon salt. Place stuffing
in a well-greased baking dish. Place fish on top of stuffing.
Pour remaining 1/4 cup butter over fish and sprinkle with 1
teaspoon salt. Bake in a moderate oven, 350°, for 25 to 30
minutes or until fish flakes easily when tested with a fork.

(Serves 6)

Broiled Tangy Shark Steaks

Large sharks are easily steaked. Because the meat is so mild, you can serve it with a variety of sauces.

2 pounds shark steaks, fresh or frozen
½ cup catsup
¼ cup cooking oil
3 tablespoons lemon juice
2 tablespoons vinegar
1 teaspoon salt
1 teaspoon Worcestershire sauce
½ teaspoon powdered mustard
½ teaspoon onion powder
¼ teaspoon paprika
⅛ teaspoon garlic powder
3 drops liquid hot pepper sauce

Thaw steaks if frozen. Place steaks in a single layer in a shallow baking dish. Combine remaining ingredients. Pour marinade over fish and let stand for 30 minutes in refrigerator, turning once. Remove fish, reserving marinade for basting, and place on a well-greased broiler pan. Broil about 4 inches from source of heat for 4 to 5 minutes. Turn and baste with marinade. Cook for 4 to 5 minutes more or until fish flakes easily when tested with a fork.

(Serves 6)

Shark 'n Spaghetti

Shark can be used in sauces as well, so try it in your spaghetti sauce instead of expensive ground meat.

2 pounds shark steaks, fresh or frozen
2 cups sliced onions
2 cloves garlic, minced
¼ cup cooking oil
1 can (1 pound, 12 ounces) tomatoes
1 can (8 ounces) tomato sauce
1 can (4 ounces) sliced mushrooms, drained
1½ teaspoons salt
1½ teaspoons basil
1 teaspoon crushed rosemary
6 servings hot, cooked spaghetti
Parmesan cheese, shredded

Thaw fish if frozen. Cut shark steaks into 1-inch pieces. Cook onions and garlic in oil in a 6-quart Dutch oven until tender. Add tomatoes, tomato sauce, mushrooms, ½ teaspoon salt and herbs. Cover and simmer for 20 minutes or until flavors are blended. Uncover and simmer for 10 minutes or until sauce is thickened. Add fish and remaining 1 teaspoon salt. Simmer, uncovered, for 8 to 10 minutes or until fish flakes easily when tested with a fork. To serve, spoon over spaghetti and sprinkle generously with Parmesan cheese.

(Serves 6)

Snapping Turtle

You've heard the saying, "Never judge a book by its cover." If you judged the inside by how the outside looked, no one would ever have tried to eat snapping turtle. It is one of the nastiest looking and meanest acting animals around. It's called a snapping turtle with good reason. Beware of the jaws! There are two species: the common snapping turtle and the huge alligator snapper found further south. Both act and taste the same. These, by the way, are freshwater turtles and *not* endangered species. Rather, they endanger ducklings and anything else alive that can fit in their mouths. If you see a mother duck with her brood of little fuzzy babies, and the brood gets smaller every day, it probably means a snapping turtle is enjoying some tasty repasts.

Snapping turtles can weigh fifty pounds or more. You can catch them on setlines and in traps made of stout chicken wire and baited with fish. Unlike the endangered giant sea turtles, snappers have quite different meat in each part. The neck meat is whitest, the legs slightly darker and the back and tail darkest of all. The tail meat is excellent.

Frying is the most popular way of cooking these turtles. However, if you fry, you must parboil first until fork tender and then prepare as you would chicken. My favorite alternative is to use a crockpot or pressure cooker. This tenderizes the turtle meat and gives you a wide choice of recipes.

This thick turtle soup is a meal in itself and—pardon the pun—a snap to fix.

Turtle Scotch Broth

1 pound turtle meat
3 carrots, cut into small pieces
3 turnips, cut into small pieces
1 onion, chopped into small pieces
$^1/_3$ cup pearled barley
1 teaspoon salt
1 tablespoon instant parsley flakes
1 can ($10^1/_2$ ounces) beef broth
2 soup cans water

Place vegetables and barley in crockpot; sprinkle with salt and parsley flakes. Place turtle meat on top and add beef broth and water. Cover and cook on low heat for 8 to 10 hours. Lift out meat, remove from the bone and cut into small pieces. Return meat to crockpot and correct seasoning.

(Serves 4)

Barbecued Turtle in Pressure Cooker

You can use almost any pressure cooker recipe for chicken with your snapping turtle.

2 pounds turtle meat	2 tablespoons vinegar
Paprika	1/2 cup water
1/2 cup chili sauce	Salt and pepper to
1 onion, minced	taste

Sprinkle turtle pieces with paprika and place in pressure cooker. Combine remaining ingredients and pour over turtle meat. Close cover securely and cook at 15 pounds pressure for 15 minutes or until tender. Cool cooker and reduce pressure at once. Remove meat from bone and cut into bite size pieces. Return meat to sauce in cooker and thicken with flour or cornstarch. Serve barbecued turtle meat over buns or hot, cooked rice.

(Serves 4)

Whitebait

Many tidal areas contain a vast number of silversides, also
known as spearing. These minnows, with a broad silver
stripe down each side, are easily caught in a bait seine and
give you the raw material for a delicious feast of whitebait.
Because these small fish spoil quickly, they must be iced
at once and cooked as soon as possible. All you do is wash
them gently to remove sand, drain and dry with paper
toweling. Do not remove heads, tails or insides. If this
sounds unappealing, cook a few and try them, or serve as
an appetizer so everyone can snack and then decide.
You'll find whitebait served in some outstanding restaurants along both coasts and available in fish markets overseas. It is considered a delicacy, and the following recipes
are used by professional chefs in preparing this extra special treat.

Deep Fried Whitebait

Use a deep fryer with basket. Place a few of the whitebait
in the basket and sprinkle with flour seasoned with salt and
pepper. Shake basket to remove excess flour. Place basket
in hot oil, 375°, and cook just a few seconds until crisp and
brown. Drain on absorbent paper and serve on platter
with fresh parsley and lemon wedges.

247

Sautéed Whitebait

Here's an alternate method for fixing whitebait.

Roll whitebait gently in flour seasoned with salt and pepper. In a heavy skillet or electric frypan, melt enough butter to cover bottom. Place whitebait in single layer in skillet and cook just long enough to brown on both sides, about 3 to 5 minutes. Place on a platter with parsley and lemon wedges.

Microwave Cookery

Fish

Fish and wild game have a common quality—overcooking ruins them. Overcooked fish are dry and tasteless, and all game, whether it's upland birds, waterfowl or big game, come out dry and tough. This is why the fast cooking process of the microwave oven is excellent for fish and game. It helps retain natural juices and delicate flavor. Fish cooked in the microwave oven is especially good.

What is microwave cooking? The oven sends microwave energy into food, causing the liquid or moisture cells to vibrate against each other millions of times per second and create heat. This heat is then conducted through the food, and microwave cooking results.

Although these recipes are tested in a 650-watt countertop oven, cooking times will vary according to the wattage of your oven and the amount of power (voltage) coming into your house. It is always advisable to check whether your food is done before the recommended cooking time has elasped. Do not overcook!

When preparing fish in the microwave oven, arrangement has a lot to do with uniformity of the cooking process:

1. Fish fillets or fish steaks should be of uniform thickness.
2. It is best to place thicker pieces along the outer edge of the baking dish, since they will take longer to cook.
3. If several small dressed fish are being cooked at a time, alternate in this manner: head, tail, head, tail.

If you have small, whole fish (about one half pound each) such as trout, bass, pickerel, catfish, croaker or others, then use this recipe for easy baking.

Small Whole Baked Fish

To cook fresh, whole fish, make three slashes across the entire body of the fish on both sides. Brush cavity and both sides of fish generously with melted butter. Sprinkle only cavity with salt and favorite seasoning to taste. Cover with waxed paper and cook 2 minutes on high power for each fish. Two $1/2$-pound fish will take 4 minutes, three fish 6 minutes, etc. Remove from microwave and let stand, covered, for a few minutes. Test for doneness. Fish should flake easily when tested with a fork and not be too soft to the touch. The dorsal fin should come out cleanly.

Poached Whole Fish

Fish is easily poached in the microwave oven, and here's all
you do.
  Thaw fish if frozen. Place fish in a single layer in a baking dish. Cover with either waxed paper or a heavy duty
plastic wrap. If the latter is used, turn back one corner to
allow steam to escape. Cook 4 to 6 minutes on high power,
for one pound of fish, or until fish flakes easily when tested
with a fork. Drain. Remove skin and bone and flake fish.
The cooking time will vary according to the amount of fish
being poached.

Barbecued Fillets

When cooking any oily fish, it is important to use acidic ingredients to break down the fat and oils. That's why lemon and lime juice, vinegar, wine and tomatoes are used in many recipes involving bluefish, shad and the mackerel family, which includes all tunas, bonitos and albacore. I use this barbecue recipe for bluefish or mackerel fillets, and it's a favorite with my family.

6 fish fillets, fresh or frozen
½ cup barbecue sauce

1 bag (5 ounces) barbecued or regular potato chips, crushed
Lime wedges (garnish)

Thaw fish if frozen. Dip fish in barbecue sauce and roll in crushed chips. Place fish in a single layer in a well-greased baking dish. Cook, uncovered, on high power in microwave oven for 8 to 10 minutes or until fish flakes easily when tested with a fork. Garnish with lime wedges.

(Serves 6)

Fillets Amandine

1 pound fish fillets, fresh or frozen	1 tablespoon lemon juice
4 tablespoons butter	Salt to taste
1/4 cup sliced almonds	Lemon wedges

Thaw fish if frozen. Place butter, almonds and juice in an oblong baking dish. Microwave on high power for 5 to 7 minutes or until almonds are golden, stirring several times. Remove almonds with slotted spoon and set aside. Dip fillets into butter mixture, coating both sides; salt. Arrange fish in a single layer, with thicker portions of fillets to the outside of dish. Cover with waxed paper. Microwave at high power for 4 to 5 minutes, giving dish one half-turn during cooking, or until fish flakes easily when tested with a fork. Remove fish to a warmed platter and spoon almonds over top. Serve with lemon wedges.

(Serves 3)

Fix-Ahead Italian Fish Fillets

6 fish fillets, fresh or
  frozen
  (8 ounces) spaghetti
  sauce with mushrooms
  ($^1/_2$ can)

$^1/_2$ teaspoon oregano
$^1/_2$ package (4 ounces)
  Mozzarella cheese,
  shredded

Thaw fish if frozen. Poach fillets in microwave by placing
in a single layer in baking dish and then covering with
plastic wrap, folding one corner back for steam to escape.
Cook on high power for 4 to 6 minutes per pound or until
fish flakes easily with fork—do not overcook. Cool fish and
then refrigerate until ready to complete recipe. When
ready to do the final cooking, place cooked fillets in a
single layer in a baking dish. Combine sauce and oregano.
Spoon sauce on each portion of fish and sprinkle with
cheese. Place, covered, in microwave oven and cook on
high for 3 to 4 minutes or until cheese is melted and fish is
hot.

(Serves 4 to 5)

Fillet of Sole or
Flounder with Mushrooms

1 pound of sole or
flounder fillets, fresh
or frozen
4 tablespoons butter
$1/2$ pound fresh
mushrooms, sliced

$1/2$ cup white table wine
Salt to taste
2 teaspoons
Worcestershire sauce

Thaw fish if frozen. Place butter in an oblong baking dish and microwave on high power for 2 minutes or until melted. Spread mushrooms over melted butter. Cover mushrooms with fillets and pour wine over all. Cover with waxed paper and microwave on high power for 4 to 6 minutes or until fish flakes easily when tested with a fork. Remove fish to a warmed platter and salt to taste. Add Worcestershire sauce to mushroom liquid in dish and stir. Pour over fish and serve immediately.

(Serves 3)

Fillets with Sweet and Sour Sauce

1 pound fish fillets, fresh
  or frozen
3 tablespoons cornstarch
1/4 cup cold water
1 can (8 ounces) tomato
  sauce

1 can (8 ounces)
  pineapple chunks,
  undrained
1/2 cup brown sugar
1/3 cup red wine vinegar
1/2 teaspoon onion juice

Thaw fish if frozen. Combine cornstarch and water in a deep casserole dish and stir until dissolved. Add remaining ingredients, except fish, and mix well. Microwave on high power for 3 to 4 minutes, stirring several times. Microwave on high for an additional 4 to 5 minutes or until thickened and bubbly, stirring at 1 minute intervals. Arrange fish fillets in a single layer in a baking dish with thicker portions to outside of dish. Pour sauce evenly over fillets. Cover with waxed paper and microwave on high power for 5 to 7 minutes or until fish flakes easily when tested with a fork, giving dish one half-turn during cooking.

(Serves 3)

Baked Fish Fillets in Sour Cream

1 pound fish fillets, fresh
  or frozen
½ cup sour cream
1 tablespoon dry onion
  soup mix
½ cup fine dry bread
  crumbs

1 tablespoon grated
  Parmesan cheese
1½ teaspoons chopped
  parsley
⅛ teaspoon paprika

Thaw fish if frozen. Cut fillets into serving size portions.
Combine sour cream and onion soup mix. Combine bread
crumbs, Parmesan cheese, parsley and paprika. Dip fish in
sour cream mixture and roll in bread crumb mixture.
Place fish in a single layer in a well-greased baking dish
with thicker portions to outside of dish. Cover and cook on
high power for 5 to 7 minutes or until fish flakes easily
when tested with a fork.

(Serves 3)

Fillets Orange

If you have mild-tasting fillets such as those from flounder, weakfish (sea trout) or even shark, use this recipe and
see what a difference it makes.

2 pounds fish fillets,
   fresh or frozen
½ cup frozen orange
   juice concentrate,
   thawed
1 teaspoon salt

Dash pepper
1½ cups cereal crumbs or
   toasted bread crumbs
¼ cup butter
   Orange Sauce

Thaw fillets if frozen. Cut fillets into 6 portions. Combine
orange juice concentrate, salt and pepper. Dip fish in
orange juice and roll in crumbs. Place fish in a single layer
in baking dish with thicker portions to outside of dish. Dot
fillets with butter. Microwave, uncovered, on high power
for 8 to 10 minutes or until fish flakes easily when tested
with a fork. Turn dish once during cooking process. Serve
with Orange Sauce.

(Serves 6)

Orange Sauce

2 tablespoons white wine vinegar
1½ tablespoons sugar
½ cup chicken broth
¼ cup frozen orange juice concentrate, thawed
¼ cup water
1 tablespoon grated orange peel
¼ cup white table wine
1 tablespoon cornstarch

Combine all ingredients. Microwave on high power for 6 minutes or until sauce is thickened; stir several times.

(Makes approximately 1⅓ cups sauce)

Fish Steaks in Vermouth

4 fish steaks (4 ounces each) king mackerel, striped bass or other large fish, fresh or frozen
Salt
Onion powder
2 tablespoons butter
¼ teaspoon basil
¼ cup dry vermouth
Paprika

Thaw fish if frozen. Place fish steaks in a baking dish and sprinkle with salt and onion powder. Melt butter in a small dish in microwave oven on high power for 1 minute. Add basil to melted butter and pour over fish. Then pour vermouth over steaks and sprinkle with paprika. Cover and microwave on high power for 6 to 8 minutes or until fish flakes easily when tested with a fork. Turn dish once during cooking.

(Serves 4)

Curried Fish Steaks

4 fish steaks (4 ounces each) salmon, halibut, shark or other mild fish, fresh or frozen
½ teaspoon salt
½ teaspoon instant parsley flakes

4 thin lemon slices
1 cup water
⅔ cup mayonnaise
1 tablespoon lemon juice
¼ teaspoon curry powder

Thaw fish if frozen. Place a large size (14" × 20") oven cooking bag in a 13" × 9" × 2" baking dish. Season fish steaks with salt and parsley; place one lemon slice on each steak. Pour water into bag and arrange fish in bag. Close bag with nylon tie and make 6 ½-inch slits on top. Microwave on high power for 6 to 8 minutes or until fish flakes easily when tested with a fork. Turn dish once during cooking. To make sauce, combine remaining ingredients in a small bowl and beat until smooth. Serve with fish steaks.

(Serves 4)

Microwave Fish Loaf

3 cups cooked, flaked
bluefish, salmon,
albacore or other fish
1½ cups fresh whole
wheat bread crumbs
½ cup sour cream
1 teaspoon onion juice

¼ cup chopped celery
¼ cup chicken bouillon
2 eggs, slightly beaten
1 teaspoon
Worcestershire sauce
Salt and pepper to
taste

Combine all ingredients in a bowl. Spoon mixture into a
10-inch microwave tube pan or in a round baking dish
with inverted custard cup in center. Cover and microwave
on high power for 5 minutes. Rotate dish and microwave
on high power for another 5 minutes.

(Serves 4)

Shellfish

Shellfish, such as shrimp, lobster, crab, oysters and clams, are excellent cooked in the microwave oven. If you're using canned shellfish, it is best to drain excess liquid if recipes do not specifically call for it, except in a chowder or stew.

This crabmeat recipe makes a delicious, low calorie entrée for a luncheon or light supper.

Crabmeat on Pineapple

1 pound crabmeat, fresh or frozen	$1/2$ teaspoon Worcestershire sauce
$1/4$ cup mayonnaise or salad dressing	6 large pineapple slices, drained
$1/2$ teaspoon salt	$1/2$ cup fine corn flake crumbs
$1/2$ teaspoon dry mustard	

Thaw crabmeat if frozen. Drain. Remove any remaining pieces of shell or cartilage. Combine crabmeat, mayonnaise and seasonings; mix well, but gently, with fork. Dip both sides of pineapple slices in corn flake crumbs and place in a baking dish. Place $1/3$ cup crab mixture on top of each pineapple slice. Sprinkle remaining corn flake crumbs over top of crab mixture. Heat, uncovered, on medium high or 70% power for 6 minutes or until mixture is hot.

(Serves 3 to 4)

Crab Spread

1 cup crabmeat, fresh or frozen
1 package (8 ounces) cream cheese, softened
1 tablespoon milk
2 teaspoons Worcestershire sauce
1 teaspoon onion juice
2 tablespoons toasted slivered almonds
Assorted crackers

Thaw crabmeat if frozen. Drain. Remove any remaining pieces of shell or cartilage. In a mixing bowl, combine cream cheese, milk, Worcestershire sauce and onion juice. Add crabmeat and blend well. Turn mixture into an 8-inch pie plate. Top with toasted almonds. Microwave on high power approximately 2 minutes or until hot enough to serve. Serve warm with assorted crackers.

(Makes about 2 cups)

Hot Pineapple Crab Salad

1 pound crabmeat, fresh
  or frozen
1 large fresh pineapple
$^1/_2$ cup butter

2 tablespoons lemon
  juice
$^1/_2$ teaspoon tarragon
$^1/_2$ teaspoon salt
1 avacado

Thaw crabmeat if frozen. Drain. Remove any remaining
pieces of shell or cartilage. Cut pineapple in half lengthwise through the crown. Remove fruit, leaving shells intact. Core and dice fruit (making about $2^1/_2$ cups). In a
small bowl, microwave butter on high power for 5 minutes
or until melted. Stir in lemon juice, tarragon and salt. Peel
and slice avacado. Combine with pineapple and crab in a
large bowl. Gently fold in sauce. Turn into pineapple
shells. Cover with waxed paper and microwave on high
power for 4 minutes or until heated through.

(Serves 3 to 4)

Shrimp in Sour Cream

1 pound raw shrimp,
  peeled and deveined,
  fresh or frozen
1/4 cup finely chopped
  onion
1/4 cup butter

1 can (4 ounces) sliced
  mushrooms, drained
1 tablespoon flour
1/4 teaspoon salt
  Dash cayenne pepper
1 cup sour cream

Thaw shrimp if frozen. Place onion and butter in
1 1/2-quart casserole. Place shrimp around the outside of
bowl and add mushrooms in the center. Sprinkle in flour,
salt and pepper. Cover with plastic wrap. Microwave on
high power for 4 minutes. Stir. Recover and cook for 2
minutes on high power. Stir in sour cream. Cook 1 minute
on high power or until heated thoroughly, not allowing
mixture to boil. Serve over cooked rice.

(Serves 4)

Sweet and Sour Shrimp

2 pounds peeled, deveined, cooked shrimp, fresh or frozen
1½ cups apple juice
½ cup diagonally sliced carrots
½ cup vinegar
⅓ cup sugar
¼ cup catsup
2 tablespoons cooking oil
1 tablespoon soy sauce
¼ teaspoon salt
¼ cup apple juice
2 tablespoons cornstarch
1 teaspoon onion juice
2 cups hot cooked rice
½ cup slivered almonds, toasted

Thaw shrimp if frozen. In a large bowl, combine 1½ cups apple juice, carrots, vinegar, sugar, catsup, oil, soy sauce and salt. Stir until sugar is dissolved. Cover and microwave on high power for 15 minutes or until carrots are cooked, but still crunchy. Dissolve cornstarch in ¼ cup apple juice. Add cornstarch mixture and onion juice to carrot mixture. Cover and microwave on high power for 2 minutes longer or until sauce has thickened. Add shrimp and microwave 1 or 2 minutes more on high power or until hot enough to serve. Add almonds to rice. Serve shrimp sauce over rice.

(Serves 6)

Peaches and Scallops

1 pound scallops, fresh
  or frozen
3 slices bacon
2 tablespoons melted
  butter
2 tablespoons lemon
  juice

$^1/_4$ teaspoon salt
12 canned peach halves
$^1/_4$ teaspoon cinnamon
$^1/_4$ teaspoon cloves
$^1/_4$ teaspoon mace
$^1/_4$ teaspoon salt

Thaw scallops if frozen. Rinse with cold water to remove
any shell particles. Cut scallops into $^1/_2$-inch pieces, making
sure pieces are equal in size. Cut bacon in fourths, crosswise. Place bacon on a paper plate and cover with paper
toweling. Microwave on high power for $2^1/_2$ minutes or
until bacon is crisp. Place butter in a bowl and microwave
on high power for 1 minute. Add scallops, lemon juice and
salt to melted butter. Drain peach halves and place cut side
up in an oblong baking dish. Combine spices and salt and
sprinkle over peaches. Place about 2 tablespoons of scallop
mixture in center of each peach. Place a piece of bacon on
each peach. Microwave, uncovered, on high power for 6 to
7 minutes, turning dish once during cooking.

(Serves 6)

Scalloped Oysters

1 pint oysters, fresh or frozen	1 tablespoon minced parsley
¼ cup butter	¾ cup milk
1 teaspoon instant minced onion	2 cups Ritz cracker crumbs
1 teaspoon salt	½ cup grated Cheddar cheese
1 teaspoon lemon juice	

Thaw oysters if frozen. Drain. Remove any remaining pieces of shell particles. Combine butter, onion, salt, lemon juice and parsley in a 1½-quart casserole dish. Cover and microwave on high power for 2 minutes. Place oysters in a small bowl. Cover and microwave on high power for 2½ minutes or until edges begin to curl; drain. Add oysters, milk and 1½ cups of Ritz cracker crumbs to butter mixture. Mix well. Combine remaining ½ cup cracker crumbs with cheese and sprinkle over casserole. Microwave, uncovered, on high power for 4 minutes or until mixture is hot.

(Serves 4)

Seafood Casserole

³/₄ pound scallops, fresh
  or frozen
¹/₂ pound crabmeat, fresh
  or frozen
¹/₄ pound peeled,
  deveined, cooked
  shrimp, fresh or
  frozen
  6 tablespoons butter
1¹/₄ cups milk

¹/₄ cup flour
  1 teaspoon salt
¹/₈ teaspoon white pepper
  2 tablespoons sherry
  2 tablespoons butter
1¹/₂ cups soft, torn bread
  crumbs
¹/₄ cup shredded
  Cheddar cheese
  Paprika

Thaw seafood if frozen. Drain. Remove any remaining
pieces of shell or cartilage. If large scallops and shrimp are
used, cut in half or quarter. Place 6 tablespoons butter in a
2-quart round casserole and microwave on high power for
3 minutes or until melted. Add scallops to melted butter
and microwave, covered, on high power for 3 to 4 minutes
or until scallops are opaque. Remove scallops from dish.
Stir milk, flour, salt and pepper into butter. Cover and microwave on high power for 5 to 6 minutes, stirring often
during cooking process. Add scallops, crabmeat, shrimp
and sherry. Spoon into individual baking shells, casseroles
or ramekins. In a small bowl, microwave on high power 2
tablespoons butter for 1¹/₂ minutes or until melted. Add
bread crumbs and cheese and mix well; sprinkle over seafood mixture. Microwave on high power for 4 to 5 minutes
or until hot enough to serve. Sprinkle with paprika.

(Serves 6)

Microwave Bouillabaisse

1 pound fish fillets, fresh or frozen
½ pound raw, peeled, deveined shrimp, fresh or frozen
1 can (8 ounces) minced clams, undrained
½ cup chopped celery
½ cup chopped onion
¼ cup butter
1 can (1 pound, 4 ounces) tomatoes
1 cup water
1¼ teaspoons salt
¼ teaspoon thyme
⅛ teaspoon garlic powder
⅛ teaspoon pepper
1 bay leaf
6 slices French bread
Grated Parmesan cheese

Thaw seafood if frozen. Skin fish fillets and cut into pieces about 1-inch square. Cut large shrimp in half. In a 5-quart bowl, place celery, onion and butter. Cover and microwave on high power for 4 minutes. Add fish, shrimp, clams, tomatoes, water, salt, thyme, garlic powder, pepper and bay leaf. Cover and microwave on high power for 15 minutes or until fish flakes easily when tested with a fork. Stir once during cooking process. Remove bay leaf. Sprinkle cheese over bread; toast. Arrange toast in large individual soup bowls and cover with bouillabaisse.

(Serves 6)

Game

Energy saving translates into money. That's why the microwave oven can more than pay its way in your kitchen. You'll find it works well with all seafood and some game. The microwave simply cannot handle all game, much of which is tough enough to require long, slow cooking. I cannot recommend the microwave for wild rabbit, squirrel, wild duck or large big game roasts. These are best prepared by other methods.

Here you will find those recipes that are proved by my own personal experience. Some of the new browning/tenderizing microwave agents now available are excellent. They do help in microwave game cooking, and I have suggested them where they will do the most good.

Quail in Wine

4 quail
Micro-Shake, poultry
flavor of similar
microwave browning
agent
1/2 cup white table wine

2 tablespoons currant
jelly
1 teaspoon Dijon style
mustard
1 teaspoon cornstarch

Rinse quail with water. Place quail, breast side up, in a baking dish with breasts toward outside of dish. Sprinkle quail with Micro-Shake. Pour wine around (not over) birds. Cover with waxed paper. Microwave on high power for 4 minutes. Give dish a half-turn and microwave another 4 minutes or until meat is fork tender. Remove birds to a warmed platter and cover with foil. Add currant jelly and mustard to wine liquid in dish. Microwave on high power for 1 1/2 minutes; stir and microwave 1 1/2 minutes more. Stir until jelly is completely dissolved. Stir in cornstarch and microwave on high power for 1 1/2 minutes; stir and cook 1 1/2 minutes longer. Pour sauce over quail and serve immediately.

(Serves 2)

Barbecued Quail

4 quail
1 cup canned whole
  cranberry sauce
¹/₄ cup catsup
4 teaspoons cornstarch
1 tablespoon brown
  sugar

2 tablespoons lemon
  juice
1 tablespoon prepared
  mustard
1 tablespoon
  Worcestershire sauce
1 tablespoon vinegar

Combine all ingredients, except quail, in a square baking
dish. Place quail, skin side down, in dish; turn skin side up
to coat with sauce. Cover with waxed paper and microwave
on high power for 8 to 10 minutes. After the first 5 minutes of cooking, turn dish and baste quail. When done
(fork tender), stir sauce and spoon some over quail. Serve
remaining sauce at table.

(Serves 2)

Pheasant with Orange Glaze

1 pheasant
(2 to 2½ pounds) cut
into serving size
portions

Micro-Shake, poultry
flavor or similar
microwave browning
agent
Orange Glaze

Rinse pheasant pieces with water. Sprinkle Micro-Shake on skin side of pheasant portions, covering surface. Place pieces on a roasting rack, skin side up, in an oblong baking dish. Put thicker portions to outside of dish. Cover with waxed paper and microwave on medium high, or 70% power, for 15 minutes. Give dish a half-turn and microwave on medium high for 8 minutes or until meat is fork tender. Cover with foil while making Orange Glaze.

(Serves 3)

Orange Glaze

½ cup frozen orange
juice concentrate,
thawed
2 teaspoons cornstarch

¼ teaspoon ground
allspice
1 tablespoon brown
sugar

Mix cornstarch with orange juice concentrate. Add remaining ingredients and stir thoroughly. Microwave on high power for 1½ to 2 minutes or until thick, stirring once or twice with fork or whisk. Brush warm glaze over pheasant pieces and serve immediately. Garnish with orange slices with a dab of currant jelly in center of each slice.

Italian Venisonburgers

½ pound ground
venison, no fat added
½ pound ham sausage
2 tablespoons grated
Parmesan cheese
2 tablespoons catsup

¼ teaspoon oregano
Micro-Shake, garlic
and onion flavor, or
similar microwave
browning/tenderizing
agent

Mix all ingredients except Micro-Shake. Form meat mixture into patties. Sprinkle Micro-Shake liberally over all surfaces. Place patties in a glass baking dish or on a microwave roasting rack. Cover with waxed paper and microwave on high power for 7 to 8 minutes, turning dish after 4 minutes.

(Makes 4 patties)

Tasty Venison Loaf

1 pound ground venison
(no fat or less than
15%)
1 egg
1/2 teaspoon onion
powder
1 teaspoon
Worcestershire sauce
1/4 cup catsup
1/4 cup bread crumbs
Micro-Shake, natural
flavor or similar
microwave browning/
tenderizing agent

Mix first 6 ingredients together. Shape meat mixture in doughnut shape in a round baking dish with inverted custard cup in center. Sprinkle top of meat lightly with Micro-Shake. Cover with paper toweling. Microwave on high power for 7 to 8 minutes, rotating dish and draining after 4 minutes.

(Serves 4)

Individual Glazed Venison Loaves

1 pound ground venison
(no fat or less than
15%)
$1/3$ cup milk
$1/3$ cup bread crumbs
1 egg
1 teaspoon instant
minced onion
$1/4$ cup catsup
$1/2$ teaspoon salt

$1/4$ teaspoon sage
Dash pepper
$1/4$ cup dark brown sugar,
firmly packed
$1/3$ cup catsup
$1/4$ teaspoon nutmeg
$1/2$ teaspoon dry mustard
2 drops Worcestershire
sauce

Pour milk in mixing bowl; add bread crumbs and soak for
3 minutes. Add meat, egg, onion, catsup, salt, sage and
pepper. Mix well and divide mixture equally into 4 individual casseroles or pans. Smooth mixture for even surface. Place casseroles in a circle in microwave oven.
Microwave on high power for 6 minutes. Interchange position of casseroles halfway through cooking time. In a
small bowl, combine last 5 ingredients. Spoon on meat-
loaves. Microwave on high power for 2 more minutes.

(Serves 4)

Venison Stuffed Green Peppers

1 1/2 pounds ground
venison (no fat or less
than 15%)
6 medium green
peppers
1 teaspoon salt
1 tablespoon
Worcestershire sauce

1/3 cup instant rice,
uncooked
1 egg, beaten
1 can (10³/₄ ounces)
tomato soup, divided
2 teaspoons instant
minced onion

Cut a slice across the stem end of each pepper and scoop
out seeds and membrane. Combine ground venison, salt,
Worcestershire sauce, rice, egg, ³/₄ cup soup and onion.
Mix lightly. Fill each pepper with about ¹/₂ cup of venison
mixture. Place filled peppers in a round casserole dish.
Pour remaining soup over filled peppers. Cover with plastic wrap. Microwave on high power for 15 to 18 minutes.
Let stand, covered, for 2 or 3 minutes.

(Serves 3 to 4)

Super Venison Liver Slices

1 pound venison liver,
sliced ¹/₂ to ³/₄-inch
thick
4 slices bacon
²/₃ cup fine bread crumbs

1 tablespoon minced
parsley
1 teaspoon paprika
¹/₂ teaspoon salt
¹/₈ teaspoon pepper
¹/₃ cup Italian dressing

Place bacon slices around sides of a 9-inch square baking dish. Cover with paper toweling. Microwave on high power for 3 to 4 minutes. Remove cooked bacon to paper toweling. Combine crumbs, parsley, paprika, salt and pepper. Dip liver slices, on both sides, into Italian dressing; dredge in seasoned crumbs to coat thoroughly. Place liver slices in bacon drippings. Microwave on high power for 2 minutes; turn liver slices and microwave on high power 2 minutes more or until liver is done. Do not overcook or liver will become tough. Place bacon slices on top of liver and serve immediately.

(Serves 4)

Venison-Vegetable Stew

1 pound boneless
venison stew meat, cut
into $^1/_2$-inch cubes
Micro-Shake, natural
flavor or similar
microwave browning/
tenderizing agent
$^1/_2$ teaspoon paprika
$^1/_8$ teaspoon basil

$^1/_2$ teaspoon onion
powder
$^1/_2$ cup thinly sliced celery
2 medium carrots, thinly
sliced
2 medium potatoes,
peeled and cut into
$^1/_2$-inch cubes
1 can (6 ounces)
vegetable juice cocktail

Place meat in a 2-quart casserole. Moisten meat with water
and sprinkle Micro-Shake over top of meat. Pierce meat
liberally with fork; turn over and repeat. Cover casserole
tightly with plastic wrap. Microwave at 50% power for 8
minutes, stirring halfway. Sprinkle paprika and basil over
meat. Top with vegetables and pour juice over all. Cover
and microwave on high power for 5 minutes. Reduce power to 50%, or medium low, and microwave 25 to 30 minutes or until vegetables are tender, stirring once. Thicken
juice in dish with 1 teaspoon cornstarch dissolved in small
amount of water.

(Serves 3 to 4)

Venison Barbecue

1 pound cooked venison roast, thinly sliced
1 can (8 ounces) tomato sauce
1 medium onion, finely chopped
1/8 teaspoon garlic powder
1 tablespoon chili powder
1 tablespoon prepared mustard
1 tablespoon cider vinegar
1 teaspoon salt
1/4 teaspoon hot pepper sauce
1 can (15 1/2 ounces) red or kidney beans, drained
8 hamburger buns, heated

Combine tomato sauce, onion, garlic powder, chili powder, mustard, vinegar, salt and hot pepper sauce in a 2-quart baking dish. Cover with waxed paper and microwave on high power for 5 minutes, stirring once. Stir in cooked venison and kidney beans. Microwave on high power, covered, for 7 minutes, stirring once. Serve on heated buns.

(Makes 8 servings)

Outdoor Grill Cookery

Game

Charcoal Broiled Big Game Chops or Steaks

12 venison chops or several steaks, cut 1-inch thick

1 cup melted butter
Salt and pepper

Brush chops or steaks on both sides with melted butter and place on grill. Keep grill high enough from coals to prevent too rapid cooking. Cook about 8 minutes, turn and baste generously with melted butter. Grill 6 minutes more or until meat is rare or medium rare. When done, remove from fire and salt and pepper to taste.

(Allow 2 chops or ¹/₂-pound steak per serving)

Spitted Small Game Birds

Small upland birds such as woodcock, snipe, dove or quail can be spit-cooked over a charcoal grill but do need the protection of an outer covering during most of the cooking. Otherwise these small, delicate birds will become hard, dry and tasteless. I've found that cabbage leaves are the easiest and best to use for this purpose.

Quail, woodcock or dove, drawn, plucked and left whole
Melted butter to which favorite herbs have been added

Cabbage leaf for each bird
String
Salt

Brush outside of birds with melted, herbed butter. Place 1 or 2 birds on a skewer. Wrap each bird with a cabbage leaf and tie it on well with a piece of string. Place skewers 3 to 5 inches from source of heat and turn frequently. Although cooking times will vary according to the heat of your fire, quail will take between 12 and 15 minutes; smaller birds, such as woodcock and dove, will require 10 to 12 minutes. Then unwrap birds and brush with melted butter several times while gently browning birds 3 to 5 minutes. Salt birds after cooking.

(Allow 2 quail or 4 or more woodcock or dove per serving)

Fish

There are at least three good reasons for cooking fish on your outdoor grill. One is the price of steak and other meat products that you might be grilling. The others are that grilled fish is superb eating and relatively non-fattening.

However, grilling fish does require some care, since fish is more fragile than meat, especially when cooked. Therefore, use a well-greased, hinged hamburger grill to hold your steaks and fillets, and be sure that whole fish placed over the charcoal are well basted.

You can wrap your fish or fillets in aluminum foil. The result won't be browned or crusty, but it will be moist and flavorful.

Here are some facts you'll want to consider before you start to grill fish:

1. Allow frozen fish to thaw completely before cooking.
2. Grease your grill well so fish cannot stick to it.
3. Be careful not to overcook your fish and dry them out.
4. Try to use a medium hot fire of about 300° to 375°. How can you tell? If you can hold the palm of your hand for four or five seconds a couple of inches above your fire, the temperature is in the correct range.

Back in the days when we lived at the Jersey Shore, one of the big events was the November Cartoppers' Picnic. This was a group of anglers who launched their small aluminum boats directly into the ocean and proceeded to battle striped bass and bluefish with little regard to wind and weather. The favorite cook at these affairs was Coach Ippolito, a local high school football mentor who excelled at preparing fish. With plenty of beer and other beverages flowing, Coach would grill fish in several different ways. Here are three recipes that give you a choice of using a hinged grill, a barbecue grill or wrapping in aluminum foil.

Grilled Trout or Other Small Whole Fish

6 pan-dressed trout or other small, whole fish, fresh or frozen
1/4 cup melted fat or oil
1/4 cup sesame seeds

2 tablespoons lemon juice
1/2 teaspoon salt
Dash pepper

Thaw fish if frozen. Place fish in well-greased, hinged wire grills. Combine remaining ingredients. Baste fish with sauce. Cook about 4 inches from moderately hot coals for 5 to 8 minutes. Baste with sauce. Turn and cook for 5 to 8 minutes longer or until fish flakes easily when tested with a fork.

(Serves 6)

Mustard-Grilled Small Whole Fish

4 to 6 pan-dressed small whole fish, fresh or frozen
1/4 cup prepared yellow mustard

1/4 cup cooking oil
1 teaspoon sugar
1/2 teaspoon salt
Dash pepper
Sliced bacon

Thaw fish if frozen. Combine mustard, oil, sugar, salt and pepper. Wrap a piece of bacon around each fish and fasten with tooth picks. Place fish directly on grill over moderately hot coals. Baste with sauce and grill 5 to 8 minutes. Turn fish over, baste again and cook 5 to 8 minutes longer or until fish flakes easily when tested with a fork.

(Serves 4 to 6)

Foil Wrapped Small Whole Fish

Whole pan-dressed
fish (1 to 3 pounds
each), fresh or frozen
Butter
1 small onion, thinly
sliced

Salt and pepper
Favorite herbs: basil,
dill, thyme, parsley or
others

Thaw fish if frozen. For each fish use a piece of heavy duty aluminum foil that is a little longer than the fish. Place a small amount of butter in center of foil and arrange several onion slices on it. Place the fish over onion slices. Spinkle cavity of fish with salt and pepper. Arrange remaining onion slices and herbs over fish. Sprinkle with salt and pepper and dot with butter. Bring foil up over fish, leaving some air space. Seal edges and both ends with double fold. Place sealed packages on grill over a moderately hot fire. Cook a 1-pound fish about 15 minutes, a 2-pound fish about 25 minutes and a 3-pound fish about 35 minutes, turning 2 or 3 times. After opening packages, spoon juices over each serving.

(Allow $1/2$ pound fish per serving)

Whole Stuffed Fish

If you have a fish that weighs about three or four pounds, you can stuff it, wrap in foil and then grill with first-rate results.

1 whole pan-dressed fish (3 to 4 pounds), fresh or frozen	$^{1}/_{4}$ cup butter
Salt and pepper	2 cups herb-seasoned stuffing mix
Lemon juice	$^{1}/_{4}$ cup chopped parsley
Melted butter	4 ounces blue cheese, crumbled
$^{1}/_{2}$ cup chopped celery	1 tablespoon lemon juice
2 tablespoons chopped onion	

Thaw fish if frozen. Season cavity lightly with salt, pepper and lemon juice. Spread a little butter in center of a large sheet of heavy duty aluminum foil and lay fish on it. To prepare stuffing, sauté celery and onion in $^{1}/_{4}$ cup butter until tender. Add stuffing mix; toss to absorb all butter. Blend in parsley and blue cheese. Moisten stuffing with lemon juice and about $^{2}/_{3}$ cup water. Fill fish with stuffing. Draw fish skin together to close opening; bind with soft string. Spread top of fish with a little butter. Sprinkle lightly with salt, pepper and lemon juice. Bring ends of foil up loosely over fish and seal with double fold. Close ends by double folding. Place wrapped fish on grill over moderately hot coals. Grill about 10 minutes on first side. Turn, grill second side 10 minutes. Turn again and grill 10 minutes more.

(Allow $^{1}/_{2}$ pound fish per serving)

Sam's Dolphin Steaks

Here in Virginia we have a neighbor, Sam Uhler, whose job involved participating in trial runs with nuclear submarines. It wasn't all work. They would get at least one day's offshore fishing, and Sam would come home laden with dolphin steaks (from the fish, not the mammal). His excellent recipe will work with any other steaks from non-oily fish. For example, you could use cod, halibut, pike, red snapper, catfish or white sea bass.

> 2 pounds boneless, dolphin steaks or other similar fish, fresh or frozen
> 1/2 cup butter, melted
> 1/4 cup lemon juice
> Salt and pepper
> Quick Hollandaise Sauce

Thaw fish if frozen. Before placing fish on the grill, brush steaks with a mixture of melted butter and lemon juice. Reserve most of this melted butter for basting during grilling. Sprinkle steaks with salt and pepper. Place a piece of heavy duty foil over a moderately hot grill, but not completely covering it. After putting fish steaks on foil, baste with butter/lemon mixture. Cook on one side for 8 minutes or until milky juices appear. Turn, baste again and cook for 8 to 10 minutes more or until fish flakes easily when tested with a fork. Serve with Quick Hollandaise Sauce.

(Serves 6)

Quick Hollandaise Sauce

½ cup butter
Juice of ½ lemon

⅛ teaspoon salt
3 egg yolks

In small saucepan, heat butter with lemon juice and salt until bubbly. Add slowly to egg yolks, beating constantly.

(Makes about ¾ cup)

If you are laying a hinged hamburger grill atop your regular charcoal or gas grill, fish steaks must be basted to protect against drying out. This is why the following recipes have varied sauces.

Oriental Grilled Fish Steaks

With this sauce, you might use swordfish, king mackerel, salmon or lake trout.

2 pounds fish steaks, fresh or frozen	2 tablespoons chopped parsley
1/4 cup orange juice	1 tablespoon lemon juice
1/4 cup soy sauce	1/8 teaspoon garlic powder
2 tablespoons catsup	1/2 teaspoon oregano
2 tablespoons cooking oil	Paprika

Thaw fish if frozen. Place steaks in a single layer in a shallow baking dish. Combine remaining ingredients except for paprika. Pour sauce over fish and let stand for 30 minutes, turning once. Remove fish, reserving sauce for basting. Place fish in well-greased, hinged wire grills. Cook about 4 inches from moderately hot coals for 8 minutes. Baste with sauce. Turn and cook for 7 to 10 minutes longer or until fish flakes easily when tested with a fork. Sprinkle with paprika.

(Serves 6)

Zesty Grilled Fish Fillets

Now we get to the oilier fish such as mullet, mackerel and bluefish. This recipe has an acid type basting mixture which helps to make the fish less fatty.

2 pounds fish fillets, fresh or frozen
1/4 cup French dressing
1 tablespoon lemon juice
1 tablespoon grated onion
2 teaspoons salt
Dash pepper

Thaw fish if frozen. Combine remaining ingredients. Baste fish with sauce. Place in well-greased hinged wire grills. Cook about 4 inches from moderately hot coals for 8 minutes. Baste with sauce. Turn and cook 7 to 8 minutes longer or until fish flakes easily when tested with a fork.

(Serves 6)

Fillets in a Packet

Maybe you're looking for a recipe that's good with every fish fillet, regardless of species. Here it is.

2 pounds fish fillets, fresh or frozen	6 tablespoons chopped onion
1/3 cup melted butter	Salt and pepper
1/4 cup lemon juice	Thyme
6 tablespoons chopped celery	

Thaw fish if frozen. Cut fillets into 6 portions. Tear off 6 lengths of heavy duty aluminum foil large enough to permit adequate wrapping. Place 1 tablespoon each celery and onion on each piece of foil; place fish on top. Combine butter and lemon juice; divide evenly over each fish portion. Sprinkle with seasonings. Bring two sides of foil together and fold down loosely in double folds allowing for heat circulation and expansion. Fold short ends up and over again; crimp to seal. Grill over moderately hot coals 15 minutes, turning once, or until fish flakes easily when tested with a fork.

(Serves 6)

Barbecued Fillets

Cod, hake, whiting and some other cold water fish haven't much flavor. This basting sauce adds zip that makes so much difference in dining pleasure.

2 pounds fish fillets, fresh or frozen
2 tablespoons chopped onion
2 tablespoons cooking oil
1 can (8 ounces) tomato sauce
2 tablespoons cream sherry
$1/2$ teaspoon salt
$1/4$ teaspoon oregano
$1/8$ teaspoon garlic powder
3 drops liquid hot pepper sauce

Thaw fish if frozen. Cook onion in oil until tender. Add remaining ingredients, except fish, and simmer for 5 minutes, stirring occasionally. Cool. Place fillets in a single layer in a shallow baking dish. Pour sauce over fish and let stand for 30 minutes, turning once. Remove fish, reserving sauce for basting. Place fish in well-greased, hinged wire grills. Cook about 4 inches from moderately hot coals for 8 minutes. Baste with sauce. Turn and cook for 7 to 10 minutes longer or until fish flakes easily when tested with a fork.

(Serves 6)

Shellfish

If you've ever attended an old fashioned oyster roast or clambake, you have discovered shellfish are wonderful when cooked outdoors. Here are some mouth-watering ways of preparing them on your grill.

Grilled Soft-Shelled Crabs

12	dressed soft-shelled crabs, fresh or frozen	1	teaspoon lemon juice
1	tablespoon dehydrated parsley flakes	¹/₄	teaspoon nutmeg
¹/₂	cup cooking oil	¹/₄	teaspoon soy sauce
			Lemon wedges

Thaw crabs if frozen. Place crabs in well-greased, hinged wire grills. Combine remaining ingredients except lemon wedges. Baste crabs with sauce. Cook about 4 inches from moderately hot coals for 8 minutes. Baste with sauce. Turn and cook 7 to 10 minutes longer or until lightly browned. Serve with lemon wedges.

(Serves 6)

Grilled King Crab Legs

3 packages (12 ounces each) precooked, frozen king crab legs
1/2 cup butter, melted
2 tablespoons lemon or lime juice
1/2 teaspoon paprika
Melted butter

Thaw crab legs if frozen. Combine butter, lemon juice and paprika. Baste crabmeat with sauce. Place crab legs on a grill, flesh side down, about 4 inches from moderately hot coals. Heat for 5 minutes. Turn and baste with sauce. Heat 5 to 7 minutes longer. Serve with melted butter.

(Serves 6)

Oyster Roast

36 shell oysters
Melted butter

Wash oyster shells thoroughly. Place oysters on a grill about 4 inches from hot coals. Roast 10 to 15 minutes or until shells begin to open. Serve in shells with melted butter.

(Serves 6)

Grilled Spiny Lobster Tails

6 spiny lobster tails (8 ounces each) fresh or frozen	2 tablespoons lemon juice
1/4 cup melted butter	1/2 teaspoon salt
	Melted butter

Thaw lobster tails if frozen. Cut in half lengthwise and remove swimmerettes and sharp edges. Cut 6 squares of heavy duty aluminum foil, 12 inches each. Place each lobster tail on one half of each square of foil. Combine butter, lemon juice and salt. Baste lobster meat with sauce. Fold other half of foil loosely over lobster tail and seal edges by making double folds in the foil. Place packages, shell side down, about 5 inches from hot coals. Cook for 20 minutes. Remove lobster tails from the foil. Place lobster tails on grill, flesh side down, and cook for 2 to 3 minutes longer or until lightly browned. Serve with melted butter.

(Serves 6)

Grilled Shrimp in Foil

3 pounds shrimp, fresh or frozen
2 cans (4 ounces each) sliced mushrooms, drained
²/₃ cup butter, melted
¹/₂ cup chopped parsley
¹/₄ cup chopped onion
2 tablespoons lemon juice
2 tablespoons chili sauce
1 teaspoon salt
Dash Worcestershire sauce
Dash liquid hot pepper sauce

Thaw shrimp if frozen. Peel, devein and wash. Cut 6 squares of heavy duty aluminum foil, 12 inches each. Divide shrimp into 6 portions. Place each portion of shrimp on one half of each square of foil. Place mushrooms on top of shrimp. Combine remaining ingredients. Pour sauce over mushrooms, dividing evenly among portions. Fold other half of foil loosely over shrimp and seal edges by making double folds in the foil. Place packages about 4 inches from moderately hot coals. Cook about 20 minutes or until shrimp is tender. To serve, cut a crisscross in top of each package and fold the foil back.

(Serves 6)

Scallops on the Grill

2 pounds scallops, fresh or frozen	2 teaspoons salt
1/2 cup cooking oil	1/4 teaspoon white pepper
1/4 cup lemon juice	1/2 pound sliced bacon
	Paprika

Thaw scallops if frozen. Rinse with cold water to remove any shell particles. Place scallops in a bowl. Combine oil, lemon juice, salt and pepper. Pour sauce over scallops and let stand for 30 minutes, stirring occasionally. Cut each slice of bacon in half lengthwise and then crosswise. Remove scallops, reserving sauce for basting. Wrap each scallop with a piece of bacon and fasten with a toothpick. Place scallops in well-greased, hinged wire grills. Sprinkle with paprika. Cook about 4 inches from moderately hot coals for 5 minutes. Baste with sauce and sprinkle with paprika. Turn and cook for 5 to 7 minutes longer or until bacon is crisp. (Serves 6)

Clambakes

Many years ago, you could buy lobsters along the Maine coast for anywhere from fifty cents to one dollar each. Now they are almost prohibitively expensive. If you live where you can set your own lobster pots, or buy local lobster reasonably, you can treat yourself and friends to a real clambake.

New England Clambake
(Individual Serving)

12 steamer clams
1 (1 pound) lobster
½ small broiler/fryer
 chicken
1 ear corn
1 potato, cut lengthwise
 in eighths

1 small onion, quartered
Salt and pepper
Melted butter
1 yard square cheese
 cloth for each package
Seaweed, if available
 along the beach

Scrub clams. Rinse and split lobster. Remove sharp bones from chicken. Shuck corn. Tear off enough large squares of heavy duty aluminum foil to fit under cheesecloth square. If you have seaweed, put a handful on the cheesecloth; top with chicken, then lobster and clams. Tuck in corn, onion, potato wherever there is room. Shake on pepper and salt. If you haven't used seaweed, add 4 tablespoons water to each package. Tie cheesecloth up over the food, then close aluminum foil into airtight package. Place packages on grill about 4 inches from moderately hot coals and cook 45 minutes to 1 hour. Open a package at end of 35 minutes to test chicken for doneness; reclose and continue cooking, if not tender. Prepare melted butter and pour into individual dishes for each person.

Farther south, you can obtain crabs more readily than lobsters and have a crab-clambake. This one is for six people, but you can easily adjust it for any number.

Chesapeake Bay Crab-Clambake Menu

CRAB-CLAMBAKE

HUSH PUPPIES

TOMATO WEDGES

WATERMELON

Crab-Clambake

6 dozen soft-shelled clams	6 ears of corn in the husks
12 small onions	12 live, hard-shelled blue crabs
6 medium baking potatoes	Lemon wedges
	Melted butter

Wash clam shells thoroughly. Peel onions and wash potatoes. Parboil onions and potatoes for 15 minutes; drain. Remove corn silk from corn and replace husks. Cut 12 pieces of cheesecloth and 12 pieces of heavy duty aluminum foil, 18″ × 36″ each. Place 2 pieces of cheesecloth on top of 2 pieces of foil. Place 2 onions, a potato, ear of corn, 1 dozen clams and 2 crabs on cheesecloth. Tie opposite corners of the cheesecloth together. Pour 1 cup of water over the package. Bring foil up over the food and close into airtight package. Make 6 packages. Place packages on grill about 4 inches from hot coals. Cover with hood or aluminum foil. Cook for 45 to 60 minutes or until onions and potatoes are cooked. Serve with lemon wedges and melted butter poured into individual dishes.

(Serves 6)

Tar Heel Hush Puppies

Speaking of Hush Puppies, you never know what you'll find in the way of a recipe. While giving a game cooking exhibition at Morehead City, North Carolina, I happened to eat in a local restaurant that served marvelous hush puppies. Here's the recipe direct from the Sanitary Fish Market Restaurant.

1 pound fine corn meal	1 egg
1 tablespoon salt	1 tablespoon sugar
Pinch soda	1 cup buttermilk

Mix all ingredients, adding water last to make batter a thick consistency. Drop rounded tablespoonfuls into deep hot oil, 375°, and cook until golden brown, 2 to 4 minutes.

(Serves 6)

Kabobs: Fish, Shellfish and Game

Roasting meats on sharp sticks or metal skewers goes back to those days when mankind first discovered fire. Long before pots, skillets or ovens, cooking was done over open fires. Then around the time of the Roman Empire, or probably even earlier in the vast rangelands of Central Asia, metal skewers, relatively light in weight and easily packed, came into use.

Since then kabobs have come a long way. Today they can be cooked on a charcoal or gas grill. There is no limit to the variety of kabob combinations you can create. Here are a few basic points to follow to insure marvelous eating.

1. Use skewers, with handles, that are long enough to hold all food.
2. Drain foods well before placing them on your skewers.
3. When combining meat with vegetables or fruits, use relatively small pieces of meat and do not crowd the foods on your skewer. This permits better heat circulation and more even cooking.
4. Parboil in advance those solid vegetables which take longer to cook than anything else on your skewers.
5. Barbecue kabobs over a medium to hot fire and baste frequently.

Fish Fillet Kabobs

Fish fillets of any firm-meated fish can be used for kabobs.
However, the skewers should then be secured in one or
more well-greased, hinged, wire grills to reduce the risk of
your fillets breaking into pieces and falling into the fire.

2 pounds fish fillets, fresh or frozen	1 can (1 pound) whole potatoes, drained
1/3 cup clear French dressing	1 1/2 teaspoons salt
	Dash pepper
3 large firm tomatoes	1/3 cup melted butter or oil

Thaw fillets if frozen. Skin them, if not already skinned,
and cut into strips of 1 inch by 4 inches wide. Place these
fish strips in a shallow baking dish and pour the French
dressing over them, letting them stand for 1/2 hour. Meanwhile, wash tomatoes, remove the stem ends and cut into
sixths. Remove fish strips from the dressing, reserving
liquid for basting, and roll the fillets. Place the rolled fillets
on skewers alternately with tomatoes and potatoes until
skewers are filled. Then secure your kabobs in one or
more well-greased, hinged, wire grills. Add salt, pepper
and remaining dressing to fat, mixing thoroughly. Baste
kabobs with this seasoned fat and French dressing mixture. Turn and repeat, after basting, on opposite side.
Cook until fish flakes easily when tested with a fork.

(Serves 6)

Shark Teriyaki Kabobs

Although this recipe calls for shark steaks, you might like to try chunks of striped bass, swordfish, king mackerel, dolphin or others.

2 pounds shark steaks or other fish steaks, cut in 1-inch chunks
1 can (1 pound) pineapple chunks, undrained
1/2 cup soy sauce
1/2 cup cream sherry (optional)
2 tablespoons brown sugar

1 teaspoon ground ginger
1 teaspoon dry mustard
1/8 teaspoon garlic powder
1 green pepper, cut in 1-inch squares
Cherry tomatoes, mushrooms, onions (optional)

Thaw fish if frozen. Drain pineapple chunks reserving 1/4 cup of juice. Prepare marinade by combining pineapple juice, soy sauce, sherry, brown sugar, ginger, mustard and garlic powder. Pour marinade over fish chunks. Cover and refrigerate fish for at least 1 hour. Drain fish and reserve marinade. Thread fish chunks, pineapple chunks and green pepper squares alternately on skewers. Include cherry tomatoes, fresh mushrooms and onion wedges if desired. Cook over hot coals for 5 minutes. Baste with marinade. Turn and cook for 5 minutes more or until fish flakes easily when tested with a fork.

(Serves 6)

Eel Kabobs

Because of their high fat content, eels are wonderful in kabobs.

2 pounds eel, cleaned, skinned and cut in 1½ to 2-inch lengths
1 cup soy sauce
1 tablespoon cream sherry
4 tablespoons sugar
Salt

Mix soy sauce, sherry and sugar and boil for 2 minutes. Then place pieces of eel on skewers and season with salt. Cook about 4 to 6 inches from hot coals for 20 minutes, brushing frequently with sauce and turning until evenly browned.

(Serves 3 to 4)

Scallop Kabobs

For something totally different, try either the scallop or shrimp kabobs.

1 pound scallops, fresh or frozen	1 green pepper, cut into 1-inch squares
1 can (13½ ounces) pineapple chunks, drained	¼ cup salad oil
	¼ cup lemon juice
	¼ cup chopped parsley
1 can (4 ounces) button mushrooms, drained	¼ cup soy sauce
	½ teaspoon salt
	12 slices bacon

Thaw frozen scallops. Rinse with cold water to remove any shell particles. Place pineapple, mushrooms, green pepper and scallops in a bowl. Combine oil, lemon juice, parsley, soy sauce and salt. Pour sauce over scallop mixture and let stand for 30 minutes, stirring occasionally. Fry bacon until cooked but not crisp. Cut each slice in half. Using long skewers, alternate scallops, pineapple, mushrooms, green pepper and bacon until skewers are filled. Cook about 4 inches from moderately hot coals for 6 minutes. Turn and cook for 4 to 6 minutes longer.

(Serves 6)

Skewered Shrimp

2 pounds large shrimp,
  cooked, peeled and
  deveined
¹/₂ cup cooking oil
¹/₄ cup soy sauce

¹/₄ cup lemon juice
1 medium onion, finely
  chopped
¹/₂ teaspoon ground
  ginger

Thaw shrimp if frozen. Combine all ingredients in a bowl.
Place shrimp in marinade and toss well so all are coated.
Cover and place in refrigerator for several hours. Thread
shrimp on skewers and grill about 4 inches from moderately hot coals for 4 to 6 minutes, basting constantly with
marinade. Turn and cook 4 to 6 minutes longer or until
shrimp change from translucent to opaque.

(Serves 4)

Big Game Liver Kabobs

The liver from big game animals is most delicious, and cooking it quickly over hot coals keeps it tender.

Big game liver, sliced and cut in cubes of 1-inch by 1-inch	Zucchini, sliced in $^1/_2$-inch pieces
Salt and pepper	Mushroom caps
Canned whole potatoes, drained	$^1/_2$ cup melted butter
	$^1/_2$ teaspoon mixed sweet herbs or your favorite herbs

Sprinkle liver cubes with salt and pepper. Place cubes on skewer alternately with potatoes, zucchini and mushrooms. Melt butter and add herbs. Place skewers 3 to 5 inches from source of heat and baste frequently with herbed butter while rotating skewers to insure even cooking. These liver kabobs will take about 10 to 12 minutes to cook, but do not overcook, or the liver will become dry and tough. The liver cubes should be light pink in the middle.

(Allow $^1/_3$ pound of liver per serving)

Big Game Steak Kabobs

Whether it's venison, elk, moose or other big game, you'll
need to use the tenderloin, chops or steaks for any kind of
grilling, including kabobs.

Big game tenderloin,
cut in 1-inch cubes
1 cup vegetable oil
1 cup Burgundy wine
1 onion, cut in small
pieces

6 slices bacon, fried and
crumbled
Cherry tomatoes
Canned whole onions,
drained
Green peppers, cut in
1-inch squares

Combine oil, wine, onion and bacon in a bowl. Place meat
cubes in this mixture and marinate at room temperature
for 4 to 5 hours. Then place cubes on long skewers, alter-
nating with the vegetables. Cook over hot coals, basting
with marinade frequently, until meat reaches desired state
of pink. Overcooking these cubes will cause them to become dry and tough. To insure even cooking, rotate
skewers often.

(Allow ⅓ pound boned tenderloin per serving)

Venison Meatball Kabobs

1½ pounds ground venison (less than 15% fat added)
¾ cup oatmeal, uncooked
1 teaspoon salt
⅛ teaspoon pepper

1 tablespoon instant minced onion
½ cup chili sauce
18 cherry tomatoes
4 large ears sweet corn
12 pieces green pepper
6 button mushrooms

Prepare meatballs by combining ground venison, oats, salt, pepper, onion and chili sauce. Shape this mixture around cherry tomatoes to form 18 venisonburgers with a tomato center. Meanwhile, cut each ear of corn in 3 pieces and cook these in boiling, salted water for 5 minutes. Finally, alternate venisonballs, corn and green peppers on six 12-inch skewers. Place a mushroom at the tip of each skewer and brush corn with melted butter. Cook the kabobs over hot coals for about 4 mintues before turning. Brush corn regularly with melted butter. Turn twice to cook a total of 12 minutes or until done to your taste.

(Serves 6)

Smoked Fish

There are only two methods of smoking fish—cold smoking and hot smoking. We'll deal only with hot smoking, since cold smoking requires a specially built, expensive smoke unit.

Excellent smoked fish can be produced in hooded or covered electric, gas or charcoal grills. All you need to do is adjust the temperatures according to your recipes. Although the procedure is identical for all types of grills, it is advisable to use an oven thermometer.

Wood chips from apple, oak, alder, hickory or cherry trees give a wonderful flavor to fish. Prepare them by soaking one pound of hardwood chips in two quarts of water for several hours or overnight.

While you're smoking fish, keep the heat low. If using a charcoal grill, fewer briquets are necessary than when you're broiling a steak. Spread $1/3$ of the wet chips evenly over the briquets. They'll produce smoke and lower the temperature. Be sure to add your remaining chips as needed.

Very low temperatures, 150° to 175°, are not absolutely essential in smoke fish cookery but give the fish a stronger flavor. Good results can also be had by using higher temperatures up to 300°. This reduces cooking time, since your fish takes on a smoky flavor quickly.

Plain Smoked Fish

1 quart water
¹/₄ cup salt
2 tablespoons sugar

Sweet basil leaves
(optional)
1 to 2 pounds fresh or
frozen whole fish or
fillets

Thaw fish if frozen. Mix water with salt and sugar until both dissolve. Pour mixture into an oblong glass baking dish or other shallow glass or pyrex container. Place fish in brine (do not stack). Marinate fish in refrigerator for 30 minutes. One hour before smoking, remove fish from brine and rinse thoroughly in clear, cold water. Then put them on a wire rack to air-dry.

Now place your fish, skin side down, on a well-greased grill about 4 to 6 inches from the smoking chips. Fat fish such as mackerel, bluefish, true albacore or salmon are best for smoking, but lean fish can be smoked with good results if basted frequently with cooking oil.

Close hood on grill and open vent slightly to keep smoke and air circulating. Smoke your fish approximately 1 hour at 150° to 175°, or 30 to 45 minutes at 200°. You'll know the fish is done when the cut surface is golden brown and the flesh flakes easily when tested with a fork.

Storage

Smoked fish can be held, loosely wrapped, in the refrigerator, with no loss of quality for 3 days. To freeze smoked fish, wrap loosely and allow to cool in refrigerator. Then rewrap in moisture-vapor proof wrapping and place in freezer. Smoked fish will keep 3 months in the freezer.

Smoked fish is delicious served plain or on crackers. You might also like to try it in salads, in an omelet or as a spread for hors d'oeuvres.

Smoky Fish Salad

2 cups flaked, smoked fish
6 cups salad greens
1½ cups cooked peas, drained
1 cup julienne Swiss cheese
1 cup thin red onion rings (optional)

⅓ cup mayonnaise or salad dressing
1 tablespoon sugar
¾ teaspoon salt
¼ teaspoon pepper
¼ cup cooked, crumbled bacon
6 cherry tomatoes

Combine flaked fish with salad greens, peas, cheese and onion. Then mix together mayonnaise, sugar, salt and pepper. Pour this dressing over salad. Toss lightly and chill. Before serving, sprinkle with bacon and garnish with cherry tomatoes.

(Serves 6)

Smoked Fish Western Omelet

1 cup smoked, flaked
  fish
2 packages (1¼ ounces
  each) Western style
  omelet seasoning mix

1 cup water
8 eggs, beaten
4 tablespoons butter or
  cooking oil

Combine seasoning mix and water. Add eggs and fish and beat until well mixed. In a 10-inch heavy skillet or electric frypan, melt butter, tilting skillet in all directions to coat bottom and sides of pan. Pour half of the omelet mixture into skillet. As mixture sets, lift edges with a spatula, allowing uncooked portion to run under cooked portion of omelet. When bottom of omelet is lightly browned and top is soft and creamy, fold sides over and slide from skillet onto plate. Cut omelet into thirds. Repeat procedure for remaining mixture.

(Serves 6)

Smoked Fish Italian Style

If you prefer, you can smoke an entire fish entrée or a complete dinner.

2 pounds fish fillets, fresh or frozen	2 cups finely crushed herb-seasoned stuffing mix
1 cup Italian salad dressing	
2 teaspoons salt	$\frac{1}{4}$ cup chopped parsley
	$\frac{1}{2}$ teaspoon oregano

Thaw fish if frozen. Cut fillets into serving size portions. Place in a single layer in a shallow baking dish. Pour Italian dressing over fish and marinate 30 minutes in refrigerator. Remove fish from dressing and sprinkle with salt. Combine stuffing mix, parsley and oregano. Roll fish in herbed mixture. Place fish on a well-greased grill inside smoke oven. Cook in a slow oven, 200°, for about 45 to 60 minutes or until fish flakes easily when tested with a fork.

(Serves 6)

Smoked Fish-Vegetable Dinners

2 pounds fish fillets,
 fresh or frozen
2 teaspoons salt
2 cans (4½ ounces each)
 deviled ham
1 can (1 pound) whole
 potatoes, drained
1 can (1 pound) whole
 onions, drained

1 package (8 ounces)
 frozen mixed
 vegetables, partially
 defrosted
2 tablespoons lemon
 juice
1 can (10¾ ounces)
 condensed tomato
 soup

Thaw fish if frozen. Cut fillets into serving-size portions.
Cut 6 pieces heavy-duty aluminum foil, 12″ × 12″ each.
Grease lightly. Place equal portions of fish on each piece of
foil. Season with salt. Spread ham equally on top of fish.
Divide remaining ingredients equally among the packages
of fish, using the soup last. Bring the foil up over the fish
and seal the edges by making double folds in the foil to
confine the juices. Place the packages on the grill inside the
smoke oven. Cook in a slow oven, 200°, for 15 minutes;
open packages by cutting a crisscross in the top of each
package and fold foil back. Continue to cook for 10 to 15
minutes longer or until fish flakes easily when tested with a
fork.

(Serves 6)

Smoked Oysters

If you've eaten smoked oysters from a gourmet shop, you know how excellent smoked shellfish can be. It is simple to smoke them yourself at home.

36 shell oysters	1/2 teaspoon liquid hot pepper sauce
1/2 cup butter	
1/4 cup chopped onion	1/2 teaspoon dry mustard
2 tablespoons chopped parsley	1/2 teaspoon salt
	1/2 teaspoon Worcestershire sauce

Shuck and drain oysters; place on deep half of shells. In a small saucepan, melt butter and sauté onion until tender. Add remaining ingredients and spoon sauce over oysters. Place oysters on grill inside the smoke oven and cook in a slow oven, 300°, for 20 to 25 minutes or until the edges of the oysters begin to curl.

(Serves 6)

Smoked Skewered Scallops

1½ pounds scallops, fresh
    or frozen
¼ cup soy sauce
¼ cup salad oil
1 cup apple juice
¼ cup steak sauce

1 teaspoon
    Worcestershire sauce
1 teaspoon salt
½ cup chopped parsley
1 pint cherry tomatoes

Thaw frozen scallops. Rinse with cold water to remove any shell particles. Place scallops in a shallow baking dish. Combine remaining ingredients except parsley and tomatoes. Pour sauce over scallops and let marinate for 30 minutes, stirring occasionally. Drain well. Roll scallops in chopped parsley. Using skewers, alternate scallops and cherry tomatoes. Place scallops on a well-greased grill inside smoke oven. Cook in a slow oven, 300°, for 10 to 15 minutes or until scallops are done and have a golden smoke color.

(Serves 6)

Smoked Butterfly Shrimp

2 pounds unpeeled,
fresh jumbo shrimp
1¹/₂ cups butter-flavored
cooking oil

Seafood seasoning or
seasoned salt
Cocktail Sauce

You butterfly shrimp by using scissors or sharp knife to
make a deep cut through the top shell without cutting
completely through the flesh. Remove sand vein, rinse and
spread in butterfly fashion. Place shrimp, shell side down,
on grill over low coals and wet chips. Brush generously
with oil and sprinkle with seasoning. Cook at moderately
low temperature, approximately 200° for 15 minutes,
basting once or twice with oil. Turn shrimp and continue
cooking 4 to 5 minutes longer. Serve with Cocktail Sauce.

(Serves 6)

Cocktail Sauce

³/₄ cup chili sauce
1 tablespoon lemon juice

1 tablespoon
horseradish
¹/₂ teaspoon salt

Combine all ingredients and chill.

(Serves 6)

Shrimp-Oyster Creole Dinners

1 pound raw, peeled and deveined shrimp, fresh or frozen
1 pint oysters, fresh or frozen
6 slices bacon, diced
1 cup sliced onions
1 cup sliced celery
1 cup green pepper strips
1 can (1 pound) tomatoes, undrained
1 cup chicken broth
1 tablespoon vinegar
2 teaspoons salt
1 teaspoon sugar
1 teaspoon chili powder
$1/8$ teaspoon garlic powder
1 bay leaf, crushed
$1/4$ teaspoon pepper
1 cup cooked green peas
$1^1/2$ cups precooked rice
Chopped parsley

Thaw shrimp and oysters if frozen. Drain oysters and remove any remaining pieces of shell particles. Cook bacon until crisp; remove from pan. Cook onion, celery and green pepper in bacon fat until tender. Add tomatoes and tomato liquid, chicken broth, vinegar, salt, sugar, chili powder, garlic powder, bay leaf, pepper and bacon. Let simmer for 5 minutes and then add peas. Place $1/4$ cup rice in each of 6 well-greased, 10-ounce aluminum foil containers. Place an equal amount of creole sauce on top of rice. Divide shrimp and oysters among the six containers. Place containers on grill inside smoke oven. Cook in a slow oven, 300°, 15 to 20 minutes or until shrimp are done and have a golden smoke color and the edges of oysters have curled. Garnish with chopped parsley.

(Serves 6)

Accompaniment Recipes in Menus

Hors D'Oeuvres

Barbara's Hot Cheese Dip

1½ to 2 pounds Swiss or Monterey Jack cheese
1 can (10½ ounces) white sauce or make your own

½ can (4 ounces) diced green chilies

Grate cheese and blend with white sauce and chilies. Place mixture in a casserole and put in a 325° oven. Heat for 15 minutes; stir and bake another 15 minutes. Remove from casserole and place in a fondue pot or chafing dish and keep warm over low heat. Serve with firm chips such as tortilla or corn chips.

Sherry Cheese Spread

1 package (8 ounces)
  Wispride Cheddar
  cheese
1 package (8 ounces)
  cream cheese

¹/₄ to ¹/₂ teaspoon ginger
  Cream sherry

Allow Wispride and cream cheese to become room temperature. Blend these together with ginger. Add sherry until the right spreading consistency is reached. Refrigerate until ready to use and then serve with assorted crackers.

(Makes 2 cups)

Meat Spread

1 can (12 ounces) corn
  beef
1 package (8 ounces)
  braunschweiger
¹/₂ cup mayonnaise

2 tablespoons vinegar
1 teaspoon onion
  powder
1¹/₂ teaspoons dry mustard

Combine all ingredients, mixing well. Chill. Serve with party rye bread.

(Makes about 3 cups)

Guacamole Dip

1 ripe avocado, mashed
¹/₂ teaspoon fresh, grated
   lemon peel
1 tablespoon fresh,
   squeezed lemon juice
¹/₂ teaspoon instant
   minced onion

¹/₄ cup dairy sour cream
¹/₄ teaspoon salt
¹/₄ teaspoon chili powder
   Dash hot pepper sauce
¹/₂ teaspoon garlic salt
1 small tomato, diced

Thoroughly combine mashed avocado, lemon peel, juice and onion; blend until smooth. Add remaining ingredients and mix well. Serve with raw vegetables such as carrots, cauliflower, broccoli, yellow turnip or others.

(Makes 2 cups)

Chutney Cheese Spread

1 package (8 ounces) cream cheese
1/4 cup colonial chutney
1/4 cup finely chopped almonds

1/4 teaspoon curry powder
1/4 teaspoon dry mustard

Allow cheese to become room temperature. Combine all ingredients and mix well. Refrigerate until ready to use. Serve with assorted crackers.

(Makes 1 1/4 cups)

Sesame Cheese Sticks

1 cup packaged pie crust mix
Dash salt
1/2 cup grated sharp Cheddar cheese

2 tablespoons cream sherry
1 tablespoons sesame seeds

Combine pie crust mix, salt and cheese, mixing lightly with a fork. Add sherry and mix until all ingredients are evenly moistened; shape dough into a ball. Roll to a 6-inch square on lightly floured board. Sprinkle sesame seeds evenly over dough and roll lightly with rolling pin to press seeds into dough. Cut into strips 3-inches by 3/4-inch. Arrange on ungreased baking sheet and bake at 450° for 8 to 10 minutes. Remove to a wire rack to cool before storing in an airtight container.

(Makes about 2 dozen)

Soups

Harvest Soup

1 can (1 pound, 4 ounces) chunk pineapple in syrup	1 can (1 pound) solid pack pumpkin
1½ cups diced celery	1 bay leaf
½ cup diced onion	½ teaspoon thyme
2 tablespoons butter	½ teaspoon curry powder
2 cans (14½ ounces each) chicken broth	½ teaspoon salt

Drain pineapple reserving all syrup. In a medium saucepan, sauté celery and onion in butter until vegetables are tender-crisp. Stir in reserved syrup, chicken broth, pumpkin, bay leaf, thyme, curry powder and salt. Simmer, uncovered, 30 minutes. Add pineapple and cook until heated through.

(Makes 2 quarts)

Brandied Beef Soup

2 cans (10½ ounces each) condensed beef broth
2 soup cans water
4 tablespoons brandy
½ cup heavy cream

¼ teaspoon vanilla
Dash ground nutmeg
¼ teaspoon grated orange rind

In a large saucepan, combine broth, water and brandy. Heat; stir occasionally. Meanwhile, in a small bowl, combine cream, vanilla and nutmeg. Beat until cream *just* mounds. Fold in orange rind. Serve cream mixture on soup.

(Makes about 5 cups)

Peanut Butter Soup

1/2 cup natural, creamy peanut butter	1/4 cup milk
	Sugar to taste
2 cups water	3 to 4 tablespoons
4 teaspoons cornstarch	chopped nuts or
4 teaspoons water	toasted sesame seeds

Mix peanut butter with 1/2 cup water using a whisk until smooth. Add another 1/2 cup water and stir again until the mixture is smooth. Boil the remaining 1 cup water. Add peanut butter mixture, stirring constantly, and cook over low heat until it boils. Mix cornstarch and water and then pour paste slowly while stirring until soup thickens. Add milk and sugar and heat through. Serve hot with sprinkles of chopped nuts or toasted sesame seeds.

(Serves 3 to 4)

Stracciatella Soup

1 can (10³/4 ounces) condensed chicken broth	2 tablespoons grated Parmesan cheese
1 soup can water	1 tablespoon chopped parsley
1 egg	

In saucepan, combine chicken broth and water; bring to a boil. Beat egg with cheese and parsley; gradually pour into simmering soup, stirring gently until egg is set. Serve immediately.

(Makes about 3 cups)

Starches

Sherried Rice

1 cup uncooked regular rice
2 cans (4 ounces each) sliced mushrooms, undrained

1 can (10½ ounces) beef broth
¼ cup sherry
¼ teaspoon salt
¼ cup butter, melted

Combine all ingredients in a 1½-quart casserole. Bake, covered, in a 350° oven for 45 minutes or until rice is fluffy.

(Serves 6)

Banana Sweet Potatoes

2 cans (1 pound, 2 ounces each) vacuum packed sweet potatoes
³/₄ cup mashed banana
¹/₄ cup butter, softened
1 teaspoon grated orange peel
1 teaspoon salt
2 egg yolks
2 egg whites, stiffly beaten

Mash potatoes on low speed of electric mixer. Add banana, butter, orange peel and salt. Beat until fluffy. Add egg yolks; beat well. Carefully fold stiffly beaten egg whites into potato mixture. Turn into a greased 1¹/₂-quart casserole. Bake, covered, at 350° for 20 minutes; uncover and bake 25 minutes longer or until thoroughly hot.

(Serves 8)

Note: Any leftovers are especially good heated in the microwave.

Brandy Sweet Potatoes

6 medium size sweet
  potatoes, cooked
1/4 cup orange juice
1/4 cup brandy
1 teaspoon grated
  orange peel

1 tablespoon cornstarch
1/4 teaspoon salt
2 tablespoons butter,
  melted
1/3 cup firmly packed
  brown sugar

Place sweet potatoes in a greased, 2-quart baking dish.
Combine remaining ingredients and cook, stirring constantly, until thickened. Pour sauce over sweet potatoes
and bake in a 350° oven for 30 minutes or until thoroughly
hot.

(Serves 4 to 5)

Dusty Potatoes

3/4 cup dry bread crumbs
1 teaspoon nutmeg
1/2 teaspoon salt
1/4 teaspoon pepper

4 medium potatoes,
pared, cut into
quarters
1/4 cup butter, melted

Combine bread crumbs, nutmeg, salt and pepper. Dip potatoes in melted butter and then roll in bread crumb mixture. Place in a greased shallow pan. Bake in a 350° oven for about 1 hour or until potatoes are brown and crisp.

(Serves 4)

Barley with Mushrooms

4 beef bouillon cubes
3 cups boiling water
2 tablespoons butter
1 cup sliced fresh
mushrooms

1 tablespoon lemon juice
1 cup pearl barley
1 teaspoon dill seeds
Pepper to taste
1 teaspoon paprika

Dissolve beef bouillon cubes in boiling water. Melt butter in a large heavy saucepan. Add sliced mushrooms and lemon juice. Sauté 1 minute and then stir in barley, hot bouillon, dill seeds and pepper. Simmer, tightly covered, over low heat for 35 to 40 minutes, until barley is tender and much of the liquid is absorbed. Do not overcook; the barley should be coated with a creamy sauce. Stir in paprika 5 minutes before serving.

(Serves 6)

Cheesy Grits

4 cups boiling water
1 teaspoon salt
1 cup uncooked grits
2 eggs, beaten
$^1/_2$ cup butter, melted

1 cup shredded
Cheddar cheese
Dash liquid hot pepper
sauce
$^1/_8$ teaspoon paprika

Combine water and salt and bring to a boil. Stir in grits, cover, and cook over low heat. Regular grits will take 20 to 30 minutes; quick grits will cook in $2^1/_2$ to 5 minutes. In a small bowl, combine remaining ingredients. Add a small amount of hot grits to egg mixture, stirring well. Stir egg mixture into remaining grits. Spoon mixture into a well-greased, 2-quart casserole. Bake in a 350° oven for 30 to 45 minutes.

(Serves 6 to 8)

Joan's Potato Salad

5 cups cooked, sliced potatoes
2 teaspoons salt (more if needed)
2 teaspoons sugar
1 tablespoon celery seed
2 teaspoons vinegar
1/2 cup mayonnaise
1/2 cup sour cream
4 hard-cooked eggs, quartered

Sprinkle potatoes with seasonings and vinegar. If you wish, also add 1 cup sliced celery and 1/2 cup sliced, sweet pickle. Add mayonnaise and sour cream and toss to mix. Fold in eggs. Chill well and serve the same day.

(Serves 8)

Corn Meal Fritters

1 cup corn meal
1/2 teaspoon baking soda
1/4 teaspoon salt
2 eggs, beaten
1 1/4 cups buttermilk
1 tablespoon vegetable oil

Combine corn meal, soda and salt. Add eggs, buttermilk and oil; beat until smooth. Drop tablespoonfuls of batter onto a hot, greased griddle or in a large heavy skillet. After fritters brown on bottom, turn quickly and lightly brown on other side.

(Makes 12 to 16 fritters)

Hot Breads

Sweet Potato Muffins

These unusual muffins are served at Christiana Campbell's Tavern in Williamsburg, Virginia.

1¼ cups sugar
1¼ cups cooked, mashed sweet potatoes, fresh or canned
½ cup butter, room temperature
2 large eggs
1½ cups flour
2 teaspoons baking powder

1 teaspoon cinnamon
¼ teaspoon nutmeg
¼ teaspoon salt
1 cup milk
½ cup chopped raisins
¼ cup chopped walnuts or pecans
2 tablespoons sugar mixed with ¼ teaspoon cinnamon

Thoroughly grease 24 muffin cups (paper liners may be used instead). Preheat oven to 400°. Beat sugar, sweet potatoes and butter until smooth. Add eggs and blend well. Sift together flour, baking powder, spices and salt. Add alternately with milk to sweet potato mixture, stirring just to blend. Do not overmix. Fold in raisins and nuts. Spoon into muffin cups and sprinkle each with sugar/cinnamon mixture. Bake for 25 to 30 minutes or until muffins test done. Serve warm. Muffins may be frozen and reheated.

(Makes 24 muffins)

Herbed Cheese Muffins

2 cups flour
$1/4$ cup sugar
1 teaspoon baking powder
$1/2$ teaspoon baking soda
$3/4$ teaspoon salt
$1/4$ teaspoon savory, crushed
$1/8$ teaspoon thyme
$1^1/2$ teaspoons dried parsley flakes
$1/3$ cup shredded Cheddar cheese
1 egg, beaten
1 cup buttermilk
$1/4$ cup oil

Preheat oven to 400°. Sift flour, sugar, baking powder, baking soda and salt into a bowl. Add savory, thyme, dried parsley flakes and Cheddar cheese; mix. Combine egg, milk and oil; add all at once to dry ingredients and stir just until flour is moistened. Batter will be lumpy. Grease muffin cups with a vegetable spray. Fill $2/3$ full. Bake for 23 to 25 minutes. Remove muffins from pan immediately.

(Makes 12 large muffins)

Cheese Biscuits

2 cups sifted flour
3 teaspoons baking powder
½ teaspoon salt
4 tablespoons cold shortening
½ cup grated Cheddar cheese
¾ cup milk

Preheat oven to 450°. Sift dry ingredients together; cut in shortening and add cheese. Add milk to make a soft dough. Place on a floured board and knead lightly a few seconds, using as little flour as possible on board. Roll out ½-inch thick and cut with floured biscuit cutter. Place on greased baking sheet and bake about 12 minutes.

(Makes 12 2-inch biscuits)

Rich Biscuits

2 cups self-rising flour
2 teaspoons sugar
1 carton (1 cup) whipping cream

Preheat oven to 450°. Combine all ingredients; mix well. Turn dough out on a lightly floured board and knead 10 or 12 times. Roll dough to ½-inch thickness and cut with floured biscuit cutter. Place biscuits on a lightly greased baking sheet and bake for 10 to 12 minutes.

(Makes about 1½ dozen)

Blueberry Muffins

3 cups flour
1/2 cup sugar
4 teaspoons baking
   powder
1 teaspoon salt

2 eggs
1/2 cup cooking oil
1 cup milk
2 cups fresh blueberries

Preheat oven to 400°. In a large bowl, combine flour, sugar, baking powder and salt; mix well. In a small bowl, beat eggs and add oil and milk. Add liquid mixture to dry ingredients and stir just until flour is moistened. Fold in blueberries. Grease 24 muffin cups (paper liners may be used instead). Fill 2/3 full. Bake for 20 to 25 minutes.

(Makes 24 muffins)

Super Yeast Rolls

1 cup milk	$^1/_4$ cup sugar
$^1/_4$ cup water	$1^1/_4$ teaspoons salt
$^1/_4$ cup sour cream	1 teaspoon grated lemon
3 tablespoons shortening or oil	peel
3 to $3^1/_2$ cups flour	1 package active dry yeast
1 cup rolled oats	1 egg

In a medium saucepan, heat first four ingredients until very warm (120° to 130°). In a large bowl, combine warm liquid, 1 cup flour, oats, sugar, salt, lemon peel, yeast and egg; beat 2 minutes at medium speed. By hand, stir in remaining flour. On well-floured surface, knead about 5 minutes. (Dough will be soft and slightly sticky.) Place in a greased bowl. Cover; let rise in warm place until light and doubled in size, 45 to 60 minutes. Grease 18 muffin cups. Punch dough down. Divide into 18 pieces; shape into balls. Place in greased muffin cups. Cover; let rise until light and doubled in size, 35 to 45 minutes. Preheat oven to 375°. Bake 15 to 20 minutes or until golden brown. Cool 5 minutes; remove from pan.

(Makes 18 rolls)

Vegetables

Vegetable Medley

½ pound small white
   onions, peeled
½ pound carrots, scraped
   and cut in half
½ pound celery stalks,
   cut in half

½ cup water
1 tablespoon butter
  Dash pepper
¾ teaspoon salt

Place a small size (10″ × 16″) oven cooking bag in a 2-quart
casserole dish. Combine all ingredients in bag. Close bag
with nylon twist tie; make 6 ½-inch slits in top. Cook in a
350° oven for 45 to 60 minutes or until vegetables are
tender.

Baked Spinach with Pecans

2 packages (10 ounces
  each) frozen chopped
  spinach, thawed and
  well drained
1 cup sour cream

½ cup coarsely chopped
  pecans
2 tablespoons grated
  Parmesan cheese
1 tablespoon dehydrated
  onion soup mix

Grease a 1-quart baking dish. Combine all ingredients in
mixing bowl and blend well. Turn into baking dish and
bake, uncovered, in a 350° oven for 20 to 30 minutes or
until thoroughly hot.

(Serves 4)

Green Beans Napoli

3 slices bacon
1 cup solid pack tomatoes
1 onion, diced
½ teaspoon salt
¼ teaspoon mace
¼ teaspoon allspice

Dash cayenne pepper
1 bag (16 ounces) frozen French cut green beans, thawed
½ cup grated Cheddar cheese

In a heavy skillet or electric frypan, fry bacon until crisp; break into bits. Leave amount of bacon fat in skillet that you like for flavor. Add to skillet all ingredients except beans and cheese. Bring to a boil and simmer about 20 minutes. This sauce can be made a day ahead and refrigerated. Just before dinner, place thawed beans in a large saucepan, cover with sauce and heat only until beans are tender. Sprinkle with Cheddar cheese and serve.

(Serves 4 to 6)

Carrots with Water Chestnuts

1 pound carrots, peeled
and sliced $^1/_2$-inch
thick
2 tablespoons butter
$^1/_2$ can (8$^1/_2$ ounces) water
chestnuts, drained and
thinly sliced

$^1/_2$ teaspoon thyme
$^1/_4$ teaspoon ginger
3 tablespoons white table
wine
1 tablespoon snipped
parsley

Cook carrots in small amount of boiling salted water or in
a pressure cooker until crisp-tender. Drain and set aside.
In a saucepan, melt butter; add water chestnuts, thyme
and ginger. Cook and stir for 2 minutes. Add wine, parsley
and cooked carrots; cook and stir until heated through
out.

(Serves 4 to 6)

343

Curried Peas

2 teaspoons cooking oil
2 teaspoons margarine
1 cup minced onion
1 clove garlic
1 slice fresh ginger root
1/4 teaspoon caraway seed
1/2 teaspoon salt
Dash pepper
Dash tumeric
1/4 cup tomato purée
2 packages (10 ounces each) frozen peas
Dash ground coriander
1/8 teaspoon cumin
1/8 teaspoon cayenne pepper
1 1/4 cups sliced mushrooms

In a heavy skillet, heat oil and margarine. Sauté onion until soft. Liquefy garlic and ginger in blender with a little water and add to onion. Add caraway, salt, pepper and tumeric; cook about 8 minutes, stirring to keep from sticking. Add tomato purée and heat. Add peas and simmer about 5 minutes. Add coriander, cumin and cayenne; simmer 10 minutes. Add mushrooms, cover, and cook just until mushrooms are done.

(Serves 6 to 8)

Yellow Squash Casserole

1½ to 2 pounds yellow
   squash, sliced
1 teaspoon instant
   minced onion
1 tablespoon minced
   parsley
1 egg, slightly beaten

¼ cup milk
½ cup cottage cheese
½ teaspoon salt
1 teaspoon sugar
¼ cup finely chopped
   pecans

Parboil squash, drain and mash. Add all other ingredients
except nuts. Place in a greased, 2-quart casserole and
sprinkle pecans over top. Bake in a 350° oven for 25 to 30
minutes or until top is brown.

(Serves 4 to 6)

Carrot-Rice Bake

3 cups shredded carrots
3 cups cooked rice
1 1/2 cups shredded
   Cheddar cheese
   1/2 cup milk
2 beaten eggs

2 tablespoons chopped
   onion
1 teaspoon salt
1/4 teaspoon pepper
1/2 cup shredded
   Cheddar cheese

Combine carrots, rice, 1 1/2 cups cheese, milk and eggs. Stir in onion, salt and pepper. Pour mixture into a greased 9" × 13" baking dish. Sprinkle remaining 1/2 cup cheese on top. Bake in a 350° oven for 50 to 60 minutes.

(Serves 6)

Marinated Broccoli

1 bunch fresh broccoli,
   broken into pieces
$1/2$ to $3/4$ bottle Italian
   dressing

2 green onions, sliced
$1/4$ pound mushrooms,
   thinly sliced
6 radishes, thinly sliced

Combine all ingredients in a large bowl and refrigerate for
3 to 4 hours. Do not marinate longer or broccoli will become limp.

(Serves 6 to 8)

Kay's Tomato Casserole

2 eggs
4 tablespoons butter,
   melted
1 tablespoon instant
   minced onion
$1/2$ teaspoon salt
$1/4$ teaspoon pepper

2 cans (1 pound each)
   tomato wedges
$1 1/2$ cups herb seasoned
   stuffing
$1/2$ cup shredded
   Cheddar cheese

Beat eggs slightly and add butter, onion, salt and pepper.
Add tomatoes and stuffing to egg mixture. Pour into a
$1 1/2$-quart casserole and sprinkle with cheese. Bake in
a 375°oven for 45 minutes.

(Serves 4 to 5)

Asparagus Casserole

2 cans (14½ ounces each) asparagus spears (reserve liquid)
1 can (8½ ounces) water chestnuts, thinly sliced
3 hard-cooked eggs, sliced
4 tablespoons butter
6 tablespoons flour
½ cup milk
1½ cups liquid from asparagus
½ teaspoon salt
1½ cups shredded sharp Cheddar cheese
1 jar (2 ounces) pimientos
1 cup dry bread crumbs

Grease an oblong (11½" × 7½" × 2") baking dish. Drain asparagus, reserving liquid, and arrange in bottom of baking dish in a single layer. Place sliced water chestnuts over asparagus and sliced eggs over all. Melt butter in a medium saucepan and add flour, stirring until well blended. Add milk slowly, stirring constantly. When well blended, add asparagus liquid and cook, stirring constantly, until thickened. Add salt and cheese to sauce and stir until cheese melts; add pimientos. Pour sauce evenly over asparagus mixture; top with bread crumbs. Bake in a 375° oven for about 35 minutes or until bubbly and brown.

(Serves 8 to 10)

Port Cranberry Sauce

1 cup sugar (up to 2 cups sugar can be used)
1/2 cup water
1 stick cinnamon

2 thin slices lemon
1/2 cup port wine
1 pound fresh cranberries

In a medium saucepan, combine sugar and water and boil for 3 minutes. Add rest of ingredients and cook 5 minutes longer or until cranberries begin to pop. Let cool and refrigerate several hours or overnight.

(Serves 6 to 8)

Cranberry Mousse

1 cup cranberry juice
  cocktail

1 package (3 ounces)
  raspberry flavored
  gelatin

1 can (16 ounces) whole
  cranberry sauce

1 cup heavy cream,
  whipped

In a saucepan, heat cranberry juice to boiling; stir in raspberry gelatin until dissolved. Stir in cranberry sauce. Chill until mixture is thickened. Fold in whipped cream and pour into serving bowl or mold. Chill until firm.

(Serves 6 to 8)

Spinach/Mushroom Salad

4 slices bacon

1 package (10 ounces)
  fresh spinach, washed
  and trimmed

$1/3$ pound mushrooms,
  thinly sliced

$1/4$ cup vegetable oil

2 tablespoons red wine
  vinegar

1 tablespoon Dijon-style
  mustard

1 teaspoon fresh lemon
  juice

Dash salt

Fry bacon until crisp; crumble and reserve. Combine spinach and mushrooms in a large serving bowl; refrigerate covered. Combine remaining ingredients in a glass jar with tight-fitting lid; cover and shake. At serving time, pour dressing over salad; toss to coat. Sprinkle reserved bacon.

(Serves 4 to 6)

Molded Pineapple Salad

1 can (1 pound, 4 ounces) sliced pineapple
1 cup water
1 package (3 ounces) lemon flavored gelatin
1/4 cup diced celery
1/4 cup diced cucumber
2 tablespoons prepared horseradish
1/2 pint (1 cup) heavy cream, whipped

Drain pineapple, reserving syrup. Stand pineapple slices along sides of a 6-cup ring mold. Boil 1 cup water; add to gelatin. Stir until dissolved. Add 3/4 cup reserved syrup. Let set in refrigerator until mixture is the consistency of unbeaten egg whites. Toss together celery, cucumber and horseradish. Fold into gelatin. Whip cream and fold into gelatin mixture. Pour mixture over pineapple slices into ring mold. Chill until firm. To unmold, carefully run a knife around edges. Place mold in a large pan of warm water for 10 seconds and invert on serving platter.

(Serves 8 to 10)

Cherry Mold

1 package (3 ounces)
   cherry flavored gelatin
1 cup boiling water
1 can (21 ounces)
   prepared cherry pie
   filling
1 package (3 ounces)
   lemon flavored gelatin
1 cup boiling water

1 package (3 ounces)
   cream cheese, softened
1/3 cup salad dressing
1 can (8 ounces)
   crushed pineapple,
   undrained
1/3 cup miniature
   marshmallows
1/2 cup heavy cream,
   whipped

Combine cherry gelatin and 1 cup boiling water and stir until gelatin is dissolved; stir in cherry pie filling. Pour into top of a 6-cup mold and chill. Combine lemon gelatin and 1 cup boiling water and stir until gelatin is dissolved. Stir in softened cream cheese, salad dressing, crushed pineapple with juice and marshmallows. Fold in whipped cream. Pour mixture on top of cherry layer and chill until firm. To unmold, carefully run a knife around edges. Place mold in a large pan of warm water for 10 seconds and invert on serving platter.

(Serves 10 to 12)

Sherried Fruit

Josie Smith of Williamsburg, Virginia, brought this dish to a game dinner, and it was so delicious that I asked her for the recipe.

1 can (1 pound) pear chunks
1 can (1 pound) sliced peaches
1 can (1 pound) apricot halves
1 can (1 pound) pineapple chunks
1 can (1 pound) plums, pitted and halved
1/2 cup butter
1/2 cup brown sugar
2 tablespoons flour
1 cup cream sherry
1 jar (15 ounces) apple rings

Drain first 5 fruits well and place in a greased casserole. In a saucepan, melt butter; add sugar, flour and sherry and stir constantly until thickened. Pour over fruit. Drain and add apple rings. Bake in a 350° oven for 30 minutes or until hot and bubbly.

(Serves 10 to 12)

Comb of the Rooster Salad

2 tomatoes, diced
1 large avocado, peeled and diced
1 cucumber, peeled and diced

2 tablespoons olive or vegetable oil
2 tablespoons lime or lemon juice
1 teaspoon garlic salt

Combine tomatoes, avocado and cucumber in a serving bowl and refrigerate until serving time. Combine remaining ingredients in a glass jar with tight-fitting lid; cover and shake. At serving time, pour dressing over salad, tossing lightly so as not to mash.

(Serves 4)

Barbara's Chinese Beans

1 can (1 pound) cut green beans
1 can (1 pound) cut wax beans
1 can (5 ounces) water chestnuts, sliced
1 can (4 ounces) button mushrooms

$1/2$ cup red onion rings, thinly sliced
$1/3$ cup sugar
$1/3$ cup wine vinegar
2 tablespoons vegetable oil
2 tablespoons soy sauce
$1/2$ teaspoon celery salt

Drain and combine vegetables in a bowl. In a small bowl, combine sugar, vinegar, oil, soy sauce and celery salt. Blend ingredients well; pour dressing over vegetables, mixing lightly. Let stand in refrigerator several hours or overnight. Toss occasionally.

(Serves 6 to 8)

Jim's Roquefort Cheese Salad

Jim Koontz enjoys cooking. One evening when he and his wife came for dinner, Jim brought me some of his tasty Roquefort dressing.

Assorted greens
Tomato wedges
Zucchini slices
Mushroom slices
Carrot slices
Pitted ripe olives
Jim's Roquefort
Cheese Dressing

Tear greens in bite-size pieces into lettuce-lined bowl. Add tomatoes, zucchini, mushrooms, carrots and olives; toss lightly. Serve with Jim's Roquefort Cheese Dressing.

Dressing

$^1/_3$ cup fresh lemon juice
1 tablespoon tarragon vinegar
1 teaspoon salt
$^1/_2$ to 1 teaspoon pepper
$^1/_8$ teaspoon cayenne pepper
1 teaspoon paprika
$^2/_3$ cup olive or vegetable oil

* * * *

8 ounces blue cheese
8 ounces (1 cup) sour cream
$^1/_2$ cup Dressing

Place 7 ingredients for Dressing in a glass jar with tight-fitting lid; cover and shake. In a processor or blender, place blue cheese, sour cream and $^1/_2$ cup Dressing. Process until smooth; dressing will be thick. Pour over greens and vegetables just before serving.

Desserts

Ice Cream with Chestnut Sauce

20 whole chestnuts $^1/_4$ cup apple cider
 1 cup honey $1^1/_2$ tablespoons brandy

With a sharp knife, make an "X" in each chestnut. Place chestnuts in a saucepan and cover with cold water. Bring to a full boil and continue boiling for 20 minutes. Peel skins from chestnuts and cut in half. In a saucepan, combine honey, cider and chestnuts. Bring to a full boil and add brandy. When cooled, refrigerate. Serve sauce over scoop of vanilla ice cream.

(Makes about $1^1/_2$ cups sauce)

Lemon Cookies

1 cup sugar
1 cup butter (or
    ¹/₂ butter and
    ¹/₂ margarine),
    softened
1 package (3 ounces)
    cream cheese, softened
1 egg yolk

¹/₂ teaspoon lemon
    extract
2¹/₂ cups flour
1 cup finely chopped
    walnuts
¹/₂ teaspoon salt
1 teaspoon grated lemon
    rind

Combine sugar, butter and cream cheese; cream until light
and fluffy. Add egg yolk and lemon extract; beat well. Stir
in flour, walnuts, salt and lemon rind; mix well. Cover and
chill at least 2 hours. Shape teaspoonfuls of dough into
2-inch logs by rolling between palms of hands. Place
cookies on ungreased baking sheets and bake at 350° for
10 to 12 minutes or until lightly browned. When cooled,
store in an airtight container or freeze.

(Makes 10 dozen)

Brandied Apple Cake

6 tablespoons brandy
4 cups peeled, chopped
  apples
2 cups flour
1 teaspoon salt
2 teaspoons baking soda
2 teaspoons cinnamon
1 teaspoon nutmeg

$^1/_2$ teaspoon ground
  cloves
1 cup chopped walnuts
1 cup raisins
2 eggs
2 cups sugar
$^1/_2$ cup vegetable oil

Sprinkle brandy over apples and set aside. In a large bowl, combine flour, salt, soda, cinnamon, nutmeg and cloves. Stir in walnuts and raisins. Combine eggs, sugar and oil; beat well and blend into flour mixture. Stir in apples. Pour batter into a greased 13″ × 9″ × 2″ pan. Bake in a 375° oven for 35 minutes or until cake tests done.

(Serves 12)

Burgundy Pears

3 ripe, firm pears,
  preferably Anjou
2 cups Burgundy wine
$^1/_3$ cup honey

1 small bay leaf
1 whole clove
1 small cinnamon stick

Cut pears in quarters; remove core and peel. Combine wine, honey, bay leaf, clove and cinnamon stick in a saucepan and bring to a boil. Add pears and let cook, uncovered, for 30 to 45 minutes or until tender. Let pears cool in cooking liquid and then refrigerate.

(Serves 4)

Cranberry Bread

Joyce Robinson of Millinocket, Maine, served us this flavorful, moist bread made from wild cranberries she had picked.

Juice and grated rind
from 1 orange
2 tablespoons vegetable
oil
1 egg, beaten
2 cups flour
1 cup sugar
1 1/2 teaspoons baking
powder
1/2 teaspoon baking soda
1/2 teaspoon salt
1/2 cup chopped nuts
1 cup raw cranberries,
cut in half

To orange juice add boiling water to make 1 cup liquid. Pour liquid into a bowl; stir in oil and egg. Place dry ingredients (except nuts and cranberries) in a large mixing bowl. Add liquid mixture to dry mixture and stir just until blended. Stir in nuts, cranberries and grated orange rind. Spoon batter into a greased and floured 9″ × 5″ × 3″ loaf pan. Bake in a 350° oven for 1 hour.

(Makes 12 to 16 servings)

Pumpkin Nut Cake

1⅓ cups vegetable oil
1 can (1 pound)
   pumpkin
2 cups sugar
2 eggs, beaten
3 cups flour
1 teaspoon salt

2 teaspoons baking
   powder
2 teaspoons baking soda
2 teaspoons pumpkin
   pie spice
½ cup chopped pecans

In a large mixing bowl, combine oil, pumpkin, sugar and eggs; beat well until blended and light. Combine dry ingredients and gradually add to pumpkin mixture; beat well. Add nuts. Spoon batter into a well-greased, 10-inch tube pan. Bake in a 350° oven for 1 hour or until cake tests done.

(Makes 16 to 20 servings)

Pecan Pie

Phyllis Smith makes a superb pecan pie, so I'm passing on
to you her recipes for the pie and crust.

1/2 cup butter, softened	1 teaspoon vanilla
1 cup sugar	3/4 cup broken pecan
3 large eggs	pieces
3/4 cup King dark corn	16 pecan halves
syrup	1 unbaked 9-inch pie
1/4 teaspoon salt	crust

Cream butter and sugar; add eggs and beat until fluffy.
Add corn syrup, salt, vanilla and broken pecans. Pour into
a 9-inch unbaked crust. Place pecan halves around top
edge of pie. Bake in a 375° oven for 20 minutes; reduce
heat to 350° and bake until a crack appears on top. Total
cooking time is approximately 1 hour.

(Serves 6 to 8)

Pie Crust

2 packages (9 ounces each) Jiffy pie crust mix

Follow directions on box for each package. Substitute 4 scant tablespoons cold milk plus 1 tablespoon oil for 4 to 5 tablespoons cold water. Roll out 3 bottom crusts. Use one for Pecan Pie and freeze 2 remaining crusts.

Frances' Coconut Pound Cake

Frances and Carter Day manage Cedar Run Shooting Preserve in Catlett, Virginia. One day before hunting there, Frances served us this elegant cake.

1 cup Crisco or similar solid shortening
2 cups sugar
1 teaspoon vanilla
1 teaspoon coconut extract

1 teaspoon butter flavoring
6 eggs
2 cups flour
1 teaspoon salt
1 can (3½ ounces) flaked coconut

Glaze:

¼ cup sugar	1 teaspoon coconut
2 tablespoons boiling water	extract

Cream shortening and sugar until fluffy. Add flavorings. Add eggs one at a time, beating well after each. Add flour and salt gradually. Fold in coconut. Spoon batter into a well-greased and floured 10-inch tube pan and bake in a 350° oven for 70 minutes. Just before removing cake from oven, combine ingredients for glaze. Remove cake from oven and immediately pour glaze mixture over top of cake. Return cake to oven for 3 minutes. Let cake cool and then turn out on a cake platter. Top of cake will resemble a macaroon.

(Makes 16 to 20 servings)

Mother's Caramel Custard

½ cup granulated sugar
3 eggs
3 tablespoons sugar

2 cups milk, scalded
1 teaspoon vanilla

Melt ½ cup sugar in a 2-quart pyrex dish over very low heat. Spread caramel evenly over bottom of dish and ½-inch up sides. Put aside to cool. In a large bowl, beat 3 eggs with 3 tablespoons sugar until light and fluffy. Slowly add scalded milk and when well blended, add vanilla. Pour mixture over caramel in pyrex dish. Place baking dish in a pan of water with 5 or 6 layers of paper toweling under dish (this keeps caramel syrup liquid). Bake in a 325° oven about 45 minutes or until custard is set. Custard is done when knife comes out clean at side of dish.

(Serves 6)

Mother's Angel Berry Pie

6 egg whites
¼ teaspoon salt
2 cups sugar, divided
1 tablespoon vinegar
1 teaspoon vanilla

1 cup heavy whipping
cream
Fresh strawberries or
fresh red raspberries

In a large bowl, beat egg whites with salt until stiff. Add
1 cup sugar to beaten egg whites at full speed of mixer.
Then add second cup sugar, using low speed of mixer,
alternately with vinegar. Add vanilla. Sprinkle a 10-inch
pie plate with confectioners sugar. Pour meringue mixture
into sugared pie plate, piling higher in center. Bake 1 hour
in a 300° oven. Let pie cool—it will fall somewhat. Whip
cream and spread, gently, over baked meringue. Cover
top with sliced fresh strawberries or fresh red raspberries.
Do not cover with whipped cream and fruit until just before serving, since meringue pie should *not* be placed in
the refrigerator.

(Serves 8 to 10)

Blueberry Dumplings

2½ cups fresh blueberries
⅓ cup sugar
Dash salt
1 cup water
1 tablespoon lemon juice
1 cup flour

2 tablespoons sugar
2 teaspoons baking powder
¼ teaspoon salt
1 tablespoon butter
½ cup milk

Bring first 4 ingredients to a boil; cover and simmer 5 minutes. Add lemon juice. Combine dry ingredients and cut in butter until it resembles coarse meal. Add milk all at once and stir only until flour is dampened. Drop tablespoonfuls of batter into bubbling blueberry sauce, making 6 dumplings (don't let them overlap). Cover tightly and cook over low heat for 10 minutes without peeking. Serve hot plain or with a dab of vanilla ice cream.

(Serves 6)

Banana Split Dessert

1½ cups graham cracker
    crumbs
½ cups melted butter
2 cups confectioners
    sugar
½ cup butter, softened
2 eggs
1 teaspoon vanilla
3 or 4 bananas, sliced

1 can (1 pound, 4
    ounces) crushed
    pineapple, drained
    well
1 carton (12 ounces)
    whipped topping
½ to ¾ cup chopped
    nuts
Maraschino cherries
Small can of chocolate
    syrup (optional)

Mix crumbs and ½ cup melted butter; spread on bottom
of a 9″ × 13″ pan or dish. Beat confectioners sugar, ½ cup
softened butter, eggs and vanilla for 10 minutes. Spread
over crumbs. Arrange bananas over egg mixture. Sprinkle
pineapple on top of bananas. Cover with whipped topping
and sprinkle nuts on top. Chill well before serving. Place a
cherry on each piece and drizzle with chocolate syrup.

(Serves 12 to 16)

367

Tables

Substitutions

INGREDIENT CALLED FOR	SUBSTITUTION
1 cup self-rising flour	1 cup all-purpose flour plus 1 teaspoon baking powder and $^1/_2$ teaspoon salt
1 cup cake flour	1 cup all-purpose flour less 2 tablespoons
1 teaspoon baking powder	$^1/_2$ teaspoon cream of tartar plus $^1/_4$ teaspoon baking soda

1 tablespoon cornstarch	2 tablespoons all-purpose flour
1 tablespoon tapioca	1½ tablespoons all-purpose flour
1 whole egg	2 egg yolks plus 1 tablespoon water
1 cup commercial sour cream	1 tablespoon lemon juice plus evaporated milk to equal 1 cup
1 cup yogurt	1 cup buttermilk or sour milk
1 cup sour milk or buttermilk	1 tablespoon vinegar or lemon juice plus sweet milk to equal 1 cup
1 cup honey	1¼ cups sugar plus ¼ cup liquid
1 ounce unsweetened chocolate	3 tablespoons cocoa plus 1 tablespoon butter or margarine
1 clove fresh garlic	1 teaspoon garlic salt or ⅛ teaspoon garlic powder
1 teaspoon onion powder	2 teaspoons minced onion
1 tablespoon fresh herbs	1 teaspoon ground or crushed dry herbs
1 pound fresh mushrooms	6 ounces canned mushrooms

Equivalents

Ingredient Called for	Equivalent
1 pound all-purpose flour	4 cups
1 pound granulated sugar	2 cups
1 pound powdered sugar	3½ cups
1 pound brown sugar	2¼ cups firmly packed
1 cup uncooked long grain rice	3 to 4 cups cooked rice
1 cup (4 ounces) uncooked macaroni	2¼ cups cooked macaroni
4 ounces uncooked noodles	2 cups cooked noodles
7 ounces uncooked spaghetti	4 cups cooked spaghetti
1 cup soft breadcrumbs	2 slices fresh bread
1 cup egg whites	Whites of 6 or 7 large eggs
1 cup egg yolks	Yolks of 11 or 12 large eggs
1 cup whipping cream	2 cups whipped cream
1 cup shredded cheese	4 ounces cheese
1 lemon	2 to 4 tablespoons lemon juice plus 2 teaspoons grated rind

| 1 orange | 6 to 8 tablespoons orange juice plus 2 to 3 tablespoons grated rind |
| 1 pound shelled pecans or walnuts | 4 cups chopped nuts |

Before and After Measurements

INGREDIENT	AMOUNT BEFORE PREPARATION	AMOUNT AFTER PREPARATION
Apples	3 medium	3 cups sliced
Bacon	8 slices cooked	1/2 cup crumbled
Bananas	3 medium	2 cups mashed
Biscuit mix	1 cup	6 biscuits
Bread	1 pound loaf	12 to 16 slices
Bread	1 1/2 slices	1 cup soft crumbs
Cabbage	1 pound head	4 1/2 cups shredded
Carrots	1 pound	3 cups shredded
Cheese, American or Cheddar	1 pound	4 to 5 cups shredded
Coffee	1 pound	About 40 cups perked
Corn	2 medium ears	1 cup kernels
Crackers		
chocolate wafers	19 wafers	1 cup crumbs
graham crackers	14 squares	1 cup fine crumbs
saltine crackers	28 crackers	1 cup finely crushed
vanilla wafers	22 wafers	1 cup finely crushed
Cream, whipping	1 cup (1/2 pint)	2 cups whipped
Dates, pitted	1 pound	2 to 3 cups chopped
Green pepper	1 large	1 cup diced
Lettuce	1 pound head	6 1/4 cups torn
Lemon	1 medium	2 to 3 tablespoons juice and 2 teaspoons grated rind
Lime	1 medium	1 1/2 tablespoons juice
Macaroni	1 cup	2 1/4 cups cooked
Mushrooms	3 cups raw (8 ounces)	1 cup sliced, cooked

Noodles	3 cups	3 cups cooked
Nuts, shelled		
almonds	1 pound	$3^1/_4$ cups chopped
peanuts	1 pound	2 to 3 cups nutmeats
pecans	1 pound	$4^1/_2$ to 5 cups halves
walnuts	1 pound	4 cups chopped
Oats, quick-cooking	1 cup	$1^3/_4$ cups cooked
Onion	1 medium	$^1/_2$ cup chopped
Orange	1 medium	$^1/_3$ cup juice and 2 tablespoons grated rind
Peaches	4 medium	2 cups sliced
Pears	4 medium	2 cups sliced
Potatoes, white	3 medium	2 cups cubed cooked or $1^3/_4$ cups mashed
Potatoes, sweet	3 medium	3 cups sliced
Rice, long-grain	1 cup	3 to 4 cups cooked
Rice, pre-cooked	1 cup	2 cups cooked
Spaghetti	7 ounces	about 4 cups cooked
Strawberries	1 quart	4 cups sliced

Acknowledgments

The following sources were consulted:

Mrs. Sue Turner, Merchandising Specialist, II, Seafood Marketing, Florida Department of Natural Resources

Gulf and South Atlantic Fisheries Development Foundation, Inc.

Seafood Marketing Authority, Maryland Department of Economic and Community Development

Food Industries Development Section, North Carolina Department of Natural and Economic Resources, Division of Economic Development

United States Department of Interior, Bureau of Commercial Fisheries

Extension Division, Virginia Polytechnic Institute and State University

North Carolina State Extension Service, Carteret County, North Carolina

The following recipes are from Barbara Nusbaum of Los Angeles, California: Barbara's Chinese Beans, Cherry Mold, Comb of the Rooster Salad, Curried Peas, Green Beans Napoli, Hot Cheese Dip

373

Index

375

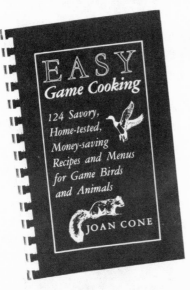

$4.95

JOAN CONE'S *Easy Game Cooking*

The little best-seller that made Joan Cone famous is now available in a spiral-bound edition. EASY GAME COOKING contains Mrs. Cone's first batch of recipes that were so good they made hunters and cooks call out for more. You can use the order form below to request either EASY GAME COOKING ($4.95) or the newer book, FISH & GAME COOKING ($7.95). Order several for yourself or for friends. Together they make a classic pair.

ORDER FORM

EPM Publications, Inc. (703) 356-5110
Box 490 • McLean, Virginia 22101

Please send me _____ **copies of** _____ **at $** _____

Subtotal _____

Virginia residents, add 4% sales tax _____

Add $1.25 postage and handling for the first book, 75¢ for each additional book _____

I enclose check ☐ money order ☐ for **TOTAL** _____

Name _____

Address _____

City _____

State _____ Zip _____

All orders over 10 pounds will be sent by UPS and shipping charges will be billed separately. **Canadian residents,** *use U.S. Dollar World Money Order or check drawn on U.S. funds in U.S. Bank.*

Use this form to order other outdoor books from EPM

QUANTITY   AMOUNT

_____ copies of STILLROOM COOKERY by Grace Firth.
How to cool or preserve your catch the way grand-
ma did. Updated recipes for delicious smoked,
pickled and dried fish and game as well as cheeses,
sausages, beer and other thirst-quenchers to go with
them.
Hardcover $9.95 $_____

_____ copies of CATCHING FRESHWATER STRIPED
BASS by Pete Elkins. The first book on how to land
the exciting new hard-fighting, tasty striper which
is now found in 28 states. Practical tips on tactics,
tackle and striper hot-spots from a pro.
Hardcover $9.95 $_____

_____ copies of THE CRAFT OF DISMANTLING A
CRAB by Robert H. Robinson and Daniel G. Cos-
ton, Jr. (illustrator). How to operate on oysters,
muscle in on mussels, put leverage on a lobster, and
be king over crabs and clams. Yummy recipes from
chowder to cioppini offer alternatives to a raw deal.
Spiralbound $4.95 $_____

_____ copies of YEN FOR A YACHT by Robert Woodbury. The personal story of a bank executive who
left the rat race to become a charter boat captain in
the Caribbean. Bob Woodbury tells what drove him
to do it, how it worked out, and why he gave it up 3
years later. Wish-fulfillment for dreamers, how-to
for doers.
Hardcover $9.95 $_____

Subtotal $_____

Virginia residents add 4% sales tax $_____
Add $1.25 postage and handling for the first
book, 75¢ for each additional book $_____

I enclose check ☐ money order ☐ for TOTAL $_____

All orders over 10 pounds will be sent by UPS and shipping charges will
be billed separately. *Canadian residents,* use U. S. Dollar World Money
Order or check drawn on U. S. funds in U. S. bank.

EPM PUBLICATIONS, INC.
Box 490, McLean, VA 22101   *Phone: (703) 356-5111*

Name _____

Address _____

City _____ State _____ Zip _____